BELIEFS AND DECISION RULES IN PUBLIC GOOD GAMES

BELIEFS AND DECISION RULES IN PUBLIC GOOD GAMES
Theory and Experiments

by

THEO OFFERMAN
University of Amsterdam,
CREED

KLUWER ACADEMIC PUBLISHERS
DORDRECHT / BOSTON / LONDON

A C.I.P. Catalogue record for this book is available from the Library of Congress.

ISBN 0-7923-9991-9

Published by Kluwer Academic Publishers,
P.O. Box 17, 3300 AA Dordrecht, The Netherlands.

Sold and distributed in the U.S.A. and Canada
by Kluwer Academic Publishers,
101 Philip Drive, Norwell, MA 02061, U.S.A.

In all other countries, sold and distributed
by Kluwer Academic Publishers,
P.O. Box 322, 3300 AH Dordrecht, The Netherlands.

Printed on acid-free paper

Printed in the Netherlands

Acknowledgements

This book is based on four years of research as a PH-D student at CREED, University of Amsterdam. CREED provides a stimulating environment for experimental researchers. Doors are literally open for discussion. The presence of people with different backgrounds makes discussion very rewarding.

Some people deserve special mention. My supervisor Arthur Schram was involved at all stages of my research project. He especially had a profound influence at the editorial stage. His efficient and effective way of working provided much relief in hard times. My other supervisor, Frans van Winden, helped with the fine-tuning of the manuscript. He convinced me to throw a whole chapter out of the book. In the end, it is quite hard to part from so much sweat and blood.

Joep Sonnemans also contributed to all parts of this book. He stimulated me to develop experimental designs which make more direct tests of hypotheses possible. The considerable contributions of both Joep and Arthur are reflected in the fact that they are the co-authors of most of my papers at this project. Of the many other people who gave valuable suggestions and comments, I wish to mention Mark Olson, Hans van Ophem, Randolph Sloof (for extensive comments on chapter 2), Nanne de Vries and Jörgen Wit in particular. I am grateful to Otto Perdeck for writing the computer programs of the experiments. Teresia Collier made my English sound less Dutch.

Gerti Vos provided loving and moral support. Her positive attitude guaranteed my ongoing lust for life. I also received much social support from my parents, family and friends. Sharing a room with Isidoro Mazza was always very agreeable. I will never forget his strange ideas about soccer.

Doing research costs money. I want to thank the Netherlands Organization for Scientific Research for funds for the experiments. The Tinbergen Institute and CREED proved very helpful and provided facilities of various kinds.

Tilburg, May 1997

Contents

Part I: Introduction

1. Experimentation in the social sciences

1.1 Introduction	3
1.2 The experimental method	7
1.3 Disputes about how to use the experimental method	11
1.4 Outline of this book	17

2. Theoretical foundation

2.1 Step-level public goods: definition and relevance	19
2.2 Decision rules	22
2.3 Game theoretic models	35
2.4 Learning models	49
2.5 Summary	62

3. Basic experimental tools

3.1 Introduction	67
3.2 The decomposed game technique	68
3.3 The scoring rule	72
3.4 Conclusions	77

Part II: Experimental results

4. Decision rules

4.1 Introduction 81

4.2 Experimental design and procedures 82

4.3 Experimental results 89

4.4 Conclusions 120

5. Beliefs and learning

5.1 Introduction 125

5.2 Experimental design and procedures 129

5.3 Experimental results: spotlight on expectations 131

5.4 Experimental results: spotlight on choices 143

5.5 Simulations of the interaction between players 154

5.6 Conclusions 162

Part III: Evaluation of the results

6. Towards a positive theory of public good games

6.1 Introduction 169

6.2 Environmental effects 170

6.3 Value orientations 172

6.4 Decision rules 177

6.5 Expectation formation and learning 181

6.6 Conclusions 188

Appendix A: Mathematical proofs 191

Appendix B: Experimental instructions 211

References 219

Subject index 231

Author index 237

PART I: Introduction

Part I provides an introduction to this study of players' beliefs and decision rules in public good games. The experimental method will be used to obtain data in order to test theoretical ideas about beliefs and decision rules. Chapter 1 discusses some methodological issues concerning experimentation in the social sciences. In particular, this chapter focuses on the relationship between experimental economics and social psychology. Chapter 2 provides an overview of psychological and economic ideas concerning players' beliefs and decision rules in public good games. This chapter forms the theoretical foundation of the book. Chapter 3 discusses some basic experimental tools which will be used in the experiments to be reported in part II. These basic experimental tools make up two procedures, to obtain a measure of a player's social orientation and a measure of her or his beliefs.

1. Experimentation in the social sciences

1.1 Introduction

The study of human behavior is an area where economics and psychology overlap. Although both disciplines are concerned with the same human beings, they often have different points of view on how people make choices and the motivation behind it. Psychology has a broader interest in human behavior than economics. It does not limit its scope to human choices in relation to the allocation of scarce resources as economics does. Nevertheless, psychologists and economists often study human behavior in the same research areas. Examples of such research areas are the voluntary provision of public goods and bargaining. This does not necessarily imply that there is always a fruitful exchange of ideas between scholars of the two disciplines in these areas. This first section will sketch some of the differences in theorizing between the two approaches which may have prevented a thorough exchange of ideas. However, it will also point to an important similarity between the two fields which may make an interdisciplinary approach fruitful. Finally the relatively recent emergence of the field of experimental economics and its relationship to psychology will be discussed.[1]

Striking in economic approaches is the high degree of unity in the analysis created by the extensive use of the rationality assumption. In a world of uncertainty this assumption says that people maximize their expected utility. In game settings this rationality assumption is not sufficient to derive predictions about players' choices. An additional assumption is needed with respect to how people interact. For example, one may specify the players' expectations regarding other players' behavior. Usually the

[1]Unfortunately, it is impossible to avoid generalization if one wants to discuss the broad topics of this first chapter. For reasons of clarity a clear contrast between economic and psychological ideas is pursued here. The consequence is probably that many readers, economists as well as psychologists, have a more balanced view than attributed to them here.

assumption is that players' expectations are accurate so that their choices are in equilibrium. These parsimonious assumptions about decision rules and expectations allow for rigorous, deductive reasoning. Often, economists are not so interested in the question whether the assumptions made are descriptively accurate (Caldwell, 1982, p.139-172) or in the processes which might lead human beings to particular choices. Economists are usually outcome oriented. From an empirical point of view, it is not surprising that it is easy to attack the gigantic attempt to explain all economic behavior with only one or two elegant principles. In fact, economists as well as psychologists have recorded anomalies or biases in many areas of economic behavior (Frey, 1992; Hogarth and Reder, 1987).

On the other hand, psychological approaches are marked by an extensive use of the inductive method. This has led to a patchwork of different theories and paradigms. This patchwork is less elegant from the theoretical perspective, but it has the advantage that each part has some empirical support. Psychologists put relatively less weight on parsimony and more on realism or empirical accuracy than economists do. Most psychologists do not believe that there is one sovereign principle like utility maximization, from which all human behavior can be predicted deductively. This does not mean that psychologists believe that people are not rational. They rather view rationality in terms of the processes it employs (Simon, 1987). Psychologists are process oriented. They emphasize the necessity to study cognitive processes for a good understanding of human behavior. Moreover, they think that concepts like expectations, attitudes, learning, emotions and individual perceptions of aspects of the environment are not only relevant for an explanation of behavior but also measurable.[2]

Nevertheless, an important common aspect of the economic and psychological approach lies in their methodological starting point. Most economists build their theories of human behavior on methodological individualism. The main exception might be Marx, whose ideas on this subject are ambiguous (see Olson, 1971, p.102-110). The main idea of methodological individualism is that "all explanation of social phenomena must be given in terms that are reducible to propositions which contain reference to individuals alone and not to social wholes" (Dowding, 1991, p.10). Only

---

[2]In fact, this study concentrates on the sub-field social psychology. For convenience, the discussion uses terms like 'psychology', where 'social psychology' would be more accurate.

individuals act. It is not sufficient to show that a group of people assembles and makes a decision merely because the group has a collective interest to do so, an explanation of group behavior sometimes encountered in sociology or political science (Olson, 1971, p.111-131). Frequently, free-rider incentives are present to benefit from the efforts of other group-members, incentives to be overcome in one way or another before any action profitable for the group as a whole is undertaken. For example, in this approach the rise of labor unions could be explained as the result of a process in which individuals are forced or bribed to become members of the union, but not as the direct result of the existence of a latent collective interest for workers to be represented by a union.

In social psychology the behavior of individuals in relation to the group(s) to which they belong is studied. Although no explicit reference is made to methodological individualism, the starting point of psychology is quite similar to that of economics. The ultimate goal is to study how an individual observes, thinks and behaves in a group and not how the group behaves or thinks as an aggregate. Most social psychological studies concentrate either on the influence of (the functioning of) other individuals on the perceptions and behavior of an individual or on the individual functioning relative to other people (Buunk and Meertens, 1988, p.26).

In principle, what counts as a proper explanation in one discipline, is also considered a proper explanation in the other. Scholars who do not take any notice of what is going on in the other discipline risk spending much time re-inventing the wheel. This study will have an open eye for developments in both economics and psychology, and will make efforts to integrate insights obtained in one discipline into the other.

It is an open question whether the two fields will actually converge in the areas where they overlap as time passes. Probably, there will always remain interest in realistic theories explaining behavior in a specific context as well as a separate interest in general theories explaining behavior in a set of contexts. However, the rise of experimental economics provides an incentive for cooperation between economists and psychologists, as they start using the same tools to gather information on human behavior.

Social psychology has an older tradition in experimentation than economics. An early experiment in social psychology was carried out by Tripplet in 1897 (Buunk and

Meertens, 1988, p.31). He investigated the positive influence of the mere presence of other individuals on the performance of an individual riding a bike, a phenomenon which has been called social facilitation in more recent times. An early experiment in economics was carried out in 1931 by Thurstone (Roth, 1993). His experiment showed that subjects' (hypothetical) choices between hats, coats and shoes can adequately be represented by indifference curves. It lasted until the nineteen sixties before a serious start with experimental economics was made. The American pioneer was Smith, later followed by Plott. Smith started a systematic study of the convergence patterns in markets and the effects of institutions on these patterns. At about the same time, Selten started to carry out oligopoly experiments in Germany (Friedman and Sunder, 1994).

Two rather different experimental movements developed from these initial efforts. American experimental economics is relatively closest to mainstream economics. Usually the experiments do not question the descriptive validity of the core assumptions of the economic paradigm. Many American scholars are outcome oriented. For example, game theoretic models often generate multiple Nash equilibria. These American scholars regard the experimental method as a useful device for empirical equilibrium selection. The descriptive validity of the Nash equilibrium concept itself is not questioned, however.

German experimental economics developed more in the direction of psychology. Here, systematic biases against the economic framework are taken more seriously. German scholars propose the view that individuals are only boundedly rational. As a consequence, they shift their attention to theories that describe how people learn. German experimental economics is more process oriented. A point of criticism of American scholars towards German scholars is that their efforts did not succeed in finding a unified theory that outperforms the theory proposed by mainstream economics. The German reaction to such criticism tends to be that it is better to have a set of theories with empirical support than one theory without empirical support.[3]

This study will borrow elements from both the American and the German approach. It will have an open eye for the question which equilibrium tends to be selected in which institutional setting, but it will also consider the cognitive processes

[3]Note that this sketch of the German and American schools is very rough. Much interesting experimental work does not fit in either of these descriptions. For a more elaborate discussion of these issues and references the reader is referred to Friedman and Sunder, 1994.

and learning exhibited by individuals.

One important difference between German experimental economics and psychology lies in the matter of how experimental methods should be applied. German experimental economists have the same ideas about the use of experimental tools as their American colleagues. The next section will discuss some methodological issues concerning the use of experimental methods by psychologists and economists. It will also provide a general discussion of the aims and limits of the use of the experimental method in social sciences, as well as its advantages and disadvantages. Section 1.3 will present some of the disputes between economists and psychologists concerning how the experimental method should be applied. Section 1.4 presents an outline of this book.

1.2 The experimental method

Several goals can be pursued with experiments. The most obvious and perhaps most important purpose of experimentation is to empirically evaluate existing theories. Experiments provide existing theories the best chance to show their predictive power, because the conditions under which a theory is supposed to hold can be precisely realized in an experimental setting. A natural extension of this aim is to use experiments for heuristic purposes. Then, the aim is to search for empirical regularities in areas where no theory exists. An important example of theory searching experiments is provided by market experiments. Much of the literature on markets is concerned with the existence and the properties of the equilibrium and not with its attainment. Some kind of meta-theory would be required to show how a set of consumers and producers actually reach the equilibrium. Experiments have filled this theoretical gap and revealed that market processes converge to the equilibrium with the speed of convergence dependent on the institutional setting (see for example Hey, 1991). In this study the experimental method is primarily used to assess theories or to search for empirical regularities.

Another role that can be fulfilled by experimentation is to advise policy-makers in areas lacking theoretical predictions. For example, Grether and Plott (1984) use experiments to provide evidence in an antitrust case. Often the question is which institution yields the most efficient allocation in an economic or political market. The emphasis of this kind of experiment lies in simulation of real world problems. For references to this type of experiment, see Friedman and Sunder, 1994.[4]

The main advantage of experiments compared to other empirical research is that the researcher has considerable control over the environment in an experiment. The institutions in a game are easy to control in a laboratory setting but not in the outside world. Thus, it is easier to assess the effects of a change in institutions in an experimental setting. The ideal procedure in an experiment allows the researcher to measure the effect of one of the independent variables on the dependent variable by varying this independent variable, while keeping the others constant. In this way causal relationships could be traced. Although actual experiments often do not succeed completely in reaching this ideal, they usually do a better job than field studies. In field studies there is virtually no control over important independent variables. This frequently gives rise to ambiguity on the issue whether the ceteris paribus condition is fulfilled or not. Experimental studies often need fewer auxiliary assumptions than field studies to evaluate theories.

Of course, some aspects are simply uncontrollable. An obvious example is subjects' personal idiosyncracies. Usually it is not possible to control subjects' expectations either. Proper random allocation of subjects to the different treatments takes care that treatment effects are not affected systematically by such uncontrolled aspects. Such procedures are usually not available in field studies.

Besides randomization, an additional useful tool is available in experiments to cope with uncontrolled effects. In an experimental setting it is easier to obtain a measurement of expectations or idiosyncracies, factors which are often considered to be 'unobservable' in field studies. Psychologists are usually more keen to obtain such measurements than economists. This study will obtain additional measurements on the expectations subjects have regarding other subjects' behavior and on their social attitude towards other people.

Another advantage of experimentation is that it provides the possibility of

---

[4]Experiments can also be used to support the education of students. For example, students tend to understand the functioning of markets faster if they are given the possibility to trade actively in an experimental market.

replication (Davis and Holt, 1993, p.14). If it is suspected that a data-set contains a lot of noise, or if there are insufficient data to draw a firm conclusion, one may repeat the experiment and create new data. With naturally occurring phenomena it may take considerable time to acquire a data-set of the desired size. Experiments are also helpful to create data in areas where it is virtually impossible to obtain reliable field data. Lobbying provides an example of this type of research (Potters and Van Winden, 1995).

Of course, there are also some objections raised against experiments. A usual point of criticism is that experiments lack realism. The argument is that people behave differently in an artificial laboratory setting than in the real world, and that as a consequence the data obtained in experiments are meaningless.

Concerns about the external validity of experiments are encountered in all disciplines where the experimental method is used to gather data. Aronson, Ellsworth, Carlsmith and Gonzales (1990) distinguish between 'mundane realism' and 'experimental realism' to clarify the discussion. Mundane realism refers to the similarity between the choices the individual is confronted with in the experiment and the choices the individual has to make in the outside world. Many experimenters would admit that the level of mundane realism is not as high as possible in their experiments. For example, subjects are often not allowed to communicate in the laboratory or if they are, communication is restricted to a set of previously specified messages. In principle the realism of an experiment could be enhanced by relaxing some of the strict procedures. This is a sensible thing to do if it is believed that a variable like communication plays a vital role in the outside world. But one should keep in mind that there is a trade-off between mundane realism and control. If one wants to enhance control over the important variables, it is unavoidable to make the laboratory setting more sterile. If one wants to make the laboratory situation more similar to reality, then one loses control over some of the relevant variables. The ultimately realistic experiment is a field study of reality itself without any control of the situation.

Whereas many experimenters would admit that the experiments have only a limited level of mundane realism, they emphasize the high level of experimental realism in the experiments. An experiment has a high level of experimental realism if subjects consider the choices they are confronted with seriously. Many experimenters report that subjects are absorbed by the problem posed to them during the experiment.

Potential gains and losses are usually substantial compared to the marginal wage rate of subjects. After an experiment spontaneous discussions often arise about the rationality of different strategies. In this way the experiment does not resemble reality, but it becomes a part of reality and a meaningful instance to test a theory or to search for a new one.

The criticism that experiments are less useful because they lack realism is weaker if the aim of the experiment is to test a theory than if the aim is to advise policy-makers. When testing a theory, experimenters replicate the conditions of the theory as precisely as possible in the laboratory. If people think that the experiment is too artificial or too simple, it means that the theory is too artificial or too simple. At least, there are no theories which state that they hold everywhere except in the laboratory (Hey, 1991).

The criticism of external validity seems to be stronger if the goal of an experiment is to simulate a part of reality without the help of theory. But especially in these areas experimenters put considerable effort into catching all important aspects of the relevant situation in the experimental setting. A more constructive argument would indicate which part of a particular experiment is artificial, so it could be taken into account in the design. It should not be forgotten that these types of experiments usually explore areas where other methods have little to say.

A different point of criticism directed specifically at the use of the experimental method in the social sciences is that these experiments lack representativeness of subjects. Students are virtually the only part of the population which are subjected to tests in experiments. The pragmatic reasons for using students are that they are relatively easy to recruit and that they do not have to be paid as much as other people. Of course, formally it is sufficient to show that the evidence obtained with a part of the population, for example students, rejects a theory, if the theory is supposed to hold for a whole population. But if an experimenter concludes that the behavior of people is compatible with the behavior predicted by theory, then representativeness of the subjects is a prerequisite. At the same time, it should be recognized that it is practically impossible to recruit a truly representative population. Thus, the discussion usually shifts to the empirical question whether differences exist between the behavior of students and of other people in particular areas.

Representativeness of the subject population is a hot issue especially if experiments reveal behavioral anomalies. Critics point out that important economic decisions are taken by experts and not by students and that experts do not fall prey to these behavioral anomalies. Of course, one may doubt whether economic decisions taken by non-experts do not affect the economic process significantly. More importantly, the behavior of experts and students has been compared experimentally in some areas. Systematic effects do not seem to exist in this respect. Professionals often fall prey to the same anomalies as students do. Sometimes professionals perform better than students, but there are also instances where they perform worse! For example, in an experiment experienced business executives from the construction contract industry were just as prone to the winners' curse (a kind of overbidding) as students were, even though the experimenters were careful to provide the experts with considerable incentives (Dyer, Kagel and Levin, 1989). Davis and Holt (1993, p.17) and Friedman and Sunder (1994, p.40-42) provide an overview of studies which control for this issue.

No experimenter would argue that experiments should replace other empirical research. On the contrary, each method can make up for the deficiencies of the other. Empirical evidence is the strongest if it is obtained from both experiments and field studies. Experiments may provide the most direct test of a theory. But if a theory survives the evidence obtained in an experiment, it is not guaranteed that the theory will also survive outside the laboratory. There is always a danger that an artificial theory is not rejected in an artificial experiment. There will always remain an important role for field studies.

1.3 Disputes about how to use the experimental method

Psychologists and economists usually have similar ideas about the advantages, disadvantages and limitations of the experimental method. But they have different views on three aspects of the experimental procedures. Economic experimenters often put considerable effort into the provision of an incentive compatible mechanism. Many psychologists do not think that such incentives are very important. Another difference is that psychologists often gather additional data via questionnaires and take these data seriously, while economists tend to be skeptical about the value of such data. A final difference is that economic experimenters tend to oppose manipulating subjects, a practice often encountered in psychological experiments.

Probably, the most important disagreement between psychological and economic experimenters concerns the question how *monetary incentives* should be treated. In a typical economic experiment, the amount of money a subject makes depends on her or his own choices and possibly on the choices made by other individuals. The reason economists tend to think that proper incentives are important is that they feel that subjects take their task more seriously when they receive money contingent on their actions. Sometimes an even stronger claim is made and the provision of incentives is regarded as an essential part of the means to induce subjects' preferences. Three conditions should hold to allow one to control preferences. *Monotonicity* requires that subjects prefer more money to less money, and that this desire does not become satiated in the course of the experiment. *Salience* requires that the payoff depends on the subject's own action and possibly on the actions of other subjects. Subjects are supposed to understand how the institutions of the environment affect their payoff. A fixed flat payment is not salient. *Dominance* requires that subjects generate utility from the payoffs they earn, and that potential effects of other influences on their utility are negligible. When these three conditions hold, the experimenter achieves control over subjects' preferences (cf. Friedman and Sunder, 1994, p.12-14).

Some economists seem to be willing to go one step further. They want to give incentives of considerable magnitude. They are afraid that people will not take a decision problem seriously, unless the magnitude of the incentive is significant. Although this fear is not a result derived deductively from the economic concept of rationality, it finds some support among economic experimenters. For example, Hey (1991, p.225-226) even regards the size of the incentives as one of the "major methodological issues that experimental economists will need to confront as an increasing matter of urgency". Sometimes it is argued that incentives should be of significant magnitude because there are costs attached to thinking. However, the introduction of such costs has a theoretical problem, because a rational individual should then evaluate whether it is worthwhile to think about the problem at all. This results in an infinite regression of whether it is worthwhile to think whether to think etc.

Psychologists are usually less careful on the matter of incentives. Sometimes they use a proper incentive scheme dependent on the decisions of the subjects, sometimes they do not. If not, they often give individuals a lump sum payment for participating, while subjects play for fictitious money or some other fictitious commodity in the experiment itself. Of course, if non-economic problems are investigated in an experiment, the use of a monetary incentive scheme need not be important or may even influence subjects in an undesired manner. If the problem at hand lies in the field of economics, however, the experimenter will have to face the skepticism of most economists. This skepticism says that the problem of choosing between options which yield different quantities of hypothetical money is not an economic problem, because hypothetical money is not a scarce resource which can be used for other purposes.

Some empirical work suggests that incentives do affect behavior, while other work reports no effect of incentives on behavior. If effects are found, the conclusion tends to be that subjects take their task more seriously with incentives (cf. Grether, 1992; Offerman and Schram, 1993; Smith and Walker, 1993; Wright and Aboul-Ezz, 1988; and references cited in these studies). Smith and Walker (1993, p.259) conclude from a survey of experimental papers that "the comparative effects of subject monetary rewards (including no rewards) shows a tendency for the error variance of the observations around the predicted optimal level to decline with increased monetary rewards". On the other hand, biases reported in psychological work tend to survive the introduction of incentives in the experimental setting. For example, the preference reversal phenomenon reported by psychologists (Lichtenstein and Slovic, 1971) does not vanish in experiments with incentives (Grether and Plott, 1979). Another point is that at present it is not so clear whether incentives allow experimenters to control preferences in all areas. Specifically the dominance condition seems to be problematic in public good games and bargaining games. Especially in these areas subjects' choices seem to be affected by concerns about the payoffs for others or concerns for being treated fairly. One may continue to defend the view that dominance and control over preferences will result if incentives are sufficiently high, but a problem of such a defense seems to be that it is impossible to reject.

In this study subjects will be motivated with proper incentives as much as possible. However, it is not assumed that incentives will allow the experimenter to control preferences in the public good experiments, given the evidence of former experiments (for an overview of public good experiments, see Ledyard, 1995). On the contrary, in the experiments additional measures will be obtained to assess the concerns subjects have towards the payoffs to others.

The second difference is that economists and psychologists tend to put different weight on data obtained from *questionnaires and oral interviews*. Economists sometimes use questionnaires to find out whether their subjects understood the instructions of the experiment, but they rarely use them to test hypotheses. Skepticism is fed by the tendency of individuals to give socially desirable answers if there is no clear monetary incentive to give a true answer, by the tendency of people to give 'yes'-answers out of love of ease and by the possibility that the order in which the questions are posed affects the content of the answers. Cognitive psychologists defend the use of questionnaires by showing that these are constructed carefully. They let people choose from a set which contains alternatives of comparable social desirability, they take account of the tendency of people to give 'yes'-answers and they test whether the order of the questions affects the answers (Koomen, 1988, p.62-64). This study will make a selective use of data obtained in questionnaires.

The third difference between experimental economists and social psychologists concerns their view on the *manipulation of subjects*. Economists tend to disapprove of the manipulation of subjects if it involves fooling them. For example, psychologists sometimes let subjects play against preprogrammed strategies while they are led to believe that they are playing against other subjects. Economists fear that the subjects will discover the trick and that, as a consequence, the roles are reversed. The subjects fool the experimenter, while the latter does not know it. The fear is strengthened by the fact that many experimental economists recruit subjects who participated in former experiments. If somebody finds out that (s)he has been fooled during one experiment, (s)he may pass over this information to other subjects, and the reputation of a laboratory will deteriorate. An additional objection against manipulation in games is that it does not allow the experimenter to study how the game would evolve naturally. If subjects play against preprogrammed strategies only, you may not get the same picture as when subjects interact.

Nevertheless, this does not mean that there are no exceptions to the rule that economists do not manipulate subjects. For example, Kim and Walker (1984) fooled subjects in a public good experiment by making them believe that one hundred subjects were involved in the game, whereas in reality only five of them were. A similar manipulation is used by Weimann (1994). In some of his public good experiments subjects play with fictitious others without knowing it.

Social psychologists tend to have less objection to the manipulation of subjects. They stress the main advantage of manipulation, which is a pragmatic one. Manipulation gives the statistical analysis of the data more power. Hence, one needs fewer observations to acquire significant results. Consider the case that a group of subjects plays a game repeatedly without any manipulation. Then, subjects' choices in period t are strictly speaking not independent of subjects' choices in period $t-1$, because subjects base their choices on a common history which they built together. If the experimenter would have let each subject play against a set of preprogrammed strategies, such dependence would not evolve. Another advantage of manipulation is that it allows one to investigate questions which could not be investigated in any reasonable other way. Assume that one wants to know what kind of behavior is triggered by a specific strategy. For example, one may be interested how players react to a player using a tit-for-tat strategy in a public good game. It may be very time (and money) consuming to wait until one of the subjects incidentally uses such a strategy.

If an experimenter has taken care to conceal the manipulation, then social psychologists have confidence that subjects will not see through it. A comparative advantage on this issue for social psychologists seems to be that they often use 'fresh' first year undergraduates as subjects only once or twice.

In the experiments in this study subjects are not manipulated. Especially in the public good games this gives rise to a statistical problem, the problem which level should be treated as the appropriate one for the tests. Consider an experimental session where in each of the t periods g groups of n players each are formed. In each group in each period a game is played. After each period all players are scrambled and allocated to g new groups of n players each. In such an experimental session the appropriate level for the test is the *session level*. One session only yields one data-point in a test (usually the average of a variable in a session is used).[5] Now consider a similar session with

---

[5]An alternative is to focus on the choices made in the first period only. These choices are independent because subjects have not built a common history yet. Such a procedure would yield $n*g$ data-points per session. However, the data in the first period may contain relatively more noise because some subjects only fully understand the rules of a game after some practice. Therefore, this

the only difference being that groups remain constant, i.e., they are not scrambled after each period. In this case there is no interaction between players of different groups, so that each session yields *g* independent data-points. The appropriate level for testing is the *group level*. It is also possible to test at the *individual level*, where each player generates one data-point and a session generates $n*g$ data-points. Or one may test at the *choice level*, where each choice made by each player serves as a data-point and a session yields $n*g*t$ data-points. Many experimenters feel that the individual level and the choice level are not appropriate for testing in games because they neglect the fact that the interaction between subjects causes the data on these levels to depend on each other.

A few qualifications are in place here. Ideally, only two possible answers can be given to the question whether data are independent: yes or no. Unfortunately, the real world is not ideal. A very purist scholar might argue that almost nothing in this world is truly independent of anything else. For example, it might be argued that there is some dependence between observations of different sessions. The students used as subjects may come from the same university, and therefore have some common history which they built together. In the real world independence seems to be a matter of degree. The level of independence of data in a session where a game with scrambled groups is played is smallest at the choice level and greatest at the session level, and the level of independence is between these two at the other test levels.

It should also be recognized that data are often assumed to be independent in field studies where the criteria described above would imply some dependence. A strict application of the criteria might lead to the conclusion that the test results of many field studies are worthless because they used dependent data. Of course, such a point of view would be very extreme.

A final qualification is that tests at the session level are usually much more conservative than tests at the choice level. Tests at the session level neglect a lot of information in the data. As a consequence, a test at the session level is not very informative if the null-hypothesis is not rejected.

At present there is no consensus among economic experimenters on how to solve these statistical problems. Some studies report tests using the choice level and others report

---

procedure is not used in this study.

tests using the session level. The approach taken in this study is to analyze the data at different levels. If the evidence is consistent at all levels, only one test result will be reported. For the conclusion that a null-hypothesis is rejected, the test results will tend to be reported at the session level (or group level if groups are not scrambled). Usually the test results are sharper at other levels. If the tests of different levels are not consistent, this will be reported.

1.4 Outline of this book

The major part of this book is devoted to the study of public goods. Existing theories about how people choose in public good games will be described and ideas will be extracted from the emerging literature on learning to formulate new theories. For analytical purposes theories are dissected to clarify their propositions for decision rules and for the interaction in a game. A decision rule describes how people choose given their expectations. Decision rules may be deterministic or stochastic. The interaction describes how people form their expectations, or, if expectations are not supposed to play a role, how people adapt their propensity to make each of the available choices in the light of the outcome of the game in the former play. This distinction is useful because some theories differ precisely in their assumptions about decision rules, whereas others differ only in their assumptions about the interaction.

The next chapter will introduce the specific public good game studied here. The scope of the literature considered is broad. The chapter will discuss theories from economic as well as from psychological origin. Traditional game theoretic models describing the interaction of players in games will be proposed. But also some relatively new theories will be sketched assuming that people learn in games. The predictions about the effects of changes in the environment on the individual propensity to contribute will be discussed for various theories. Specifically, the effects of changes in group-size, of changes in the value of the public good, of changes in the variability of the group-composition and of changes in the framing of the problem will be discussed.

In the experiments independent information is obtained on subjects' beliefs and subjects' attitudes towards others. This allows for direct testing of hypotheses on decision rules and hypotheses on the interaction between subjects. The decomposed game technique is used to obtain a measure on social attitudes and a scoring rule is used to elicit subjects' beliefs. These methods are discussed and evaluated in chapter 3.

Chapter 4 and 5 will present the experimental evidence on players' behavior and interaction in public good games. Chapter 4 will focus explicitly on the evidence obtained for decision rules. Among others, it will be seen that both the psychological route concentrating on independent measures and the economic route of estimating unobservables via maximum likelihood methods lead to the conclusion that social attitudes matter in public good games, and that they differ systematically amongst individuals. But more is needed to organize the data in a satisfactory way. It will be seen that it is unlikely that individual decisions result from a deterministic rule. Decision rules have to allow for the possibility that individuals make errors. Besides evidence on decision rules, the effects of changes in the environment on individuals' decision to contribute are investigated experimentally in this chapter.

Chapter 5 will present the results for players' expectation formation and the role for belief learning and reinforcement learning in public good games. Both a direct analysis of the expectations and an indirect analysis of the choices lead to the conclusion that subjects adapt their expectations in the course of the game systematically. The adaptation is consistent with the patterns of belief learning models discussed in chapter 2, but not with the game theoretic models. Some simulation results will be presented as well.

Chapter 6 will evaluate and summarize the results. It provides a rough sketch of the contours of a positive theory of public good games, and it discusses the potential contribution of this study to such a theory.

2. Theoretical foundation

2.1 Step-level public goods: definition and relevance

The provision of public goods provides a fruitful topic for an interdisciplinary study since it has drawn the attention of many economists as well as psychologists. It allows for a comparison of basic conceptual issues involved in the construction of theories in the two domains. This study will focus in particular on the different roles ascribed by various theories to distinct decision rules and expectations when explaining individuals' decisions to contribute to public goods. Experimental evidence will be used to assess the relative strength of different ideas. It will also be investigated whether successful ideas in one field can be translated to the other.

First, a definition of the public good game studied here is given, and its potential empirical relevance is discussed. Then it is possible to address some conceptual issues in more detail. This is useful, because these conceptual issues form the major motivation for this work.

For the provision of almost all public goods some initial expenses have to be made before any quantity can be produced. Often even the establishment of a committee to organize the provision incurs some costs itself (cf. Olson, 1971, p.22). This yields a threshold in the production, that must be crossed before the good can be supplied. The unique feature distinguishing a so-called step-level public good from other public goods is that contributions exceeding the threshold do not substantially improve its quality or quantity. Several examples conform in varying degree to this rather stylized spirit of a step-level public good. Large scale examples of these 'lumpy' goods are lighthouses, dikes, bridges, railway lines and public roads. Small(er) scale examples are a law in parliament, which may only pass if enough members are willing to vote for it, or the restoration of a public building. The provision of public goods often has a repetitive character: once they are provided, they have to be maintained. Maintenance of a public good itself is often an example of a step-level public good.

Step-level public good problems are also at the heart of many inter-group problems. A coalition fighting a war is only successful if sufficient countries participate in it. But what is sufficient, is determined by the efforts of the opposing coalition. In a two party 'winner-takes-all' election a candidate wins if sufficient supporters turn up to vote for her or him. What is sufficient is determined by the number of voters for the opponent. Such inter-group problems may be interpreted as a step-level public good game with a threshold that is endogenously determined by the efforts of the members of the other group. Thus, the study of step-level public good problems may be relevant for the study of inter-group problems as well.

The focus of this study will be on step-level public good games where n group-members simultaneously face the binary choice between contributing and not contributing their original endowment c to a public good with value $f(s)-c$ to each member. The public good is provided if and only if the number of contributions is equal to or greater than the threshold s. Contributions are never refunded, even if the sum of contributions falls short of the threshold. Contributions exceeding the threshold do not increase the value of the public good. This public good game is played repeatedly.[1]

To get a better idea of the conceptual issues and the types of questions posed in this study, compare this public good game with the following investment decision. The profitability of an investment depends on the state of the world. The number of red balls in a cage determines the state of the world. If there are s or more red balls, the decision-maker receives a payoff of $f(s)-c$. By investing an original endowment of c, the individual can add one red ball to those from the (unknown) draw. Each of $n-1$ balls is randomly drawn to be either red or white. The decision-maker knows that for each ball the probability that its color is red is the same, and that this probability is independent of former draws. The decision-maker does not know this probability θ, but (s)he could learn from former observations on states of the world about the true binomial $(n-1,\theta)$ distribution generating the states of the world. The investment of c is profitable if and only if $s-1$ of the $n-1$ balls are red (cf. table 2.1).

[1]For convenience, step-level public goods will hereinafter simply be referred to as public goods. The reader should keep in mind that the ideas proposed are developed for public goods with a step-wise production function, and that the ideas may need to be adapted to be applicable for public goods with other production functions.

Table 2.1
Payoff schemes of the public good game and the investment decision

public good game			investment decision		
# others cooperating	own decision		# red balls in cage	own decision	
	not contributing	contributing		not investing	investing
< s-1	c	0	< s-1	c	0
s-1	c	f(s)-c	s-1	c	f(s)-c
> s-1	f(s)	f(s)-c	> s-1	f(s)	f(s)-c

To a large extent the investment decision is mathematically equivalent to the decision individuals face in the public good game. Basically, the investment decision is the contribution decision stripped of its social and strategic aspects. Theories propose different assumptions about the similarities and differences between players' expectation formation process in these two situations, and about the similarities and differences in players' decision rule. These issues are addressed sequentially.

If the decisions of other players in the public good games are replaced by decisions of automata choosing contribution with unknown but constant probability θ, the investment decision is obtained. Various models differ with respect to their propositions about the expectation formation processes in these games. According to some models the process of individuals' expectation formation differs in these games precisely because the strategic aspect is present in public good games but absent in investment decisions. According to other models, individuals' expectation formation is essentially the same in these games. These models assume that individuals' cognitive limitations hinder extensive strategic reasoning. Individuals abstract from the strategic aspect of the contribution decision, and 'assume' that the distribution of others' choices is stationary. An important part of this chapter focuses on the *expectation formation process* of individuals in public good games, and some of the proposed ideas are explicitly tested in chapter 5.

Some psychologists would argue that the social aspect differentiates the public good game from the investment decision (e.g., Liebrand, 1984). They argue that the mental representation of the public good problem varies substantially amongst individuals. Some individuals try to maximize joint outcomes. Others are primarily concerned about their own payoffs. There are also those who try to earn more money than others. Given their expectations, these different types of players tend to make different decisions, or, in other words, their *decision rules* differ. This finding has proven to be fruitful to address various research questions in psychology (e.g., Van Lange and Kuhlman, 1994). Such social utility considerations are absent in the investment decision, since there no interaction exists with other players. An important part of this chapter focuses explicitly on theories proposed for decision rules. The derived hypotheses will be subjected to experimental testing in chapter 4.

The organization of this chapter is as follows: section 2.2 discusses theories on individual decision rules from psychological as well as economic origin. In this section, expectations are treated as exogenously given. Section 2.3 focuses on game theoretic models describing the interaction of individuals in public good games. Game theory is the traditional vehicle used to endogenize expectations. Game theoretic models assume that the expectation formation process differs between the public good game and the investment decision. Section 2.4 describes two types of learning. First, belief learning allows individuals to update beliefs on the basis of their observations of the development of the game. Belief learning models assume that the expectation formation process is essentially the same in the public good game as in the investment decision. Second, reinforcement learning describes the development of the game without any reference to beliefs or utility maximization. Section 2.5 provides a summary of this chapter.

2.2 Decision rules

In this section three themes will be dealt with. One theme concerns the direction of the relationship between expectations and behavior: do expectations cause behavior, or is it the other way around? Another theme focuses on an intriguing behavioral difference observed in many environments. In environments where individuals' actions contain positive externalities for other individuals more pro-social actions are often observed than in environments where individuals' actions contain negative externalities for others (e.g., Andreoni, 1995a). However, a direct comparison of contribution levels is often obscured by the fact that the environments usually differ in more than one aspect. The major theme concerns the question how people choose in public good games, given their expectations. This theme will be elaborated before the other two.

2.2.1 How do people choose in public good games?

Psychologists usually propose different ideas about people's decision rules in public good games than economists do. These ideas will be dealt with subsequently.

Psychological theories about decision rules in public good games

Here, some of the most important hypotheses from the psychological literature will be discussed. According to many social psychologists, different people pursue distinct goals when making decisions that affect others. Preferences regarding one's own well-being relative to the well-being of others appear to vary amongst individuals. An often used classification distinguishes the following *value orientations*: *competitors* want to be better off than their neighbors; *individualists* try to do best for themselves and *cooperators* pursue the best for both themselves and the others. Rare orientations are *altruism* and *aggression*: altruists want to do best for others, regardless of the outcome for themselves and aggressors want to do worst for others, regardless of the outcome for themselves.[2] The majority of people is classified either as individualistic or as cooperative (cf. Kelley and Stahelski, 1970; Kuhlman and Wimberley, 1976; Liebrand, 1984). For example, in one of the experiments reported in Liebrand (1984) 10% of the subjects are labelled competitive, 31% are labelled individualistic, 53% are labelled cooperative, and 5% are labelled altruistic. These figures tend to vary amongst subject pools, however.

Given these value orientations, social psychologists offer two classic hypotheses to account for (the relationship between) expectations and behavior. These are typically applied to prisoners' dilemma type of games (for tests of these and related hypotheses, see Liebrand, 1984; McClintock and Liebrand, 1988; Van Lange, 1992; Van Lange and Kuhlman, 1994, and references quoted there). The first is the *triangle hypothesis*

[2] These terms are generally used differently in economics. For example, altruism is usually defined as utility-interdependency.

by Kelley and Stahelski (1970), according to which individualists and competitors tend to expect that other people pursue an individualistic or competitive goal as well, while cooperators can imagine that other people may have either a cooperative or an individualistic/competitive value orientation. The rationale behind the hypothesis is that competitors and individualists misjudge the goals pursued by other individuals to some extent, because their own selfish behavior tends to elicit the same behavior of others regardless of the value orientation of these others. Cooperators usually dislike being the 'sucker' and adapt their preferred cooperative behavior to selfish behavior after a while, when they are confronted with selfish behavior.

For public good games with a step-level production function the triangle hypothesis implies that competitors will not contribute and expect the same from others. Individualists contribute if and only if they think it is individually beneficial for them to do so; they expect others to act in the same way. Cooperators will contribute as long as they don't think they are being exploited; they expect others to either act cooperatively or not, a fact to be discovered by playing the game.

The second classic psychological hypothesis concerning expectations and behavior in prisoners' dilemma type of games is the *false consensus hypothesis* proposed by Kuhlman and Wimberley (1976). According to this hypothesis, people tend to expect that other people's behavior is the same as the behavior prescribed by their own value orientation. Competitors tend to expect competitive behavior of others, individualists individualistic behavior and cooperators cooperative behavior. In this view, the direction of the causal relationship between expectations and behavior is reversed: expectations are rationalized on the basis of behavior.[3]

In the public good games, this implies that competitors will not contribute and will expect that others will not either; that individualists will contribute if it is beneficial and expect the same from others; and that cooperators will contribute and expect others to do so as well. Section 2.2.2 elaborates a procedure to distinguish

---

[3]It may be noted that in these psychological hypotheses expectations are not exogenously determined. According to the false consensus hypothesis expectations are determined by behavior. The triangle hypothesis makes a prediction about the development of expectations besides the prediction about how people choose. In fact, it might be argued that the triangle hypothesis and the belief learning models to be presented in section 2.4 are related. This relationship will be discussed in chapter 6.

empirically between the false consensus hypothesis and the triangle hypothesis.[4]

Economic theories about decision rules in public good games

Economists generally have different ideas on the way in which expectations affect behavior. According to the *expected value theory* individuals maximize expected monetary payoff. To do this an individual assigns subjective probabilities to the possible future states of the world. Each state of the world yields a monetary payoff contingent on the selected action. The individual chooses the available action for which the expected value is maximized. In the public good game there are three relevant states of the world: the state of the world where one's contribution to the public good is *futile* because the public good will not be provided whatever the individual choice, i.e., fewer than $s-1$ of the others contribute (s denotes the threshold); the state of the world where the individual contribution is *critical* for the provision of the public good, i.e., exactly $s-1$ of the others contribute; and the state of the world where the individual contribution is *redundant* for the provision of the public good because the public good will be provided whatever the individual choice, i.e, more than $s-1$ of the others contribute. Let $P(<s-1)$, $P(s-1)$ and $P(>s-1)$ denote the subjectively estimated probabilities of these three states of the world. The *expected value theory* applied to this public good game yields the *expected value hypothesis* which says that an individual will contribute if and only if (s)he estimates the probability that her or his contribution will be critical to be sufficiently high. To be more precise, if and only if (s)he estimates $P(s-1) \geq c/(f(s)-c)$ (c denotes the costs for contributing and $f(s)-c$ the value of the public good, cf. table 2.1). A straightforward corollary of this hypothesis is that a positive correlation will exist between the subjectively estimated probability of being critical and the propensity to contribute.

Quite some evidence against the expected value hypothesis as a description of behavior in public good games has been provided in the non-economic literature (e.g.,

---

[4]The application of these hypotheses to the n-person public good game with a step-level production function is quite straightforward. Nevertheless, the structure underlying the present game is more like the chicken game. This structure differs from the prisoners' dilemma game for which the hypotheses were originally developed. In the chicken game as well as in the public good game with a step-level production function, some of the Nash equilibria coincide with the Pareto optimum, allowing for the possibility that both individualists and cooperators focus on the same outcome: the threshold.

Caporael *et al.*, 1989; Dawes *et al.*, 1986; Rapoport, 1988; Suleiman and Rapoport, 1992; Rapoport does support the corollary discussed above, however). The results are typically based on public good games with a step-level production function in which subjects are asked to estimate the probabilities that their contribution will be futile, critical and redundant for the provision of the public good. These estimates are subsequently used to estimate expected net benefits from contributing. A factor which may affect the empirical results of these papers is that subjects lack a (financial) incentive to report their true expectations. This potential pitfall is avoided in the present study where subjects are rewarded for their expectations by an incentive compatible mechanism (cf. chapter 3).

Given these negative empirical results it may be fruitful to consider more general versions of the expected value hypothesis. Two obvious problems of this hypothesis are the following: first, the expected value hypothesis neglects the social aspect of individuals' decisions. It seems reasonable to allow for the possibility that people do care (positively or negatively) for the outcomes for others. Second, the expected value hypothesis may be extended to allow for the possibility that people make errors. People may err when making decisions, especially in cases where the expected benefits from contributing are more or less equal to the expected benefits from not contributing.

To amend the first problem the *expected utility theory* can be used. Again, individuals assign subjective probabilities to the potential future states of the world. Each state of the world yields some utility contingent on the action chosen, but this utility is not necessarily equal to the monetary payoff obtained. According to expected utility theory people choose the action with the highest expected utility.

A common assumption in individual decision making is that an individual's risk-attitude determines her or his utility. Usually individuals are supposed to be risk-averse. To translate such an assumption directly to the present game may be less productive for this study, since the approach neglects the social aspect of the situation. In particular, a theory assuming that utility considerations in public good games are determined by risk-attitudes cannot explain the positive amounts often observed in the one-shot public good game without a threshold, where players have a dominant strategy to contribute nothing at all (cf. Ledyard, 1995).

The public good literature suggests other ways in which individuals might transform the monetary payoff matrix to a different matrix of utilities, transformations which could potentially explain the empirical result mentioned above. The most common assumption seems to be that people care for the consumption or for the utility of other people (e.g., Warr, 1982). In the spirit of this assumption the 'material cooperators' transformation is proposed. *Material cooperators* are assumed to acquire an extra social utility x for the provision of the public good.

Another assumption in the literature is that the act of contributing makes people feel good about themselves. Contributing yields a good feeling or a warm glow (Andreoni, 1990; 1993). In the spirit of this assumption the 'warm-glow cooperators' transformation is proposed. *Warm-glow cooperators* are assumed to acquire an extra social utility y from the act of contributing.

Social identity theory says that individuals strive for a positive self-image, and that they derive their self-image partly from their view on the group to which they belong (cf. Tajfel and Turner, 1986; Taylor and Moghaddam, 1994). Caporael, Dawes, Orbell and van de Kragt (1989) apply social identity theory to the provision of public goods and propose that people contribute in order to reward the own in-group. In the spirit of this explanation the 'in-group cooperators' transformation is proposed. *In-group cooperators* are assumed to acquire an extra social utility z if they are part of the group providing the public good. The corresponding utility matrices are given in table 2.2. Although the term cooperator may suggest otherwise, x, y and z are allowed to be zero or even negative. A priori it is impossible to determine which particular way of introducing a social utility component to the payoff matrix is most fruitful. Experimental results will determine which transformation works best.

These three transformations yield three *expected utility hypotheses*. It is straightforward to show that material cooperators should contribute if and only if they estimate $P(s-1) \geq c/(f(s)-c+x)$, that warm-glow cooperators should contribute if and only if they estimate $P(s-1) \geq (c-y)/(f(s)-c)$ and that in-group cooperators should contribute if and only if they estimate $P(s-1) \geq (c-zP(>s-1))/(f(s)-c+z)$. Thus, for in-group cooperators the decision is not only dependent on $P(s-1)$, but also on one other probability.

The psychological idea that people pursue different goals in public good games can easily be incorporated in the expected utility hypothesis. Consider, for example, the warm-glow cooperators transformation: it could be assumed that one part of the population feels a 'cold prickle' whereas another part feels a 'warm glow' when

Table 2.2
Utility transformations of the payoff matrix

individualists			material cooperators		
others	no	yes	others	no	yes
<s-1	c	0	<s-1	c	0
s-1	c	f(s)-c	s-1	c	f(s)-c+x
>s-1	f(s)	f(s)-c	>s-1	f(s)+x	f(s)-c+x

warm-glow cooperators			in-group cooperators		
others	no	yes	others	no	yes
<s-1	c	0+y	<s-1	c	0
s-1	c	f(s)-c+y	s-1	c	f(s)-c+z
>s-1	f(s)	f(s)-c+y	>s-1	f(s)	f(s)-c+z

Notes: no means not contributing, yes means contributing. The case for individualists who do not transform the payoff matrix is added as a bench-mark.

contributing. That means that a part $p(y_1)$ of the population, for example the part consisting of competitors and individualists, transforms the payoff matrix with the utility component y_1, with $y_1<0$ or $y_1=0$, while the remaining part $1-p(y_1)$, the cooperators, uses utility component y_2, with $y_2>0$. However, it also seems quite possible that more than two homogeneous groups of individuals exist. In the limit case each individual will be allowed to have an own subjective transformation in the empirical estimations of chapter 4.

One problem with both the expected value hypothesis and the expected utility hypothesis is that they do not allow for errors. Under both hypotheses people give best responses to their (given) expectations. This is very demanding if cognitive limitations of the players are taken into account. The concept of quantal response allows individuals to make errors (Luce, 1959; McFadden, 1974; 1976; McKelvey and Palfrey, 1995). Let $E(\pi_j)$ denote the expected payoff for choosing feasible action j ($j=1,..,J$); U_j denotes the disturbed expected payoff of action j; the error vector

$\epsilon=(\epsilon_1,..,\epsilon_J)$ is distributed according to a joint distribution with density function $f(\epsilon)$. Then,

$$U_j = E(\pi_j) + \epsilon_j \; . \tag{2.1}$$

People choose action j for which U_j is maximized. If the expected payoffs in equation 2.1 represent the expected (monetary) values of various actions, it is said that the individual chooses in accordance with *expected value with noise theory*. If the expected payoffs in equation 2.1 represent the expected utilities, it is said that the individual chooses in accordance with *expected utility with noise theory*. In both cases the individual makes a quantal response. A particular class of quantal responses is obtained if assumptions about the distribution of the error terms are made. McFadden (1974) discusses the close correspondence between the expected utility approach and the logistic quantal response. Assume that the values ϵ_j are independently identically distributed according to the extreme value type I distribution:

$$P(\epsilon_j \leq \epsilon) = e^{-e^{-\lambda\epsilon-\gamma}} \; . \tag{2.2}$$

In the present public good game each individual chooses between either contributing ($j=c$) or not contributing ($j=nc$). With extreme value distributed error terms an individual will give a logistic quantal response. (S)he will contribute with probability p_c, such that:

$$p_c = \frac{e^{\lambda E(\pi_c)}}{e^{\lambda E(\pi_c)} + e^{\lambda E(\pi_{nc})}} = \frac{1}{1 + e^{\lambda(E(\pi_{nc})-E(\pi_c))}} \; . \tag{2.3}$$

McFadden (1974) and Maddala (1983) prove this result for the specific extreme value distribution with $\lambda=1$ and $\gamma=0$. The proof for the general case is similar. Parameter λ affects the quantal response as described in equation 2.3 and parameter γ cancels out.[5] The parameter λ can be interpreted as the level of precision or the level of rationality of the person. If λ equals zero, a person chooses each alternative with probability ½, independent of the expected payoffs. If λ approaches ∞, the individual chooses the alternative with the higher expected payoff (utility) with probability

[5]The quantal response function can easily be adapted to allow for more than two alternatives.

approaching 1. A higher λ corresponds to a higher level of precision. Individuals make errors with an increasing probability if the difference in expected payoff between the alternatives decreases and vice versa.

According to the *expected value with noise hypothesis* people give a (logistic) quantal response on the basis of the expected values of the two alternatives:

$$p_c = \frac{1}{1 + e^{\lambda\,[c-(f(s)-c)*P(s-1)]}} \quad . \qquad 2.4$$

Palfrey and Prisbey (1993) advocate such a hypothesis to explain positive contribution levels observed experimentally in a different type of public good games, public good games without a threshold. In such public good games expected value maximizing behavior is at a corner of the action-space: players maximize expected value if and only if they contribute nothing, whatever their beliefs about the behavior of other players are (in the one-shot game). Palfrey and Prisbey argue that positive contribution levels observed in such games may be due to random error but interpreted falsely as altruism as a result of the institutional setting. The only possible error is to contribute, which may be falsely interpreted as altruism.

According to the *expected utility with noise hypothesis* people give a quantal response on the basis of the expected utilities of the alternatives. It is assumed that utilities take one of the three forms proposed in table 2.2. For example, if people transform the payoff matrix as warm-glow cooperators, they will contribute with probability:

$$p_c = \frac{1}{1 + e^{\lambda\,[c-y-(f(s)-c)*P(s-1)]}} \quad . \qquad 2.5$$

Andreoni (1995b) favors such a hypothesis. He concludes from experiments that both kindness and confusion play a role in determining people's behavior in public good settings. Table 2.3 provides a summary of the decision rules discussed.

For the economic hypotheses a trade-off between parsimony and fit will have to be made. For example, the expected value hypothesis is more parsimonious than the expected value with noise hypothesis, which in turn is more parsimonious than the expected utility with noise hypothesis. At the same time, the expected utility with noise

Table 2.3
Summary of proposed decision rules

Psychological Hypotheses: value orientations play a role

behavior ⇒ expectations	expectations ⇒ behavior
false consensus	**triangle**

Economic Hypotheses: expectations ⇒ behavior

	no utility transformations, value orientations do not play a role	utility transformations, value orientations may play a role
no noise	**expected value**	**material cooperators warm-glow cooperators ⇒ expected utility in-group cooperators**
noise	**expected value with noise**	**material cooperators warm-glow cooperators ⇒ expected utility in-group cooperators with noise**

hypothesis necessarily gives a fit of the data at least as good as the expected value with noise hypothesis, which in turn gives a fit at least as good as the expected value hypothesis. Whether an increase in the fit of the data is worth the decrease in parsimony of the theory will be determined as much as possible by statistical measures.[6]

A straight comparison of the predictive power of psychological and economic hypotheses is not possible, because the former hypotheses primarily make qualitative

[6]Two other forces may drive individual decision-making. The first is that people may choose on the basis of fairness or reciprocity, its more specific representative. In that case people do not care about other people or do not feel a warm glow when they contribute, but they want to comply to a norm. Sometimes this is operationalized by the assumption that people try to match the (average) contribution level of others. Although the concept of fairness is clearly distinct from the concept of utility-interdependency proposed above, it is very hard to distinguish between these explanations at an empirical level. Here the approach of utility-interdependency is chosen, because that approach is closer to the traditional economic approach and to the psychological concept of value orientations.

The other force comes from evolutionary models and could be labelled the Pavlov-hypothesis (cf. Nowak and Sigmund, 1993). According to this hypothesis individuals tend to repeat successful choices and abandon unsuccessful choices. In section 2.4.2 a learning model based on this idea will be discussed.

predictions. Nevertheless, important aspects of psychological hypotheses will be tested (in isolation) in chapter 4 and, as already noted above, some of the psychological ideas may be incorporated in a more quantitative frame-work. The concept of value orientations can not only be used in economic hypotheses about decision rules, but also in a game theoretic framework analyzing decision rules and expectations simultaneously, as will be seen in section 2.3.2.

2.2.2 Do expectations cause decisions or vice versa?

A conceptual difference between the false consensus hypothesis and the other hypotheses concerns the idea about the causality in the relationship between expectations and choices. According to the false consensus hypothesis, the orientation determines behavior, and behavior determines the expectations about others' behavior. According to the other hypotheses behavior is determined by expectations.

The experimental evidence regarding the causal direction between expectations and behavior, as tested in prisoners' dilemmas, is mixed: some studies show that (manipulated) expectations can affect choices (e.g., Messick *et al.*, 1983). Other studies show that projection and justification are sometimes a source via which behavior affects expectations (e.g., Messé and Sivacek, 1979; Yamagishi and Sato, 1986).

According to the false consensus hypothesis the fact that a decision-maker makes a choice narrows her or his view of the world. (S)he makes a choice and reasons that there is no solid ground to conclude that other people would make a different choice. An impartial spectator would not be bothered by the false consensus effect, because (s)he does not make the choice which causes the narrow view. Therefore, a decision-maker would be more confident of her or his beliefs than a spectator would be if they were in a similar position. Such a difference in confidence would not be expected if one of the other hypotheses gives the true description of the world. Thus, a comparison of these confidence levels may shine light on the question whether expectations affect decisions or vice versa. Dawes, McTavish and Shaklee (1977) develop a procedure to investigate experimentally whether decision-makers are more confident than spectators. They find the surprising result that the confidence level of decision-makers is *less* than that of spectators. A similar procedure is implemented in one of the experiments reported in chapter 4 to see whether this result can be replicated.

2.2.3 Environments with positive versus environments with negative externalities

A problem related to public good provision is public bad prevention. In public bad games individuals can withdraw resources from a common pool (e.g., whales from the ocean). For an individual it may be advantageous to harvest a lot, but this yields negative externalities for others (whales become extinct). Public bad prevention has usually been studied in different institutional settings than public good provision. For example, a common pool resource game (for an overview, see Ostrom *et al.*, 1994) is often played as a game with many periods in which the size of the common pool is determined by its size in the last period, minus the resources taken away by the individuals and then multiplied by some known factor. A curious aspect suggested by empirical work is that individuals seem to behave more cooperatively in public good games than in experiments with negative externalities such as oligopoly experiments or common pool resource games (Andreoni 1995a, 1995b). However, as long as differences exist in the institutional setting of public good and public bad problems, it is difficult to draw hard conclusions about behavior. From a theoretical perspective, the problem of preventing a public bad can be made strategically equivalent to the problem of providing a public good.

Framing effects as such have been very popular in psychological research since the seventies. Two theories about framing effects in different areas of research are adapted to derive predictions for the particular public good and public bad game studied here: prospect theory and Pruitt's hypothesis. A well-known theory in this area is Kahneman and Tversky's (1979) prospect theory. Prospect theory describes individual decision making under risk. Its central thesis is that an individual evaluates alternatives with respect to a (subjective) reference point. Outcomes smaller than this reference point are framed as losses and outcomes greater are framed as gains. The individual's utility function is steeper for losses than for gains. Moreover, the utility function is convex for losses and concave for gains. This means that the subjective disutility of a loss is greater than the subjective utility of a gain of the same magnitude. Prospect theory has been shown to make quite accurate predictions in individual decision problems (e.g., Harless and Camerer, 1994). A disadvantage of applying prospect theory to public good situations may be that prospect theory does not take the social aspect of the situation into account. Raub and Snijders (1995) provide a rigorous application of prospect theory on n-person prisoners' dilemmas.

In a social situation like a public good game or a public bad game it is not immediately clear what the prediction of prospect theory will be. Establishing the reference points is not straightforward. An intuitively appealing possibility is that the money contributed to a public good game is perceived as a loss and the money taken in a public bad game is perceived as a gain. In that case, one would expect fewer cooperative decisions in the public good game than in the public bad game.[7]

Pruitt (1967; 1970; 1981) developed an hypothesis about the effects of framing in a prisoners' dilemma game. This hypothesis is connected with the goal-expectation theory (Pruitt and Kimmel, 1977) about cooperation in a prisoners' dilemma game. The goal-expectation theory formulates two necessary conditions for a cooperative choice: the goal of mutual cooperation and the expectation that the other player will also cooperate. Pruitt (1967, 1970) presented subjects with different decompositions of a prisoners' dilemma in which the cooperative behavior was either giving money (equivalent to a public good game), or not-taking money (equivalent to public bad game). In his studies subjects turned out to be more cooperative in the giving decomposition than in the taking decomposition. Pruitt's hypothesis is that subjects in the giving decomposition will see the game as one in which they have more influence on each other's payoffs and in which they are more interdependent than in the taking decomposition. This perception of the game enhances the goal of mutual cooperation in the giving case and causes higher cooperation rates.

Pruitt's hypothesis is about framing in a prisoners' dilemma game and cannot be applied directly to the n-person public good and public bad games studied here (which resemble chicken games). Nevertheless, a prediction in line with Pruitt's hypothesis would be that more cooperative choices will be made in a public good than in a public bad game. According to Pruitt the public good frame will elicit a higher desire for mutual cooperation then the public bad frame. A loose translation of this hypothesis to the expected utility approach would imply that the public good frame triggers higher values for x in the material cooperators transformation than the public bad frame. A related explanation states that the public good frame triggers warm glow while the public bad frame triggers cold prickle (i.e., the public good frame triggers a higher value for y for the warm-glow cooperators transformation than the public bad frame, cf. Andreoni, 1995a).

---

[7]This holds if the utility function is (almost) linear at both sides of the reference point and if it is steeper for losses than for gains.

Several social psychological studies about framing effects in social dilemmas have been carried out in a different setting than the present with symmetric step-level production function (Komorita, 1987; Komorita and Barth, 1985; Komorita and Carnevale, 1992; Van Dijk and Wilke 1995). Often, it is found that subjects cooperate more in public good (or give some) type of games and less in public bad (or take some) type of games, but the evidence is not completely consistent (cf. Brewer and Kramer, 1986 for a counter-example). In chapter 4 it will be investigated whether framing effects occur in public good games with a step-level production function, and if so, which theory explains the observations best.[8]

2.3 Game theoretic models

Game theory focuses on equilibrium conditions and characteristics of equilibrium. It is often used to analyze expectations and decision rules simultaneously. Game theoretic assumptions about the decision rule are drawn from the expected utility approach. Players' expectations about other players' behavior are required to satisfy a condition in order to be in equilibrium: players have expectations consistent with actual behavior.[9] In that case behavior is in equilibrium as well. The assumptions about decision rules and expectations are sufficient to derive equilibrium predictions for any particular institutional setting. It is useful to distinguish between static and dynamic game theoretic models. Static game theoretic predictions do not depend on the history of play. Game theoretic players will choose an action without considering available information about the history of the game. These models are especially applicable in environments where players play a game only once, or where they play a game

---

[8]The explanations of the potential framing effects proposed here treat expectations as given. Expectations may be endogenized in simple settings. For example, the explanation that material cooperators attach a different level of utility in the two frames can be incorporated in a game theoretic analysis as well as in a belief learning model, as will become clear in the next sections.

[9]Sometimes a Nash equilibrium is referred to as a rational expectations equilibrium (e.g., Nyarko *et al.*, 1994). In the game theoretic models to be described in this chapter (as well as in many other game theoretic models) players are assumed to have the same accurate expectations about the behavior of a third player. It is acknowledged that differences in private information may lead to differences in beliefs about the behavior of a third player, even if players have a common prior distribution (e.g., Aumann and Brandenburger, 1995).

repeatedly but with different players all the time. Dynamic game theoretic models allow players to make their strategies contingent on the development of the game over time. These models are especially applicable in environments where players play a game repeatedly with the same players.[10]

In this section static game theoretic models are presented describing the interaction of the players of public good games with a step-level production function. First, the Nash equilibria for homogeneous individuals with complete information are discussed. Second, the analysis is extended to allow for more than one type of individual. The psychological ideas about value orientations are taken seriously by the introduction of individualists and cooperators in the game. In these types of models players will have incomplete information about the distribution of types of players. Third, the concept of quantal response equilibria proposed by McKelvey and Palfrey (1995) is applied to allow players to make errors.

2.3.1 Game theory: homogenous individuals

The analysis in this section assumes that players are expected value maximizers who do not transform the payoff matrix. This analysis for homogeneous individuals is an extension of the analysis of Gradstein and Nitzan (1990) who study the setting where the quantity of the public good provided increases with each additional contribution. For homogeneous 'individualists' the payoff matrix coincides with the utilities matrix (cf. table 2.2). For the provision of public goods with a step-level production function numerous equilibria exist. First, equilibria in pure strategies are discussed and then attention is drawn to equilibria in mixed strategies. Recall that s denotes the threshold, that c denotes the costs for contributing and that $f(s)-c$ denotes the value of the public good. For simplicity assume: $f(s) > 2c$ (otherwise not contributing is a dominant strategy) and $s > 1$. A first Nash equilibrium is obtained if nobody contributes. Given that other players do not contribute, a player's own contribution (with irreversible costs) is not sufficient to provide the public good.

Furthermore, $\binom{n}{s}$ different Nash equilibria exist where exactly s players

---

[10]Dynamic modelling also proves valuable if only one of the players plays the game repeatedly and opponents observe this player's former actions. A well-known example is Kreps and Wilson's reputation building model for the chain-store game with incomplete information (Kreps and Wilson, 1982). In this game the (constant) monopolist may try to build a reputation for being tough to deter (different) potential entrants.

contribute. Note that a contributor does not have an incentive to deviate from her or his strategy, because (given the others' choices) a switch to non-contribution would prevent the public good being provided. Furthermore, a non-contributor does not have an incentive to deviate to contributing, because the public good is provided anyway.

These are the only pure strategy equilibria: if there are more than s contributors, at least one contributor has an incentive to withdraw her or his contribution, because this contribution is not needed to obtain the public good. If there are fewer than s but more than 0 contributors, contributors have an incentive to withdraw their contribution because their contribution is futile.

Since the players are not allowed to communicate and since they have to decide simultaneously, they face a huge coordination problem: they do not know in advance on which equilibrium others will focus. The prediction of a game theoretic model with multiple equilibria is not clear. The present public good game shares this problem with many other games. One may pursue an empirical or a theoretical solution for this problem.

The empirical solution accepts the presence of multiple equilibria as a given. It posits that experimental work may provide insight in the question whether actual players manage to coordinate their actions implicitly, and if so, which equilibrium tends to be selected (Smith, 1989). The theoretical solution selects between the equilibria on the basis of refinement criteria. Some equilibria may intuitively be more appealing to players than others.

A first criterium selects between the equilibria on the basis of *symmetry*. Given that it is impossible to implement a schedule describing who should and who should not contribute to the public good, players may discard asymmetric equilibria a priori. This criterium gets rid of the $\binom{n}{s}$ pure strategies equilibria where s of the n players contribute. The equilibrium where nobody contributes survives this refinement criterium. However, it is also possible that players focus on a Nash equilibrium in symmetric *mixed* strategies. Such an equilibrium occurs if all players contribute with the same probability p such that:

$$\binom{n-1}{s-1} p^{s-1} (1-p)^{n-s} (f(s)-c) = c \ . \qquad 2.6$$

In cases where the contribution of an individual is not critical for the provision of the public good, (s)he is better off if (s)he does not contribute ($f(s) > f(s)-c$ and $c > 0$). The contribution of an individual is critical if and only if $s-1$ of the other $n-1$ players contribute. If all individuals contribute with equal probability p such that equation 2.6 holds, the expected value of contributing is the same as the expected value of not contributing for all players. Thus, the individuals are indifferent between contributing and not contributing and a Nash equilibrium in symmetric mixed strategies is obtained.[11] Theorem 2.1 provides the conditions for which two symmetric mixed strategies equilibria exist with $0 < p < 1$. The situation is shown in figure 2.1, below. The criterium of symmetry is not sufficient to obtain a unique selection of the Nash equilibria.

Theorem 2.1

Assume that $s > 1$ and $n > s$. Let p_0^* represent the symmetric equilibrium where nobody contributes (i.e., $p_0^*=0$). If

$$\binom{n-1}{s-1} \left(\frac{s-1}{n-1}\right)^{s-1} \left(1-\frac{s-1}{n-1}\right)^{n-s} > \frac{c}{f(s)-c}, \qquad 2.7$$

two positive mixed strategies equilibria p_1^* and p_2^* with $0 < p_1^* < p_2^* < 1$ exist. In that case p_2^* yields a higher expected payoff than p_1^*, and p_1^* yields a higher expected payoff than p_0^*. □

Proofs of the theorems and lemmas in this chapter are presented in appendix A.

A second criterium to select between the three surviving symmetric equilibria is *payoff dominance* (cf. Harsanyi, 1977). According to this criterium players will focus on the equilibrium with the highest expected payoff. The three symmetric equilibria are univocally ranked by this criterium, as described in theorem 2.1. The symmetric mixed strategy with the highest contribution probability is the unique equilibrium surviving the two criteria. This seems to be the most appealing equilibrium from a theoretical perspective.

---

[11]It can also be shown that asymmetric equilibria exist with some players contributing, some players not contributing and the rest of the players randomizing with positive probability (cf. Gradstein and Nitzan, 1990, footnote 5).

Game theoretic models may also be judged in their ability to predict changes in behavior as a result of changes in the environment. Here, the effects of three different environmental changes will be considered: a change in the value of the public good, a change in group-size and a change in the variability of the group-composition.

Intuitively, one would expect that an increase in the value of the public good (ceteris paribus) would increase the individual propensity to contribute. This is a formal game theoretic result:

Theorem 2.2

Assume that $s>1$ and $n>s$ and that inequality 2.7 holds. If players focus on the payoff dominant symmetric equilibrium p_2^*, an increase in the value of the public good (or similarly, a decrease in the costs of contributing) will yield an increase in the probability of contributing. □

The proof of theorem 2.2 follows immediately from figure 2.1, and is omitted from Appendix A. Figure 2.1 displays the probability of being critical as a function of p for

Figure 2.1
Mixed strategies for homogeneous individuals

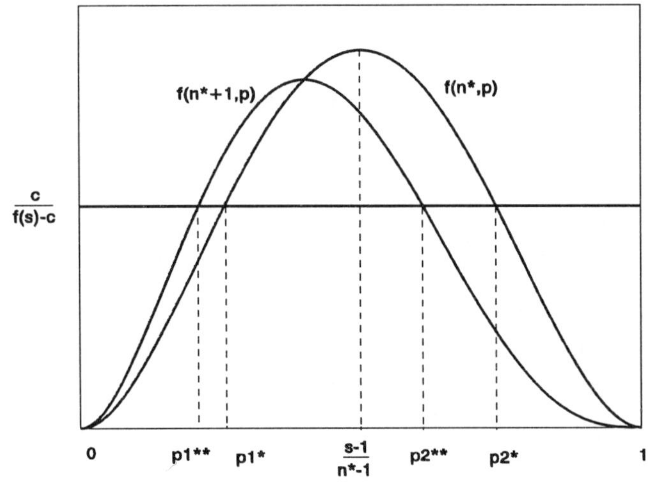

Note: $f(n^*,p)$ denotes the probability of being critical as function of contribution probability p at group-size n^*.

varying group-size. The intersections of these functions with the horizontal line $y = \frac{c}{f(s)-c}$ yield the mixed strategies equilibria for fixed group-size. An increase of the value of the public good causes a decrease of $\frac{c}{f(s)-c}$. This results in an upward shift of the payoff dominant equilibrium p_2^*: if players focus on the payoff dominant symmetric equilibrium, an increase in the value of the public good yields an increase in the equilibrium probability of contributing. However, this is not a very robust result: if players focus on the other mixed strategy equilibrium $p_1^*(>0)$, an increase in the value yields a downward shift of the equilibrium probability. In that case the opposite effect results.

Another effect which might be expected intuitively is that increasing group-size (ceteris paribus) would diminish the individual propensity to contribute. Figure 2.1 shows that the symmetric mixed strategies equilibria both shift to the left for increasing group-size. The model predicts that an increase in group-size will diminish the individual propensity to contribute, as can be seen in theorem 2.3.

Theorem 2.3

Assume that $s>1$ and $n^*>s$. If p_1^* (p_1^{**}) and p_2^* (p_2^{**}) with $0<p_1^*<p_2^*<1$ represent the two mixed strategies equilibria when the number of players is equal to n^* (n^*+1), then $p_1^{**}<p_1^*$ and $p_2^{**}<p_2^*$ (if p_1^{**} and p_2^{**} exist). □

A final effect considers the variability of the group-composition. One might expect that players will be more likely to contribute to public goods in environments where the composition of the group remains constant than in environments where the composition of the group changes all the time. However, this cannot be argued formally on the basis of the present static model. As noted above, this model is more appropriate to describe the interaction of players in environments with changing groups than in environments with constant groups. Environments with constant groups are better described by a dynamic game theoretic model. Here, the discussion is limited to an informal dynamic game theoretic argument.

In constant environments players might want to build a reputation of being (conditionally) cooperative in order to elicit cooperative choices by other group-members. Such strategic reasoning does not make sense in environments where the composition of the group changes all the time. Whether the variability of the group-composition affects individual behavior has been investigated experimentally in public good games without a threshold. The experimental results are not consistent. Andreoni (1988) finds the surprising result that subjects contribute *more* in changing than in constant groups. Weimann (1994) is not able to replicate this result. In his experiment subjects contribute on average as much in changing groups as in constant groups.

The effects of changes in the environment of the public good will be assessed in the experiments reported in chapter 4.[12]

2.3.2 Game theory: heterogeneous individuals

The social psychological concept of value orientations can be incorporated in a game theoretic analysis. Players may be allowed to have different preferences in the public good game. The interaction is modelled as a game with incomplete information. Players do not know the types of the other players with certainty. Such an assumption seems reasonable in environments where players enter a game anonymously.

The game theoretic analysis for the case of heterogeneous players is tedious. Therefore, the subject of this section does not get exhaustive treatment. A more elaborate discussion is provided in Offerman (1994). The purpose of the analysis is to give an idea of the type of results and problems which are encountered when heterogeneous players are introduced in the game. Only theorem 2.6 is quite general in its scope since it holds for all three different utility transformations discussed in section 2.2.1. The rest of the analysis is restricted to the case where all players transform the payoff matrix as material cooperators. As discussed, this may be the most common assumption in economic models.[13] For a start, it is assumed that the population can be divided into two internally homogeneous groups of individuals. Although the players receive the same amount of money if the public good is provided, they generate different utility levels from this amount. Members of the group which

---

[12]The question whether an increase in the threshold yields an increase in contributions and/or an increase in the frequency the public good is actually provided is investigated experimentally in Dawes *et al.* (1986), Isaac *et al.* (1988), Kerr (1989), Palfrey and Rosenthal (1991) and Suleiman and Rapoport (1992). Often it is found that an increase of the threshold elicits more contributions but decreases the frequency that the public good is provided. The evidence is not completely consistent (see Ledyard, 1995 for a comprehensive overview).

[13]For comparison, Palfrey and Rosenthal (1988) model the altruism component as proposed by the warm-glow transformation: individuals acquire utility from the act of contributing.

acquires the higher level of utility are referred to as cooperators and the others are referred to as individualists:

$$f_c(s) > f_i(s) \ . \tag{2.8}$$

It is assumed that individuals know their own type with certainty and have consistent expectations about the types of the others. Specifically, each individual assigns a probability q to the event that an arbitrary other individual is a cooperator and a probability $1\text{-}q$ to the event that this individual is an individualist. q is contained in the common knowledge of the players. If $f_i(s) > 2c$ and $s > 1$, then the same equilibria in pure strategies as in section 2.3.1 can be derived: one Nash equilibrium results if nobody contributes and $\binom{n}{s}$ different Nash equilibria exist with exactly s contributors.

The analysis differs for the equilibria in mixed strategies. The focus will be restricted to 'within group symmetric' equilibria. Assume that individualists contribute with probability p_1 and cooperators contribute with probability p_2. The probability of being critical is the same for all individuals and equal to:

$$P(s-1) = \sum_{k=0}^{n-1} \left(\binom{n-1}{k} q^k (1-q)^{(n-k-1)} * \sum_{i=0}^{\min(s-1,n-k-1)} \binom{n-k-1}{i} p_1^i (1-p_1)^{(n-k-i-1)} \binom{k}{s-i-1} p_2^{(s-i-1)} (1-p_2)^{(k-s+i+1)} \right) . \tag{2.9}$$

For given q, n, and s this probability is a polynomial in p_1 and p_2. If $0 < p_1 < 1$, then for a Bayesian Nash equilibrium it is required that:

$$P(s-1) * (f_i(s) - c) = c. \tag{2.10}$$

And if $0 < p_2 < 1$, then for such an equilibrium to evolve it is required that:

$$P(s-1) * (f_c(s) - c) = c \ . \tag{2.11}$$

In total, nine combinations of mixed strategies can be distinguished (cf. table 2.4). It is not difficult to see that cases 4, 5, 7 and 8 cannot occur, however. For example, in case 5 equations 2.8, 2.10 and 2.11 should hold simultaneously, yielding an inconsistent set of equations. Furthermore, cases 1, 3 and 9 degenerate to equilibria in pure strategies. Cases 2 and 6 represent the more interesting cases.

Table 2.4
Possible combinations of individualists' and cooperators' mixed strategies

	$p_2 = 0$	$0 < p_2 < 1$	$p_2 = 1$
$p_1 = 0$	case 1	case 2	case 3
$0 < p_1 < 1$	case 4 X	case 5 X	case 6
$p_1 = 1$	case 7 X	case 8 X	case 9

case 6: $0<p_1<1$ and $p_2=1$.
The Bayesian Nash equilibrium where (material) individualists contribute with probability p_1 and (material) cooperators contribute for sure is realized if the following condition is fulfilled:

$$\sum_{k=0}^{s-1} \binom{n-1}{k} q^k(1-q)^{(n-k-1)} \binom{n-k-1}{s-k-1} p_1^{(s-k-1)}(1-p_1)^{(n-s)} *(f_i(s)-c) = c \qquad 2.12$$

Theorem 2.4
Sufficient, although not necessary conditions for the uniqueness of the Bayesian Nash equilibrium in case 6 are:

$$\frac{q^{(s-1)}}{(1-q)} > \frac{(s-1)}{(n-s)} \qquad 2.13$$

$$f_i(s) > \frac{c}{\binom{n-1}{s-1} q^{s-1} (1-q)^{(n-s)}} + c \qquad 2.14$$

$$s < n; \quad 0 < q < 1 \, . \qquad 2.15$$

□

Thus, if these conditions hold, there is only one value of p_1 for which a Bayesian Nash equilibrium exists as described in case 6.

Corollary 2.1

If the conditions stated in theorem 2.4 hold, the equilibrium probability of contribution in case 6 is decreasing in c, or $d(p_1)/d(c) < 0$, and increasing in $f_i(s)$, or $d(p_1)/d(f_i(s)) > 0$.

□

case 2: $p_1 = 0$ and $0 < p_2 < 1$.

The Bayesian Nash equilibrium where (material) individualists do not contribute and (material) cooperators contribute with probability p_2 occurs if the following condition holds:

$$\sum_{k=s-1}^{n-1} \binom{n-1}{k} q^k (1-q)^{(n-k-1)} \binom{k}{s-1} p_2^{(s-1)} (1-p_2)^{(k-s+1)} * (f_c(s)-c) = c \;. \qquad 2.16$$

Theorem 2.5

Sufficient, although not necessary conditions for the uniqueness of the Bayesian Nash equilibrium in case 2 are:

$$\frac{(1-q)^{(n-s+1)}}{q} > \frac{(n-s)}{(s-1)} \qquad 2.17$$

$$f_c(s) > \frac{c}{\binom{n-1}{s-1} q^{s-1} (1-q)^{(n-s)}} + c \qquad 2.18$$

$$0 < q < 1; \quad s > 1 \;. \qquad 2.19$$

□

Thus, if these conditions hold, there is only one value of p_2 for which a Bayesian Nash equilibrium exists as described in case 2.

Corollary 2.2

If the conditions stated in theorem 2.5 hold, the equilibrium probability of contribution in case 2 is increasing in c, or $d(p_2)/d(c) > 0$, and decreasing in $f_c(s)$, or

$d(p_2)/d(f_c(s))<0.$ □

Note that corollary 2.1 and 2.2 make opposite predictions. Corollary 2.1 makes the intuitive prediction: an increase in the value of the public good or a decrease in the costs for contributing may be expected to have a positive effect on individuals' inclination to contribute.

The effect of increasing group-size is not clear-cut if two types of individuals are present because of the complex form of the first derivative of the polynomials in p_1 and p_2. Nevertheless, from a mathematical point of view the model with two types of individuals has the advantage over the model with homogeneous individuals that conditions for the uniqueness of the mixed strategies equilibrium can be derived, whereas the latter model generally yields two mixed strategy equilibria with positive probability of contributing, as can be easily seen in figure 2.1.

The more general case arises when m $(2<m\leq n)$ types of individuals are allowed in the game theoretic analysis. In this setting it is assumed that the common knowledge of the players includes consistent estimates of the payoffs to the other players besides the knowledge of the own payoff. Furthermore, players estimate the probability that an arbitrary other individual belongs to a particular type consistently. And of course, players know the values for s, n and c for sure.[14]

Theorem 2.6

If there are m different types of individuals who all use the same transformation of the utility matrix (either all players are material cooperators, or all players are warm-glow cooperators, or all players are in-group cooperators), assimilation of behavior will be the result. In a Bayesian Nash equilibrium at most one type of player will randomize. All players with a smaller social utility component than this randomizing type will not contribute and all players with a greater social utility component will contribute for sure. □

---

[14]Palfrey and Rosenthal (1988) follow a different approach: they assume a continuous common prior on the altruism component which is contained in the common knowledge of the players. Heckman and Singer (1984) argue that results may be sensitive to the particular choice of a distribution. They favor a non-parametric approach like the one chosen here if there are no compelling theoretical arguments for a particular parametric distribution.

In this setting players' beliefs are not type specific. Therefore, all players make the same predictions that their contribution will be critical, redundant or futile. For the randomizing type of individuals, the expected benefits from contributing are equal to the expected costs. For types with a smaller social utility component (than the social utility component of the randomizing type) the expected costs from contributing will exceed the expected benefits. Thus, they will not contribute. For types with a greater social utility component the expected benefits from contributing will exceed the expected costs. This induces them to contribute.

The players of such a game face a twofold coordination problem. First, it may be impossible to establish ex ante which type of player should randomize. Second, it is not certain whether a unique probability exists for the randomizers. Although this model seems to be more plausible than former models on the voluntary provision of public goods in the sense that it allows for differences in preferences, a serious drawback is that the coordination problem of the players is not solved but severed.

Another obvious drawback is that the model requires more rationality of the players than may be assumed to be realistic. It would be interesting to allow players to make errors. This approach is proposed in the next section, where McKelvey and Palfrey's concept of Quantal Response Equilibria is used to model the interaction of homogeneous players in public good games with step-level production functions.

2.3.3 Game theory: Quantal Response Equilibria

The (static) concept of Quantal Response Equilibrium is based on two ideas. The first concerns the decision rule used by players: players are assumed to give quantal responses to their expectations about the behavior of other players. They tend to choose the alternative with the higher expected value (utility), but their decisions are prone to error (cf. section 2.2.1). The second idea concerns the expectations players have about other players. On average players have consistent estimates of the quantal responses of other players. A Quantal Response Equilibrium is a fixed point of this process. This process defines a noisy equilibrium with a connection to the literature on 'purification' of Nash equilibria for example (see McKelvey and Palfrey, 1995 for a discussion).

A major contribution of McKelvey and Palfrey's equilibrium concept is that it provides an elegant solution to the zero-likelihood problem which has bothered empirical work using (many of the) traditional game theoretic concepts. The introduction of the probability of an error makes every outcome in the game possible. This is of great help in applied empirical work where, strictly speaking, a game theoretic model has to be rejected even if a non-equilibrium state of the world is observed only once in a thousand times.

Just like many other equilibrium concepts, this concept of Quantal Response Equilibrium has the problem that it potentially gives rise to multiple equilibria. For many games the concept defines multiple 'branches' or 'paths' as functions of the level of rationality λ. This is also the case in the public good game with a step-level production function. One way to select between the equilibria is to focus on symmetric equilibria only.[15] In a symmetric Quantal Response Equilibrium each individual contributes with probability p_c, and expects that each other individual in the group will contribute with the same probability p_c. An individual with rational expectations estimates the probability that her or his contribution will be critical as:

$$P(s-1) = \binom{n-1}{s-1} p_c^{s-1} (1-p_c)^{n-s} . \qquad 2.20$$

This belief is inserted in the decision rule described by equation 2.4. In a logistic symmetric equilibrium players will contribute with probability:

$$p_c = \frac{1}{1 + e^{\lambda * [c - (f(s)-c) * \binom{n-1}{s-1} p_c^{s-1} (1-p_c)^{n-s}]}} . \qquad 2.21$$

The solution of this equation can be obtained numerically for each λ.[16] The equation yields one, two or three solutions dependent on the parameters of the game and the value of λ (cf. figures 5.1-5.3 in chapter 5). If λ approaches ∞ and if convergence takes place, the Quantal Response Equilibria can be shown to approach the Nash equilibria of the underlying game (cf. McKelvey and Palfrey, 1995, theorem 2).

---

[15]McKelvey and Palfrey (1995) prove that for almost all games there is a unique branch which starts at the centroid for $\lambda = 0$ and converges to a unique Nash equilibrium as λ approaches ∞ (third property of theorem 3). This branch may also serve as a selection criterion.

[16]Here, it is assumed that players give quantal responses on the basis of the payoff matrix. Theoretically, the analysis could easily be adapted to allow for utility transformations of the payoff matrix. For example, the logistic equilibrium for homogeneous warm-glow cooperators is obtained by inserting equation 2.20 in equation 2.5.

A clear conceptual advantage of the Quantal Response Equilibrium over the equilibrium concepts used in the former sections is that it allows players to err in quite a plausible way. Nevertheless, the introduction of error is not without costs. This concept shifts cognitive burden from the decision rule to the expectation formation process. When forming expectations about other players' choices, players not only have to deduce best responses for the other players, but they also have to anticipate that these others give noisy best responses (like they do themselves). The process according to which real world players could obtain these equilibrium expectations is not clear. The next section describes some belief learning models which may give a more intuitive account of the expectation formation process.

An important feature of the game theoretic models is that *in equilibrium expectations about other group-members' behavior are consistent with reality*. For example, in the model where expected value maximizers play a symmetric mixed strategies equilibrium with positive contribution probability, players' beliefs would be characterized by the binomial distribution based on the true probability of contributing. For empirical work one may want to replace this assumption by a weaker version which says that players' beliefs should not suffer from systematic errors.

This does not imply that static game theoretic models assume that players' expectations remain constant across plays in subsequent plays of a one-shot game. In such a setting players play exactly the same game repeatedly, but they are grouped with different players all the time. Public good games with step-level production functions possess multiple equilibria. It may be that in one period players focus on one equilibrium and in another period on another.[17] It is important to note, however, that the static game theoretic models proposed here do not positively predict any specific updating pattern in expectations across periods. This contrasts with belief learning models which predict a very specific pattern in the expectations across periods, as will be seen in the next section.

The static game theoretic models considered in this section neglect the possibility that

[17]Nevertheless, in some instances one might expect constant expectations across subsequent plays of a one-shot game. If homogeneous players focus on the payoff dominant symmetric equilibrium in each play, their expectations will not be adapted across plays.

players' strategies are history dependent. This neglect may not be innocent, especially in games where a constant group of players plays a game repeatedly. In principle, it is possible to develop dynamic game theoretic models which allow players to make their strategies contingent on former outcomes of the game. The most obvious equilibrium of the repeated game is the repeated play of one of the Nash equilibria of the static game. However, the number of equilibria is considerably greater in the repeated game than in the one-shot game. For example, all kinds of cross-overs are possible: if players play a different static equilibrium in each period, they play according to a Nash equilibrium of the repeated game. Furthermore, in the repeated game trigger strategies become possible (cf. Gibbons, 1992). The number of Nash equilibria will increase enormously if the static models are turned into dynamic models. As a consequence, the coordination problem would be exacerbated considerably and the cognitive demands for the players would increase enormously. It may be more fruitful to consider simple alternatives first.

2.4 Learning models

Dissatisfaction with the plausibility or predictive power of game theoretic models has given rise to the development of learning models (e.g., Milgrom and Roberts, 1991). In this section two types of learning are discussed. The first type is belief learning. Belief learning models usually maintain the game theoretic assumption that players give (noisy) best responses to their expectations, but they drop the game theoretic assumption that expectations are (immediately) in equilibrium. According to belief learning models, expectations are formed adaptively. Players use observation on others' former play to form expectations about others' future play.

The second type of learning is reinforcement learning. Reinforcement learning models assume an even lower level of rationality for players. These models drop both the game theoretic assumption that people give (noisy) best responses and the game theoretic assumption that expectations are in equilibrium. In fact, players' expectations about other players' behavior do not play a role at all in these models. The basic idea of reinforcement learning models is that players evaluate whether their choice in the former play was a success or a failure and that they tend to repeat successes but abandon failures.

2.4.1 Belief learning

There is an increasing interest in the subject of belief learning in games. Recent experimental literature on (mainly) signaling games strongly suggests that subjects take the history of a game into account when they form expectations about the behavior of other players even when they are matched with different players from period to period. In this literature, subjects in a game give a (noisy) myopic best response using adaptively formed expectations, instead of consistent expectations as proposed by conventional game theoretic models. This experimental work is accompanied by theoretical work investigating (asymptotic) properties of various belief learning models.[18]

The central assumption in belief learning models is that players have a stationary view of the world around them. Players do not know the distribution of others' choices. But they assume that this distribution is constant in a probabilistic sense (cf. Milgrom and Roberts, 1991). Then, former observations about others' behavior contain valuable information for a player: (s)he uses this information to update beliefs about this distribution. Players disregard the possibility that other players adapt their expectations and behavior as a consequence of their own experience. However, if the model is true, other players also adapt their expectations and behavior during the game. Thus, the expectations of a player with respect to other players' behavior are generally not accurate and need to be adapted, at least until this process hits an equilibrium. In this way belief learning models deviate from game theoretic models and can be interpreted as dis-equilibrium models.

Game theory assumes a level of sophisticated strategic reasoning that may not be common to players. On the other hand, belief learning models neglect all strategic considerations that players may have. This may be more plausible in strategically complicated than in strategically transparent games. Strategically transparent games are

---

[18]For experimental work on signaling games, see Brandts and Holt, 1992; 1993; 1994; Cooper *et al.*, 1994; Partow and Schotter, 1993, Potters and Van Winden, 1995. For other experimental work, see Boylan and El-Gamal, 1993; El-Gamal *et al.*, 1994; Mookherjee and Sopher, 1994; Offerman, Sonnemans and Schram, 1995. For theoretical work, see Eichberger, 1995; Eichberger *et al.*, 1993; Fudenberg and Kreps, 1993; Jordan, 1993; Metrick and Polak, 1994; Milgrom and Roberts, 1991.

games with a few players and a unique Nash equilibrium which can be computed without serious difficulty. The prisoners' dilemma may serve as an example of this category. Games with more players and multiple Nash equilibria are strategically more complicated. In games with multiple equilibria players face a coordination problem, and unless refinements criteria are introduced, it is not clear ex ante on which equilibrium rational players should focus. The public good problem with step-level production function studied here may serve as an example of a strategically complicated game.

The naive Bayesian model

A very general belief learning model assumes that players process information using Bayes' rule. This model is labeled the naive Bayesian model. The adjective 'naive' refers to the property of the model that players neglect strategic aspects of the interaction. The model is general in the sense that it can be applied to any discrete choice game without the introduction of additional auxiliary assumptions. This model has been used by Brandts and Holt (1994) for signaling games and by Eichberger (1995) and Eichberger *et al.* (1993) for various two-player games. The relationship between the naive Bayesian model and other specific belief learning models like fictitious play will be discussed later.

Assume that a player expects a randomly selected other player to contribute with probability θ. The (uninformative) prior distribution on θ is assumed to be the uniform $[0,1]$ distribution with density $\pi(\theta)=I_{[0,1]}(\theta)$.[19] If each other randomly selected group-member contributes with probability θ, the number of contributors among the other $n-1$ group-members is binomially $(n-1,\theta)$ distributed. In the ideal case, an individual will update the prior distribution on θ using Bayes' rule for continuous distributions after observing draws from this process. Denote the k observations from the (assumed) binomial distribution by $x_1,\ldots,x_k$ and the sum of these observations by $s_k = x_1+\ldots+x_k$. Thus, x_i represents the number of other contributors in the i-th play of the game. The density of the posterior distribution of θ given these observations is denoted by

[19] It cannot be excluded that players have a different prior belief on θ, even if they have not played the game yet. Homegrown beliefs do not affect the belief learning pattern discussed below if they are (approximately) the result of the following process: originally the player had an uninformative prior distribution, but before (s)he entered the game (s)he observed some fictitious events on the behavior of the others.

$\pi(\theta \mid x_1,..,x_k)$. The posterior distributions of θ are known to belong to the family of beta distributions (e.g. Press, 1989, p.39) and can be elaborated explicitly using Bayes' rule. The beta distribution has the convenient property that it belongs to a conjugate family, i.e., the posterior distribution of a prior beta distribution is a beta distribution with adapted parameters. The density of the posterior distribution of θ is described in theorem 2.7.

Theorem 2.7

$$\pi(\theta|x_1,..,x_k) = \pi(\theta|s_k) = [k(n-1)+1] \binom{k(n-1)}{s_k} \theta^{s_k}(1-\theta)^{k(n-1)-s_k} . \qquad 2.22$$

□

The posterior distribution depends on the number of observations k and on the sum of the observations s_k (s_k is a sufficient statistic). For a Bayesian neither the order nor the separate values of the observations should affect the posterior distribution.

From the posterior distribution of θ the predictive distribution for a new observation y can be derived. The density of the predictive distribution $g(y \mid s_k)$, its mean and its variance are described in theorem 2.8.

Theorem 2.8

$$g(y|s_k) = \frac{k(n-1)+1}{(n-1)(k+1)+1} \binom{k(n-1)}{s_k} \frac{\binom{n-1}{y}}{\binom{(n-1)(k+1)}{s_k+y}} \qquad 2.23$$

$$E[y|s_k] = \frac{(n-1)(s_k+1)}{k(n-1)+2} \qquad 2.24$$

$$var[y|s_k] = \frac{(n-1)(s_k+1)\ [k(n-1)+n+1]\ [k(n-1)-s_k+1]}{[k(n-1)+2]^2\ [k(n-1)+3]} . \qquad 2.25$$

□

The naive Bayesian model is less complex than a sophisticated game theoretic model, but the computational abilities required are still enormous. It may be unrealistic to expect that individuals update expectations precisely according to this process. However, the expectation formation process of a naive Bayesian abstracting from strategic considerations can be shown to comply to some regularities. Someone following the naive Bayesian model in a less precise way may be expected to follow these regularities as well. These regularities are summarized in the following theorems.

The first regularity is that the subjective probability of a certain event should not decrease if that event was observed in the previous play of the game. This is a general result. It is not limited to the family of beta distributions.

Theorem 2.9

Given the density of the prior distribution $\pi(\theta)$ with $0 \leq \theta \leq 1$, the previous observations $x_1, \ldots, x_k$ and a new observation y it holds that:

$$g(y|x_1,..,x_k, y) \geq g(y|x_1,..,x_k) \; . \qquad 2.26$$

□

The second regularity is that the mean of a player's predictive distribution increases (remains constant/decreases) if the event observed is greater than (equal to/smaller than) the former mean of her or his predictive distribution.[20] This regularity is derived specifically for binomially distributed variables.

Theorem 2.10

Assume that the events x_1, ..., x_k summing up to s_k have been observed from an (assumed) binomial $(n\text{-}1,\theta)$ distribution with unknown θ. The new observation is x_{k+1}. It holds that:

$$E[y|s_k+x_{k+1}] \geq E[y|s_k] \Leftrightarrow x_{k+1} \geq E[y|s_k]. \qquad 2.27$$

□

[20]The main text uses loose shorthand as 'the mean of the predictive distribution' or 'the variance of the predictive distribution' instead of 'the mean of the density of the predictive distribution' or 'the variance of the density of the predictive distribution'. The latter terms are more precise but more awkward.

The third regularity is that as players gather more information, they will become more confident in their predictions, on average resulting in smaller variances of the predictive distribution. The predictive distribution converges to the binomial $(n\text{-}1, \theta)$ distribution if the number of observations goes to infinity and the others truly contribute with probability θ. To derive this result, the auxiliary assumption is needed that others' play converges to a constant probability distribution. This is not an innocent auxiliary assumption, as will be discussed later.

Lemma 2.1

$g(y \mid s_k)$ converges to $bin\ (n\text{-}1, \theta)$ if k approaches ∞ and if others contribute with constant probability θ. □

Theorem 2.11

Under the conditions of lemma 2.1 the variance of the density of the predictive distribution decreases on average. □

Intuitively, one would expect that if more information is revealed, i.e., when more events are observed, a Bayesian updater should feel more secure about the accurateness of her or his predictions. As a result the variance of the reported predictive distribution should decrease. Theorem 2.11 follows immediately from lemma 2.1: without any observations the variance of the reported distribution is equal to $(n\text{-}1)(n+1)/12$ (theorem 2.8) which is greater than the variance of the asymptotic distribution for $n \geq 2$, because the variance of the asymptotic distribution is always smaller than or equal to $(n\text{-}1)/4$. Nevertheless, it is possible that at some point the variance of the predictive distribution is smaller than the variance of the asymptotic distribution. For example, when $n=5$, $\theta=½$ and the only event observed is 0, the variance of the predictive distribution, 50/63, is smaller than the variance of the asymptotic distribution which is equal to 1.

Theorems 2.9, 2.10 and 2.11 together shall be referred to as the '*belief learning pattern*'.[21] This belief learning pattern is not positively predicted by the static game

[21] A general name is chosen to refer to this pattern, since the theorems stated could also be derived from the belief learning model of fictitious play.

theoretic models discussed in the former section. In an experimental situation where a series of one-shot public good games is played, it might be difficult to determine whether the naive Bayesian model or one of the static game theoretic models gives the more accurate description of players' expectation formation process even if expectations are elicited directly. Since both models require very much of the computational abilities of players, noise may be expected whichever model is true. In order to get an estimate of the natural amount of noise in the naive Bayesian model, one may compare players' expectations in public good games with decision-makers' expectations in a related game against nature. In the related game against nature the choices of other players in the group are replaced by the choices of automata. These *n-1* automata 'choose' to contribute with fixed but unknown probability θ, a fact known to the decision-maker. In a game against nature any possible strategic considerations are eliminated. The naive Bayesian model predicts that the expectation formation process of a player in the public good game is similar to the expectation formation process of a decision-maker in the game against nature, such that similar levels of noise may be expected. This similarity is not to be expected if one of the sophisticated game theoretic models gives the better description. Then, one would expect approximately accurate expectations in the public good game. More importantly, one would expect the belief learning pattern to emerge in the game against nature but not in the public good game.[22]

As mentioned above, players' expectations need not be accurate according to the naive Bayesian model. Systematic biases are expected if the distribution of others' choices shifts persistently in one direction. Consider the case that as time passes, fewer and fewer of the others choose to contribute. A naive Bayesian will gradually expect that fewer of the others will contribute if (s)he observes a decline in others' aggregate choices (theorem 2.10). But (s)he will adapt her or his beliefs too slowly, since (s)he maintains the false assumption that the distribution of others' choices remains constant. In such a case a naive Bayesian will systematically be too optimistic about others' behavior. Similar reasoning reveals that a naive Bayesian will be too pessimistic if the aggregate of others' choices consistently increases over time.

The naive Bayesian procedure described here is not an ad-hoc device only

[22]Note that the Bayesian updating process without strategic considerations is not naive in the game against nature.

applicable in a specific environment. It can be applied to any game where n players each have the choice between two actions. The naive Bayesian procedure is also well defined for games where n players each choose between r actions. The Dirichlet distribution (multi-variate beta) is the appropriate conjugate family to be used to calculate posterior distributions in this more general setting (Berger, 1980).

If people tend to update their expectations while abstracting from strategic considerations in the public good game, one may question whether the rate of this updating process is in line with the naive Bayesian model. The judgment of a Bayesian observer is not affected by the order of the observations. If an individual updates too slow (referred to as conservatism, or primacy) or updates too fast (representativeness, or recency), the order of the observations will affect the judgment. In former work both primacy and recency have been observed. El-Gamal and Grether (1994) find that some people tend to ignore their prior while others overweigh it. This suggests that individual differences exist regarding the pace of updating. Hogarth and Einhorn (1992) discuss many studies on order effects in belief updating, primarily from psychological origin. They suggest that the interaction between the response mode (either a judgment is made after each piece of information, or a judgment is only made after a series of information pieces), the complexity of the task (simple or complex) and the number of pieces of information (short or long series) determine whether primacy or recency will be observed. According to their criteria the decisions in the experiments reported in chapters 4 and 5 would be classified as decisions where players have a complex task of forming judgments for long series of information in a step-by-step response mode. As a consequence, declining recency would be expected in players' judgments.

Recency and primacy effects can be captured in the Bayesian approach if one allows players to weight their observations.[23] The term s_k denoting the sum of the former observations $x_1,\ldots,x_k$ in the equations of theorems 2.7 and 2.8 can be replaced

[23]Hogarth and Einhorn (1992) use the terms primacy and recency in a slightly different manner: they define these terms without explicit reference to the ideal Bayesian prediction. Recency is obtained if a decision-maker's judgment is more positive (negative) when (s)he observed the negative (positive) piece of information before the positive (negative) piece of information than in the case that (s)he observed the positive (negative) piece of information before the negative (positive) piece of information. Primacy is defined as the opposite effect.

by a weighted version sw_k.

$$sw_k = k * \frac{\sum_{j=1}^{k} (x_j * j^c)}{\sum_{j=1}^{k} j^c} \quad . \qquad 2.28$$

The parameter c allows for a wide range of rates of updating. For $c=0$ the original ideal naive Bayesian model is obtained. For $c>0$ the model attributes relatively high value to recent observations, resulting in a recency effect. For $c<0$ the model attributes relatively high value to early observations, resulting in a primacy effect. In chapter 5 this weighted sum of observations will be used in a model to assess order effects in actual judgments with the help of maximum likelihood estimations.

Other belief learning models

The naive Bayesian belief learning model has the advantage of being a model with a very general scope, which could be applied to any game where a finite number of players each chooses from a finite number of strategies. One obvious disadvantage of the model is that, if taken literally, it assumes players to have an unrealistic level of computational abilities. Alternative models exist which seem easier to implement for real world players, but which have a more ad-hoc character. These models share the property of the naive Bayesian model that players' expectations are guided in the direction of former observations.

The simplest belief learning rule is the *Cournot rule* (cf., Milgrom and Roberts, 1991). According to this rule, players believe that the former outcome of the game will occur again. Other rules look further back than the last period only. A well-known example is the rule of *fictitious play* (e.g., Fudenberg and Kreps, 1993). According to fictitious play, players' beliefs about the others' play in the next round are determined by the empirical frequency distribution of past play. A player expects that another player selects a particular action with probability equal to the observed relative frequency of that action in past play. To apply this, one has to make rather arbitrary assumptions about the prior distribution of players' beliefs before the start of the first period. In particular, the weight of the prior distribution relative to the weight of subsequent observations is indeterminate. However, the choice of the prior distribution seems to matter less as the number of observations of former play grows. Other rules exist as well. For example, Crawford (1995) studies a class of linear adjustment rules in a coordination game.

All belief learning models discussed above assume that players are rather unsophisticated in the sense that they base their beliefs on past actions of other players only. In other words, they are backward looking only. They neglect possible information about the payoffs for these others and the extent of rationality of the others completely. It is possible to extend these naive models to allow for some forward looking considerations, without a regression to the assumption of full strategic rationality used in game theoretic models. If players know the possible payoffs, the level of rationality, the particular history and the belief learning rule used by another player, or if they are willing to make (maybe inconsistent) assumptions about these aspects, they may in principle predict what this other player will choose in the next round. Sometimes it is suggested that players' beliefs are determined by a combination of a naive estimate based on former play of other players and by a limited sophisticated prediction about what others will do given their own history, possible payoffs and rationality level (cf., Milgrom and Roberts, 1991; Brandts and Holt, 1994).

The expectations generated by each of the belief learning models discussed above may be inserted in each of the decision rules discussed in section 2.2.1 (except the idea of false consensus). Players may give a best response or a quantal response. Altruism considerations may transform the payoff matrix to a different utility matrix. The decision rule in combination with a belief learning model defines the interaction between players in a game. This combination yields some straightforward general comparative statics predictions for behavior, irrespective of the particular model used. Natural questions concern the effects of changes in the environment on behavior and the evolution of play over time. The effect of increasing the value of the public good is obvious.

Theorem 2.12

Assume that a player uses one of the naive adaptive belief learning rules (the naive Bayesian model, fictitious play or the Cournot rule). Given the history of play, a player will be more inclined to contribute in the public good game if the value of the public good is increased. □

The proof of theorem 2.12 is trivial and therefore not presented in appendix A. A naive updater will not anticipate the potentially positive effect of the increased value of the public good on other players' inclination to contribute which may decrease the need of the own contribution for the provision of the public good. In fact, (s)he neglects any effects of changes in the payoffs of others on their behavior. Thus, given a certain history the expected value (utility) of contributing increases relative to the expected value (utility) of not contributing, and the probability of a contribution increases (unless, of course, players are led by the idea of false consensus).

A more difficult question concerns the effect of an increase of the group-size on individual behavior. For this effect a limiting result for the naive Bayesian model is proposed.[24]

Lemma 2.2
Let $0<\theta<1$. If $n \to \infty$, then $g(y|s_k) \to 0$ $\forall y$, i.e., if group-size grows beyond bounds, and if other players (are assumed to) contribute with probability θ, with θ strictly between 0 and 1, then the naive Bayesian's predicted probability of any specific event approaches 0. □

Theorem 2.13
Assume that the conditions stated in lemma 2.2 hold. A player will not contribute to the public good if her or his decision rule is such, that the decision depends only on the subjectively estimated probability that the contribution is critical for the provision of the public good. □

Theorem 2.13 follows immediately from lemma 2.2. This theorem implies that in extremely large groups, positive contributions can only be sustained for cut-point rules like the one for in-group cooperators, whose decision to contribute is dependent on both the probability of being critical and on the probability of being redundant. The theorem confirms the intuitive notion that larger groups generally yield higher

---

[24]A similar result can be obtained for fictitious play.

incentives to free ride.

Strict reasoning in the line proposed by naive belief learning models yield the conclusion that a change in the variability of the composition of the group does not have an effect on players' inclination to contribute. After all, according to these naive models players neglect all strategic considerations. Whether the composition of their group remains constant or not does not matter. A somewhat more balanced view is represented by sophisticated belief learning models, which allow for limited strategic anticipation. Such limited strategic anticipation may induce them to play more cooperatively when groups remain constant. A reputation for being (conditionally) cooperative may elicit cooperative actions of other group-members.

Interestingly, behavior generated by a combination of a belief learning model and a decision rule often converges to one of the Nash equilibria of the game. However, it is difficult to obtain general theoretical results. The dynamics generated by fictitious play and best response converge for two-player, finite-strategy, zero-sum games (Robinson, 1951), and for two-player, two-strategies games in general (Metrick and Polack, 1994). But Shapley (1964) already provided examples showing that two-player, finite-strategy games without the zero-sum restriction can lead to cycles of ever increasing length. The results for naive Bayesian learning combined with best response are similar: Eichberger, Haller and Milne (1993) show that two-player, two strategies games converge if players' prior distributions are of the beta-type. Eichberger (1995) gives sufficient conditions for convergence in general two-player games. But convergence results seem to be difficult to obtain for more general settings. For example, Jordan (1993) shows that in a three players matching penny game the unique equilibrium is locally unstable. The limited scope of the theoretical results obtained suggests that simulations may become a useful tool in examining properties of belief learning models. In chapter 5 (section 5.5.1) the results of simulations based on this model will be provided.

2.4.2 Reinforcement learning

Reinforcement learning models account for behavior in games without any reference to players' expectations. At the heart of reinforcement learning models is a clear evolutionary idea. Successful strategies are more likely to spread in a population than unsuccessful strategies. The popular evolutionary notion of *replicator dynamics* can be applied on the public good game studied here to describe the evolution of strategies. Let $x_c(t)$ and $x_{nc}(t)$, respectively, denote the proportion of (an infinite) population playing the strategy 'contributing' and the proportion playing the strategy 'not contributing' at period t. Players are drawn randomly from this population and allocated to groups. Let $E[\pi_c(t)]$ and $E[\pi_{nc}(t)]$ denote the expected payoff of playing 'contributing' and 'not contributing' in period t. Replicator dynamics implies that the relative proportions evolve as follows:

$$x_c(t) = x_c(t-1) * \frac{E[\pi_c(t-1)]}{x_c(t-1) * E[\pi_c(t-1)] + x_{nc}(t-1) * E[\pi_{nc}(t-1)]} . \qquad 2.29$$

The remainder of the population will play the strategy 'not contributing'. This process grasps the intuitive idea that the relative frequency of the successful strategy increases and that the rate of increase is positively related to the rate of success (cf. Miller and Andreoni, 1991; Gale *et al.*, 1995 and references cited there).

Individual reinforcement learning models have been proposed in the spirit of the replicator dynamics. Roth and Erev (1995) propose a simple learning model which can easily be applied to the public good game studied here. Before the game starts, each player i has an initial propensity $q_{i,c}(0)$ and $q_{i,nc}(0)$ to play each of the pure strategies 'contributing' and 'not contributing'. A player adapts the propensities to play the strategies by setting $q_{i,x}(t)$ equal to $q_{i,x}(t\text{-}1)+\pi_x(t\text{-}1)$ if the strategy choice x ($x=c$ or $x=nc$) generated a payoff $\pi_x(t\text{-}1)$ and by setting $q_{i,y}(t)$ equal to $q_{i,y}(t\text{-}1)$ for the strategy not chosen. The probability that player i will contribute in period t is then assumed to be:

$$p_{i,c}(t) = \frac{q_{i,c}(t)}{q_{i,c}(t)+q_{i,nc}(t)} . \qquad 2.30$$

A clear advantage of reinforcement learning is that it is simple to implement even for boundedly rational players. This type of learning does not require specific insight in the nature of the interaction of a game. In principle, reinforcement learning requires no cognitive considerations at all. It is often noted that humans share the tendency to automatically repeat successful strategies and abandon unsuccessful strategies with animals. Nevertheless, it is sometimes assumed that this type of learning results from some limited cognitive considerations. For example, Selten (1991) emphasizes that players trust the stability of the environment: what was good yesterday will be good today. Some models assume somewhat more sophistication in the reasoning of the players. According to Selten's qualitative learning direction theory, players evaluate the success of their choice in the former period, and move into the direction of the choice that might have been more successful (Selten and Buchta, 1994). Ronis, Yates and Kirscht (1989) discuss the relationship between automatic and conscious actions.

Reinforcement learning models have been used successfully to explain behavior in ultimatum games, public good games, market games, auction games, best shot games and constant sum games (Andreoni and Miller, 1995; Miller and Andreoni, 1991; Gale *et al.*, 1995; Roth and Erev, 1995; Erev and Roth, 1996).[25]

2.5 Summary

This chapter provides the theoretical underpinning for the experimental work on public good provision in chapter 4 and 5. To obtain analytical clarity theories are split to reveal their propositions for decision rules and for the interaction in a game.

Psychologists propose different ideas for decision rules than economists do. The psychological theories discussed assume that value orientations play an important role. People pursue different goals in the public good game. Two classic hypotheses use this assumption as a starting point. According to the false consensus hypothesis, people choose the action in accordance with their value orientation. Their choice causes them to expect that others will tend to choose the same action. According to the triangle hypothesis expectations affect behavior. Cooperators originally have a broad view of the world which makes them choose the cooperative action. However, if they suspect that they are matched with people who pursue individualistic or competitive goals, they adapt their preferred cooperative to individualistic behavior. Individualists have a narrow view of the world. They expect others to pursue the same goals as they do, and

---

[25]Selten (1991) identifies a third type of learning: *learning by imitation*. In some environments people are able to observe the actions and payoffs for others. Then decision-makers can not only learn from their own experiences, but also from the failures and successes of others. In principle the mechanisms described in this section are accelerated by the possibility to observe others' actions and payoffs. Ellison and Fudenberg (1993; 1995) propose models where individuals use information about the popularity of technologies in their rules of thumb for adopting new technologies.

as a consequence they choose the individualistic action.

All theories proposed by economists assume that expectations affect behavior. Economists' ideas differ in parsimony. The most parsimonious hypothesis says that people maximize their expected value. This hypothesis assumes that people neglect the social aspect of the situation. The social aspect of the game is explicitly captured by various expected utility hypotheses. Three such hypotheses are proposed on the basis of utility transformations distilled from the literature. Material cooperators feel good as a consequence of the actual provision of the good to other group-members. Warm-glow cooperators feel good by the act of contributing itself. In-group cooperators feel good by being part of the sub-group providing the public good. These expected utility hypotheses may either assume that people are homogeneous or heterogeneous. The parsimony of these hypotheses is further decreased if the possibility of noise is introduced: stochastic versions are presented. In particular, individuals will be allowed to make errors such that the probability that they choose the optimal action increases with the difference in expected value (utility) between the two actions.

A problem related to the provision of public goods is the prevention of public bads. These games can be made strategically equivalent, such that only the framing of the problem differs. Existing evidence suggests that the games are not behaviorally equivalent. Two theories originally developed for other settings than the present public good game are adapted to explain why people's decision rule might differ in the two frames. A prediction in line with prospect theory is that people will make fewer cooperative decisions in the public good game than in the public bad game. The opposite prediction is in line with Pruitt's hypothesis.

The interaction between players can be analyzed in game theoretic models or in learning models. According to game theoretic models players have rational expectations. They predict the behavior of others accurately, at least in a probabilistic sense. One stochastic and two deterministic game theoretic models have been discussed. The simplest model assumes that players maximize expected value. The equilibrium analysis has also been presented for the case where different types of material cooperators interact. A stochastic equilibrium analysis has been presented for the case where players maximize expected value but make mistakes. Arguments have been given for the position that these models do not predict a *specific* pattern in players' expectations if they play the game repeatedly with differing group-composition.

How changes in the environment affect individuals' decisions to contribute depends on the specific game theoretic model used. For example, increasing the size of a group has a negative effect on individuals' propensity to contribute if the players are maximizing expected value (theorem 2.3). Increasing the value of the public good has a positive effect on individuals' propensity to contribute if expected value maximizers focus on the payoff dominant symmetric equilibrium (theorem 2.2) or if two types of material cooperators maximize expected utility and certain conditions are fulfilled (cf. theorem 2.4 and corollary 2.1). An informal game theoretic argument has been given to argue that individuals will be more likely to contribute in environments where the composition of the group remains constant than in environments where this composition changes over time.

Belief learning models endogenize expectations differently. Players are supposed to have a stationary view of the world: they assume that other players' behavior remains constant in a probabilistic sense. With such a view of the world an individual will use observations on former play to update beliefs. In particular, the belief learning pattern is expected to emerge in players' beliefs. The mean and the variance of the predicted distribution as well as the probability of the latest event react positively to the outcome observed in the former play (cf. theorems 2.9, 2.10 and 2.11). Furthermore, whether players have accurate expectations depends on the development of the distribution of others' choices. If this distribution shifts to the left, players will be too optimistic about other players' behavior. If this distribution shifts to the right, they will be too pessimistic.

The effects of changes in the environment on individuals' decisions to contribute are more robust than for the game theoretic models with respect to the particular decision rule used. In extremely large groups players using decision rules which depend on the probability of being critical only will not contribute. Irrespective of group-size, increasing the value of the public good has a positive effect on players' inclination to contribute (given the history of play). Informal reasoning suggests that a change in the variability of the group-composition will not affect the inclination to contribute.

Reinforcement learning provides a more basic way of learning. Reinforcement learning models take account of players' behavior without any reference to expectations. The simple idea driving reinforcement learning is that successful decisions tend to be repeated and unsuccessful decisions tend to be abandoned. Of course, whether a choice was successful in the former play also depends on the former choices of other group-members.

3. Basic experimental tools

3.1 Introduction

When explaining behavior in public good games, economic as well as psychological theories appoint a central role to the beliefs people have with respect to the behavior of others and to the attitudes people have with respect to the payoffs of others. Economists and social psychologists usually pursue different approaches to account for beliefs and attitudes in public good experiments.

Economists often infer hypotheses about beliefs from choice data. For example, Palfrey and Rosenthal (1991) investigate a step-level public good game with binary contributions using only the actual decisions on contributing to derive information about beliefs. They test different models, but conclude that the data support only the hypothesis that subjects' prior beliefs are biased upwards, i.e., that they are too optimistic about others' choices to contribute. Social psychologists sometimes ask subjects to report their estimates of the probabilities that their own contribution will be futile, critical or redundant, independent of their decision to contribute or not. They do not use an incentive compatible mechanism when eliciting beliefs, however (e.g., Dawes *et al.*, 1986; Suleiman and Rapoport, 1992).

Both the 'economic' and the 'non-economic' approach have an important drawback: in the economic approach one has no independent data on beliefs, so one can never straightforwardly test the inferences made about 'homegrown' beliefs. In fact, without independent data one performs a joint test on beliefs and decision rules and the result of such a combined test is necessarily rather inconclusive. One can always maintain one's preferred hypothesis on beliefs by adapting the assumption about decision rules, and vice-versa. In the non-economic approach the lack of financial incentives might affect the care with which subjects report beliefs (cf. section 3.1). If subjects are asked to estimate the behavior of the others while they are rewarded to do so accurately, one can independently investigate the process of expectation formation and the relationship between expectations and behavior.

Similar problems exist with former work on the role of attitudes towards others in public good games. Evidence from economic as well as psychological experiments on the voluntary provision of public goods indicates that substantial differences exist in the attitudes of subjects towards contributing (e.g., Kelley and Stahelski, 1970; Liebrand, 1984; Palfrey and Rosenthal, 1988; Schram and Sonnemans, 1995; Suleiman and Rapoport, 1992). Unfortunately, some of these studies lack an independent measure of value orientation: a subject is simply believed to have a cooperative preference because (s)he is observed to contribute a lot. Naturally, these preferences cannot subsequently be used to explain the behavior which was used to derive them. Other studies obtain an independent measurement for value orientations, but do not provide subjects with proper incentives for the task on which the measurement is based.

The present study tries to avoid the problems concerning beliefs by using an incentive compatible mechanism for their elicitation. The problems concerning value orientations are avoided by measuring these independently in a short experiment preceding the public good experiments. In section 3.2 the decomposed game technique used to measure value orientations is discussed. It is explicitly investigated whether incentives affect the scores of subjects in this method. In section 3.3 the quadratic scoring rule is proposed. This rule is used for the elicitation of beliefs. Some aspects concerning the success of this method are discussed. Section 3.4 concludes.

3.2 The decomposed game technique

The *decomposed game* technique was developed by social psychologists (e.g., Griesinger and Livingston, 1973; Liebrand, 1984). This technique is used to assess individual value orientations.[1] In this method, each subject is asked to make 24 choices between two 'own-other' combinations. Each own-other combination allocates an amount of money to the decision-maker and an amount to some other subject to which the individual is linked during the 24 choices. Subjects do not know to which

---

[1]Professor Liebrand was so kind to provide the software used to measure value orientations.

other subject they are paired in this game, but they know that their partner is the same throughout the 24 decisions. During the experiment, subjects do not receive any feedback about the other's choices. At the end of the experiment, each subject is paid privately and told the (aggregate) choice of the other, without revealing the identity of this other.

The total amount to be allocated by an individual is not constant over combinations. The 24 pairs of outcomes lie equally spaced on a circle with the origin of the outcome plane serving as center and a radius of 15 units of some currency, denoted by 'francs'. The horizontal axis measures the amount of money allocated to oneself (x) and the vertical axis measures the amount of money offered to the other (y) (see figure 3.1).

Figure 3.1
The value orientation circle.

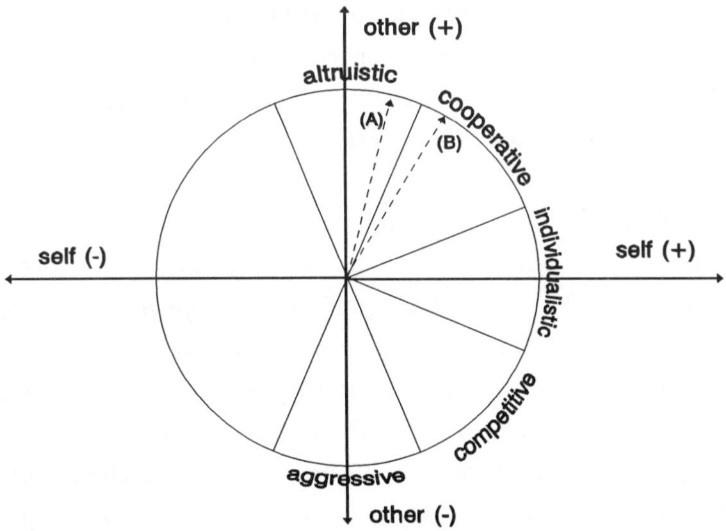

Note that $x^2+y^2=15^2$ and that $x+y$ is not constant. Each pair present the subjects with a choice between two adjacent outcomes on the circle, for example, a choice between 3.90 francs for themself and 14.50 francs for the other versus 7.50 francs for themself and 13.00 francs for the other (vector A=(3.90,14.50) versus vector B=(7.50,13.00)).

A motivational vector in the circle-space described above is defined as the vector that describes an individual's preferences regarding outcomes for her- or himself relative to the other. Adding up the individual's 24 chosen vectors yields an estimate of the individual's preferred motivational vector. Social psychologists have developed a standard classification of individuals on the basis of these vectors. Individuals with an observed vector lying between -112.5 and -67.5 degrees are classified as *aggressive*, individuals with vectors between -67.5 and -22.5 are classified as *competitive*, individuals with vectors between -22.5 and 22.5 are classified as *individualistic*, individuals with vectors between 22.5 and 67.5 are classified as *cooperative* and individuals with vectors between 67.5 and 112.5 as *altruistic*.[2]

A choice between two adjacent vectors is called consistent if and only if the alternative closest to the observed motivational vector is selected. For example, if the motivational vector is (15,0) and an individual chooses between alternative C (-10.60, -10.60) and D (-7.50,-13.00), then D would constitute the consistent choice. If a subject makes 24 consistent choices, then the revealed vector-length (the sum of the chosen vectors) can be shown to be twice the radius of the circle (i.e., 30 francs). If the subject chooses randomly, the vector-length will be small (possibly 0). This suggests that the vector-length as a percentage of the maximal vector-length can serve as a measure of the consistency of a subject.

A preliminary experiment was conducted to assess the role of monetary incentives in this method. 58 subjects were divided into two treatments, each of which was run twice. The subject pool was the undergraduate population of the University of Amsterdam. A majority of 57% of the subjects majored in economics.

In the *fictitious money* treatment 28 subjects received a lump sum payment of 15 guilders for their efforts and played for fictive francs.[3] They were asked to imagine that they were playing for real money, as is often done in psychological experiments.

In the *real money* treatment 30 subjects received a lump-sum payment of 5 guilders for showing up and they played for real money in the experiment. At the end they could exchange their total amount of francs (their own allocation to themselves

---

[2]This classification is ad hoc, though very natural. Note that the areas are of equal size and symmetric around the vectors that maximize the motivational goals.

[3]At the time of this experiment 1 guilder was worth 0.55 US-dollar.

plus the allocation of the other to them) at an exchange rate of 1 franc = f 0,30. In both treatments subjects were asked to fill out a questionnaire after they had made the 24 choices in the decomposed game technique.

Incentives may affect both the angle of the measured motivational vector and the observed level of consistency. First, the effect of real monetary incentives on revealed preferences regarding own-other outcomes is assessed. A hard-core prediction from economics would be that the introduction of real incentives will cause all subjects to reveal themselves as individualists, i.e., they will by and large pursue their self-interest. This strong prediction is not supported by the data. It turns out that both in the real money treatment and the fictitious money treatment a substantial number of individuals is not classified as individualistic. In the real money treatment 22 individuals are classified as individualistic (73.3%), 7 individuals are classified as cooperative (23.3%) and 1 individual is classified as competitive (3.3%). In the fictitious money treatment 15 individuals are classified as individualistic (53.6%), 10 individuals are classified as cooperative (35.7%), 2 individuals are classified as competitive (7.1%) and 1 individual is classified as aggressive (3.6%). Thus, incentives do not prevent other than individualistic goals being pursued, though there does seem to be a shift in the direction of individualistic goals. This shift is not statistically significant, however. A Mann-Whitney rank test does not reject the hypothesis that the ranks of the motivational angles measured in the real money treatment are equal to the ranks in the fictitious money treatment (means: 8.5° versus 10.1°; m=30, n=28: p=0.26).[4]

Second, the effect of the use of incentives on consistency is investigated. Some economists would argue that subjects in the real money treatment will exhibit more consistency in their choice-behavior than subjects in the fictitious money treatment, because they will be more motivated to consider their choices seriously. Subjects in the real money treatment appear to make significantly more consistent choices (mean=93.5%) than subjects in the fictitious money treatment (mean=85.1%; Mann-Whitney rank test, m=30, n=28: p=0.01). This result carries over to the two most frequently observed orientations: both individualists and cooperators are more

---

[4]Unless indicated otherwise, two-tailed tests are used and statistical significance is measured at the 5%-level.

consistent in the real money treatment than in the fictitious money treatment. Nevertheless, subjects in the real money treatment do not use more time to make their decisions (mean=358.4 seconds) than the subjects in the fictitious money treatment (mean=378.5). This difference is not significant (Mann-Whitney rank test) and even in the unexpected direction. This may suggest that subjects in the real money treatment are more concentrated than subjects in the fictitious money treatment.

The result that subjects differ systematically in their value orientation is corroborated by answers given in the post-experimental questionnaire. Some questions tried to elicit the value orientation of the subjects independently on a 1 to 7 scale. Subjects who are classified as cooperative on the basis of their choices report to pursue a significantly more cooperative goal than non-cooperators (means: 5.06 versus 3.44; Mann-Whitney rank test, m=17, n=41: p=0.01). 'Revealed' individualists report to pursue a significantly more individualistic goal than non-individualists (means: 6.00 versus 4.95; Mann-Whitney rank test, m=37, n=21: p=0.01). A caveat may be in place here, however: it may be the case that giving more (less) money to the other induces subjects to report a cooperative (individualistic) orientation ex post.

3.3 The scoring rule

Scoring rules provide incentive mechanisms to elicit the beliefs of decision-makers. Murphy and Winkler (1970) discuss three strictly proper scoring rules. Receiving a payoff generated by a strictly proper scoring rule induces someone maximizing expected value or someone maximizing a linear utility function to report her or his beliefs truthfully.

The quadratic scoring rule $Q_j(p)$ is an example of a strictly proper scoring rule. The general form of this rule is as follows. If an individual reports p_i (for $0 \leq i \leq n-1$, where n denotes group-size), as the probability that exactly i of the others will contribute, and if in reality j of the others contribute, then the payoff generated by this rule is equal to:

$$Q_j(p) = a + 2b * p_j - b * \sum_{i=0}^{n-1} (p_i^2). \qquad 3.1$$

This scoring rule is used in the present study.[5] The parameters *a* and *b* are both chosen to be equal to 60 cents in the experiments.[6]

The success of using this method can be evaluated. Three potential problems can be identified with the use of scoring rules. First, deviations from true judgments are not punished very severely by them. Second, subjects with a non-linear utility function may bias their reported distribution. Third, subjects may treat the reporting of beliefs and the decision in the public good game as one super-game. For example, they may use the payoff generated by the scoring rule to 'insure' themselves for a bad payoff in the public good game, or vice versa. These three problems are addressed sequentially making use of the characteristics of probability distributions reported in the experiments.[7]

An important question for empirical work is how beliefs elicited with incentives relate to beliefs elicited without incentives. This question is discussed as well.

Scoring rules share the problem of many incentive mechanisms that the objective function is rather flat around the optimum. The Becker-Degroot-Marschak mechanism for eliciting the true certainty equivalent for gambles is another notorious example with this property (Hey, 1991, p.145-146). In this study the

---

[5]The logarithmic scoring rule $L_j(p)$ and the spherical scoring rule $S_j(p)$ are other strictly proper scoring rules. The logarithmic scoring rule is believed to be the least sensitive of the three rules (Murphy and Winkler, 1970). The quadratic scoring rule is preferred in the present study to the spherical scoring rule because it seems the simpler of the two rules.

$$L_j(p) = \log(p_j); \quad S_j(p) = \frac{p_j}{\sqrt{\sum_{i=1}^{n-1} p_i^2}}.$$

[6]A sample of the instructions for subjects on the decomposed game technique and the scoring rule is reported in Appendix B. There, also, the screen asking subjects to report expectations is displayed.

[7]To evaluate the success of using the scoring rule the first three experimental treatments discussed in chapter 4 are used. In these treatments the post-experimental questionnaire addressed some issues concerning the scoring rule.

purpose of the use of the scoring rule is to elicit subjects' true beliefs, and not to test whether subjects can figure out the incentive compatibility property of the mechanism themselves. Therefore, the scoring rule was described explicitly in a handout. The handout explained that the expected payoff from this rule is maximized if probabilities are reported correctly, so that it is in the interest of a subject to report beliefs about probabilities truthfully. A proof of this statement was offered - on request - after the experiment had ended. It was emphasized that subjects did not need mathematical understanding of the equation. This procedure diminishes potential 'costs of thinking' about the mechanism, costs which might otherwise prevent subjects from reporting true beliefs.

Given this information, subjects could do three relatively easy things. They could gamble, by assigning all probability to a particular event, they could assign each event equal probability, or they could simply report their beliefs truthfully. The actual reported distributions indicate that only very few data can be interpreted as gambles. In 156 out of 3720 reported distributions (4.2%) subjects assign a probability of 100% to one of the possible events. In 47 of these cases, the allocation of 100% to the event that 0 of the others would contribute is a response to the fact that 0% contributions by the others had been observed in the previous period(s). The remaining 109 cases (2.9%) may represent gambles or otherwise implausible expectations. In only 12 cases (<0.1%) subjects attribute equal or almost equal probability to each of the possible events. The number of lazily reported distributions seems very small. The procedure used to implement the scoring rule seems to have overcome the potential problem of insensitivity.

The second potential problem is that a risk-loving or risk-averse individual does not have a linear utility function and, strictly speaking, should bias the reported probability distribution a little in order to obtain maximal expected utility. For example, a risk-averse individual will report somewhat more dispersion in the probabilities than truly expected when (s)he is rewarded with the payoff generated by a scoring rule.

Theoretically, an elegant method exists to avoid this problem. The solution is provided by the lottery mechanism proposed by Smith (1961). With this method subjects do not directly earn money with their choices. Instead, they earn lottery tickets. A lottery ticket increases a subject's probability of winning the high prize instead of the low prize in a lottery carried out at the end of the experiment. Since expected utility is linear in probabilities (according to the axioms), a subject wanting to maximize expected utility should maximize expected lottery tickets in the experiment. In other words, this mechanism should induce risk-neutrality in the experiment. However, whether the effect of this mechanism in experimental work is the same as supposed by theory is doubtful. It is not so clear that subjects understand the subtle line of reasoning in the argument and behave as risk-neutral as they are supposed to (for a discussion of this mechanism, see Davis and Holt, 1993, p.473-476). Furthermore, it does not seem easy to 'train' naive subjects to comply with the basic idea of this mechanism, since it involves an explanation of utility theory at a quite abstract level. Therefore, this mechanism is not applied in the present study.

However, risk-attitudes may form a larger theoretical than empirical problem. The usual hypothesis about risk-attitudes when people can gain money is that they are risk-averse. Only a few extreme risk-averse distributions are observed in the data, however: for groups with 7 players the probabilities are assigned such that the smallest probability is greater than 9% and the greatest probability less than 21% in only 16 cases (less than 1% of the total). For groups with 5 players only 12 cases (1%) are observed where all (5) possible events are given a probability of 20%. In all other cases with groups consisting of 5 players, the difference between the highest and lowest probability is at least 10%-points.

The hypothesis that people are risk-averse gives a bad explanation for the majority of the probability distributions reported in the public good experiments. If anything, people report probability distributions with too *small* dispersion. This result may be closely linked to the psychological finding that many people are over-confident in probability assessments (cf. Camerer, 1995). In principle, there is no tension between overconfidence and truthful reporting of probabilities. The conjecture that the small dispersion of reported distributions in the public good games is the result of overconfidence instead of a preference for risky gambles is supported by the results obtained for the related game against nature discussed in chapter 5. In these games subjects report distributions without systematic biases in dispersion. There are some (independent) indications that subjects in these investment games perceive their task as more difficult than subjects in the public good games. This may have decreased the average level of confidence. These issues will be addressed in more detail later. For the moment it is concluded that it seems unlikely that risk-attitudes have affected empirical results systematically.

The third deviation of truthful reporting distributions can occur if people perceive the decision in the public good game and the reporting of expectations as parts of one game, with related decisions. A simple example occurs if players 'insure' themselves in one game for a bad outcome in the other. Two possibilities for insuring exist in the public good experiments conducted. The first is to contribute to the public good and to give an unrealistically high estimate of the probability that fewer than s-1 of the others in the group contribute (recall that s denotes the threshold for the provision of the public good; in testing for this effect, $p_0+\ldots+p_{s-2}>80$). That way, a subject either gets a payoff from the public good, or from an accurate probability estimation. The second way to insure, is not to contribute to the public good and to report the probability that exactly s-1 of the others contribute to be unrealistically high ($p_{s-1}>70$). Only 37 reported distributions fulfil the criteria of the first way of insuring and 44 distributions fulfil the criteria of the second way (together just over 2%). In fact, some of these distributions even seem to be plausible in view of the history of the particular subject (but then, the choice whether or not to contribute is strange from an economic point of view). Thus, it is concluded that insurance in these ways is hardly taking place. This conclusion does not change, if the criteria for calling a distribution an insurance are changed.

Insurance is only a simple example of interrelated decisions. In the public good experiments reported in the next chapter three types of players are used. Some players both report their beliefs and make a decision whether or not to contribute. There are also players who only report their beliefs. And a third group only make a decision whether or not to contribute. A comparison of the choices and beliefs of these three types of players lends credence to the position that there are no clear unintended effects when players make both decisions, as will be seen in section 4.3.2. It is concluded that a very large majority of the subjects has taken the belief reporting and contribution decisions independently.

A different matter is whether the introduction of incentives improves the quality of the reported beliefs. There is some evidence that scoring rules reduce the number of extreme (Fischer, 1982) or non-sensical beliefs (Grether, 1992). This evidence is corroborated by results obtained in the post-experimental questionnaire. This included the following open question: "Suppose that we had asked your expectations about the choices of the others without payment. Do you think that your answers (the reported percentages) would have been different?" 50% of the subjects report that their estimates would have been different without incentives, primarily, that they would not have taken the estimation-task as seriously and that they would have reported distributions with less dispersion (which seems the easy thing to do).[8]

3.4 Conclusions

The results reported in this chapter suggest that proper incentives may help to increase the experimental realism perceived by subjects. With incentives subjects seem more motivated to take their task seriously. This yields more reliable measures of their attitudes towards others and of their beliefs.

The introduction of incentives in the decomposed game technique leads to higher levels of consistency in subjects' choices. On the other hand, value orientations are found to differ systematically with and without incentives. The finding in previous (psychological) studies that people pursue different goals when they interact is not an artifact caused by the use of hypothetical questions.

Scoring rules help to motivate people when they report their beliefs. Some theoretical problems connected with scoring rules turn out to be not too serious in empirical work. The insensitivity of scoring rules may prevent decision-makers from reporting true beliefs if thinking itself is costly. This problem is successfully circumvented when the incentive compatibility of the rule is explained to subjects. The actual number of lazily or incoherently reported distributions is very small. Another problem is that risk-attitudes may cause biases in the reported distributions. There is some bias in the dispersion of subjects' reported distributions in the public good games, but not in a related game against nature. This difference is better explained by a hypothesis that there is a difference in subjects' confidence levels

---

[8]The answers given in the questionnaire reveal that despite emphasis on the contrary, four subjects erroneously thought that if they contributed themselves, they should automatically add 1 to the number of others that contributed or that the event that 0 of the others would contribute logically could not occur.

than that there is a difference in their risk-attitudes. Non-sensical predictions are not numerous and the extent of abuse of the scoring rule is very limited.

These results suggest that it makes sense to obtain measurements on individual value orientations and beliefs. Incentives may improve the quality of the data. In all public goods experiments to be discussed in this study, subjects' value orientations are measured via the real money treatment of the decomposed game technique before they enter the public good game. A scoring rule is used to encourage them when predicting the future state of the world.

PART II: Experimental results

Part II provides the experimental results. The psychological as well as economic ideas discussed in chapter 2 are subjected to experimental testing. The evidence is split in two parts: chapter 4 describes the experimental results on decision rules. This chapter also examines whether differences in the experimental environment affect individual decisions to contribute to the public good. Chapter 5 describes the experimental results on beliefs. There, the main question is whether the data are better organized by game theoretic models or by belief learning models. Another matter is whether the combined results on beliefs and decision rules can account for the behavioral patterns observed in the experiments.

4. Decision rules

4.1 Introduction

The analysis of the decision-making process is split into a part on decision rules and a part on expectation formation. This chapter reports the experimental results on decision rules. In the analysis individuals' expectations concerning others' behavior are treated as exogenous. The expectation formation process will be the subject of investigation of chapter 5. In the experiments, independent measures of players' expectations with respect to other players' behavior and independent measures on players' attitudes towards others are obtained. Thus, the analysis hardly needs any auxiliary hypotheses on these issues. This procedure allows for sharp tests of decision rules.

The experiments will be used to analyze the relative merits of various decision rules directly and indirectly. To start, it is directly established which particular set of decision rules organizes individuals' choices best, given reported expectations. Hypotheses from psychological as well as from economic origin will be evaluated. Two questions concerning decision rules will be given special attention. The first is whether a decision rule needs to take account of the social aspect of interactive decision-making. The second is whether a decision rule needs a stochastic component to give a reasonable description of human behavior in public good games.

Direct evidence on decision rules is also obtained by answering the question concerning the direction in the causal relationship between expectations and behavior. According to the false consensus hypothesis, players make a choice consistent with their orientation and consequently expect others to do the same. Thus, choices determine expectations. According to the other hypotheses discussed in chapter 2, expectations determine behavior. The introduction of 'spectators', subjects who only report their expectations, in one of the treatments allows one to study the direction of this relationship.

Next, attention will be focused on indirect evidence. What are the effects of changes in the environment on players' inclination to contribute to public goods with a step-level production function?[1] In particular, the effect of an increase in the number of group-members, the effect of an increase in the value of the public good and the effect of a change in the variability of the group-composition will be assessed under ceteris paribus conditions.

A final institutional effect concerns the question whether the framing of the game has an impact on players' behavior. Uncontrolled empirical studies suggest that players behave quite aggressively in environments with negative externalities, while they behave more cooperatively in environments with positive externalities. It will be investigated whether this remarkable difference in observed behavior is due to uncontrolled differences in the strategic aspects of the environment. Individuals' behavior will be compared in two strategically equivalent frames of the public good game. Furthermore, possible explanations for the phenomenon will be examined.

The organization of this chapter is as follows: section 4.2 describes the experimental procedures and designs of the five treatments which were set up to address these themes. Section 4.3 discusses the experimental results. First, some general characteristics of the measured value orientations will be described. Then, the direct and the indirect evidence will be presented subsequently. Finally, section 4.4 concludes.

4.2 Experimental design and procedures

General framework

Subjects took part in two experiments. In the first experiment the decomposed game technique was used to obtain a measure of subjects' attitudes towards others (the design of this experiment is presented in section 3.2). Subjects were privately paid for their own, and the other's choices in this test after the second experiment had ended. Therefore, subjects did not have any information about others' orientations before the

---

[1]Note that theoretical predictions for the effects of changes in the environment depend on the hypothesis about the expectation formation besides a hypothesis concerning the decision rule. In this sense, discussion of results on this theme gives a preview of the results on expectation formation discussed in chapter 5.

start of the second experiment. In the second experiment subjects played one of the treatments of the public good game discussed below. To emphasize the distinction between experiments 1 and 2, these were conducted by different experimenters. Both experiments were computerized.[2]

The instructions of the two experiments were formulated as neutral as possible. Words like 'cooperation, defection, contributing', or 'taking away' were avoided. Instead, subjects chose between 'buying or not buying a marker', or between 'yellow and blue'. Communication between subjects was prohibited in both experiments. In the second experiment, 20 periods of one of the treatments of the public good game were played. For this experiment, a randomly appointed observer was used to ensure that no deceit was taking place.

The general structure of the decision to contribute to the public good was as follows: players were endowed with an amount c. Subjects made a binary choice between either contributing at a given irreversible cost (equal to c=60 cents) or not contributing, in which case no costs were incurred (in this second experiment, payoffs were denoted in Dutch cents). Each group-member received the value of the public good $f(s)$-c if s (=3) or more of the group-members contributed and 0 cent otherwise. Thus, if the threshold was reached, those that contributed received a net sum of $f(s)$-c, those that did not received c+$f(s)$-c = $f(s)$. It was explained to the subjects that the costs for contributing were the same for everybody as was the value of the public good, and that these would remain constant throughout the 20 periods. The amount $f(s)$ was one of the control variables in the design. Table 4.1 provides the details of the treatments and the control variables.

Strangers mode

Subjects played either in the strangers or in the partners mode (Andreoni, 1988). In the strangers mode, groups of equal size were formed randomly in each period. A subject did not know with whom (s)he was in a group in any period, but (s)he knew that the composition of the group was changing from period to period. Moreover, (s)he knew that (s)he would not be in a group with exactly the same others more than once.

[2]The program for the second experiment, the public good/bad experiment, was written in the language ESL for an OS/2 environment by CREED-programmer Otto Perdeck.

Table 4.1
Characteristics of the design

session	label of treatment	beliefs elicited?	f(s) (in cents)	#groups*size +subject mode	#spectators included
1	low-7	yes	180	3*7 strangers	0
2	low-7	yes	180	3*7 strangers	0
3	high-7	yes	245	3*7 strangers	0
4	high-7	yes	245	3*7 strangers	0
5	low-7	yes	180	3*7 strangers	0
6	high-7	yes	245	3*7 strangers	0
7	high-5	yes	245	3*5 strangers	8
8	high-5	yes	245	3*5 strangers	7
9	high-5	yes	245	3*5 strangers	8
10	high-5	yes	245	3*5 strangers	8
11	pubgood	yes	245	4*5 partners	0
12	pubbad	yes	245	4*5 partners	0
13	pubgood	no	245	4*5 partners	0
14	pubbad	no	245	4*5 partners	0

Notes: Some characteristics of the environment were kept constant in all sessions. The threshold s was always at three contributions, and the costs for contributing c were always equal to 60 cent.

In the strangers mode, the effects of changes in group-size and payoff for the public good were studied. In six out of the ten strangers sessions ('*low-7* strangers', and '*high-7* strangers'), groups consisted of seven players, in the remaining four sessions ('*high-5* strangers') they consisted of five. In three strangers sessions, the public payoff *f(s)* was set at 180 cents ('low-7 strangers'). In the remaining seven sessions this payoff was 245 cents.

Partners modes: frames

In the partners mode, four groups of five players each were formed at the start of the second experiment. A subject did not know with whom (s)he was in a group, but (s)he knew that the group-composition remained constant from period to period. The partners mode was used to study the effects of the framing of the public good. In two sessions the public good frame was used ('*pubgood* partners'). In two other sessions the public bad frame was used ('*pubbad* partners'). The only difference between pubgood partners and high-5 strangers was the subject mode used. Thus, a comparison of behavior in pubgood partners and high-5 strangers yields evidence on the question whether the variability of the group-composition affects individual contributions. For convenience, in the remainder the suffix indicating subject mode will be left out. For example, the treatment 'pubbad partners' will be referred to as pubbad.[3]

In the public good frame subjects chose whether or not to contribute their original endowment c to the public good. If enough ($\geq s$) people contributed, the public good with value $f(s)-c$ was provided. In the public bad frame, people chose whether or not to withdraw an amount c from a common pool. If too many people ($>n-s$) withdrew their endowment from the common pool, the public bad occurred, i.e., they did not obtain the public good with value $f(s)-c$. Withdrawing the amount from the common pool in the public bad game is parallel to not contributing in the public good game, and not withdrawing is parallel to contributing. The situations are strategically equivalent.

In both frames of the partners mode, subjects chose between options 'Yellow' and 'Blue', and possible earnings (per period) were 0, 60, 185, or 245 Dutch cents. Table 4.2 presents the two versions of the game used. In the public good treatment, choosing Yellow yielded an immediate loss of 60 cents. However, if 3 or more group-members chose Yellow, each of the 5 members of the group received 245 cents. In the public bad treatment choosing Yellow gave an immediate gain of 60 cents. If fewer than 3 Yellow choices were made in the group, all 5 members received 185 cents. Note that Yellow constitutes the cooperative choice in the public good frame, but that it constitutes the defective choice in the public bad frame. There, Blue is the cooperative choice. To avoid confusion, the description of the analysis of behavior in these frames will use terms like the level of cooperative behavior, and will avoid reference to Yellow and Blue. The Blue choice in pubbad will be referred to as the 'choice to contribute', or the 'cooperative choice'.

---

[3]Not all sessions used the same words to refer to the contribution decision. In the strangers treatments the decision whether or not to contribute was described to subjects as the decision whether or not 'to buy a marker'. It is awkward to use these words in the public bad frame of the partners treatments. Therefore, the partners treatments used 'Yellow' and 'Blue', as will be described below. The data were gathered within one year. The data for low-7 and high-7 were obtained in June 1993; the data for high-5 were obtained in October/November 1993 and the data for pubgood and pubbad were obtained in April 1994.

Table 4.2
The public good versus the public bad frame

	Number of yellow choices in the group					
	0	1	2	3	4	5
Group-earnings	60	60	60	245	245	245

Amount related to the yellow choice: -60 cent
Amount related to the blue choice: 0 cent

	Number of yellow choices in the group					
	0	1	2	3	4	5
Group-earnings	185	185	185	0	0	0

Amount related to the yellow choice: 60 cent
Amount related to the blue choice: 0 cent

Note: The upper table displays the choice-situation in the public good frame and the lower table displays this situation for the public bad frame.

Player types

In the fourteen sessions each subject was allocated to one of three types of players: 'full players', or simply '*players*', '*simple players*' and '*spectators*'. A subject was in the same role throughout the experiment. In each period, a (full) player had to make two decisions, decision A and decision B. Decision A was the choice whether or not to contribute to the public good (or to withdraw an amount from the common pool) as described above. Before any information about the aggregate decisions of other group-members in a period was given, each player was asked to report probabilities about how many of the others in her or his group would contribute (decision B). Thus, a player had to estimate the probability that exactly 0, exactly 1, ..., exactly *n-1* of the others would contribute. Proper incentives were provided by applying the quadratic scoring rule, described in section 3.3. Subjects made the decisions simultaneously and anonymously.

In two sessions of the pubgood and pubbad treatments only simple players were used. Simple players only made decision A, i.e., they decided whether or not to contribute. Simple players did not report their expectations regarding other group-members' behavior. A comparison of the behavior of simple and full players yields information on the question whether the elicitation of beliefs affects the choices made.

Spectators only had to make decision B. They were anonymously paired to one full player each in treatment high-5 and given all information that this player received. They were asked to estimate how many of the others in the group of the player to whom they were paired would contribute (excluding the possible contribution of this 'paired' player). They received a lump-sum payment to compensate for the diminished income due to dropping decision A. Subjects were told when period 1 began, whether they were a player or not and, if they were, whether a spectator was paired to them or not (this was the case for about half of the players). Nobody knew who was paired to whom, however, except the observer.

When everybody had made their decisions in a period, subjects were informed on how many contributions were made by their group, the resulting public payoff, and their own 'probability-payoff'. Note that subjects received only aggregate information about the others in their group. They could not keep track of the history of any other particular subject. After this information was provided, subjects proceeded to the next period. Table 4.3 presents an overview of the timing of the decisions various participants had to make in the two experiments. More details on the procedures are provided in appendix B.

Table 4.3
Timing of the decisions to be made

	Experiment 1			Experiment 2		
	Decomposed Games (DG1..DG24) determines Value Orientation			Public Good/Bad Game Contribution Decision (DEC) + Report Expectations (EXP)		
Role	Question 1	....	Question 24	Period 1	....	Period 20
Full Players (sessions 1-12)				DEC+EXP	....	DEC+EXP
Spectators (sessions 7-10)	DG1	....	DG24	EXP	....	EXP
Simple Players (sessions 13-14)				DEC	....	DEC

In all treatments subjects were asked to fill out a questionnaire after the experiment had ended. The questionnaire asked subjects to motivate their choices, and some socio-economic characteristics were elicited. In the partners mode subjects were also asked to fill out an additional questionnaire before the first period. This intended to measure the extent of subjective interdependency. After the last period the same questions were asked again. These questions were asked to acquire evidence for Pruitt's hypothesis on differences in behavior in the public good and the public bad frame. In addition, in the post-experimental questionnaire in the partners mode questions were asked about how satisfied they had felt with their decision after they had been told the outcome in various situations. Six situations were distinguished, defined by the combinations of having made a cooperative versus non-cooperative choice and the outcome that their contribution was or would have been futile, critical, or redundant. In the questions (as well as in the instructions) words like cooperative, futile, critical, and redundant were avoided.

In all sessions inexperienced subjects were used to avoid uncontrolled effects of differences in experience. No subject was allowed to participate more than once. The subject pool was the undergraduate population of the University of Amsterdam. A majority of 58% of the subjects majored in economics or econometrics; 26% of the subjects were female. The average age was 22 years old. Subjects that showed up on time for the experiment received a lump sum show-up fee of 5 guilders in case they participated and 10 guilders if they were sent off. Including this fee, an average of 48.10 Dutch guilders (= ± 26.15 US-dollars) was earned by subjects in about 2 to 2.5 hours.

A total of 311 subjects participated in the fourteen sessions. Fourteen subjects were allocated to the role of observer in experiment 2. The remaining 297 subjects were allocated to one of the three roles available. 31 of the subjects were given the role of spectator; 40 were simple players and the remaining 226 were full players. Subjects could read the computerized instructions for the experiment at their own pace. They had to answer some questions testing their understanding of the rules of the game before the experiment started. Before the public good game started, they played two practice-periods in which the behavior of other players was simulated.

4.3 Experimental results

In this section, the theories on decision rules discussed in section 2.2 will be confronted with the data obtained in the experiments. The sessions were run as planned and without any serious problems. Section 4.3.1 focuses on the question of how subjects choose in public good games, given their expectations. Section 4.3.2 discusses the experimental evidence on the direction of the relationship between expectations and decisions. Then, the focus shifts from direct hypotheses at the individual level to indirect hypotheses with respect to the treatment effects. Section 4.3.3 investigates what the effects of a change in group-size, a change in the value of the public good and a change in the variability of the group-composition are on individuals' decisions to contribute. Section 4.3.4 evaluates the effect of the framing of the game as a public good or a public bad game.

4.3.1 Experimental results on decision rules

Value orientations

The psychological theories discussed in chapter 2 attribute a central role to individual value orientations. The goals pursued by subjects are assessed by means of the choices observed in the decomposed game in experiment 1. Using their choices, 61% of the subjects are classified as individualists and 30% as cooperators. Given that the number

Table 4.4
Some characteristics of the subjects

	low-7	high-7	high-5	pubgood	pubbad	total
individualists (earnings)	77.8% (14.06)	60.3% (29.76)	56.7% (25.28)	45% (26.23)	57.5% (19.67)	60.9% (22.25)
cooperators (earnings)	15.9% (14.10)	33.3% (30.02)	31.7% (23.88)	42.5% (23.68)	30% (18.18)	29.7% (23.37)
competitors	0%	3.2%	10%	10%	10%	6%
others	6.3%	3.2%	1.7%	2.5%	2.5%	3.4%

Notes: For individualists and cooperators the average earnings in guilders for the contribution decision in the second experiment (decision A) are shown in parentheses in guilders. The category 'others' includes subjects who are not classified because their consistency level is smaller than 33%, as well as 1 aggressor (low-7).

of subjects who pursue a different orientation than these two is so small, the analysis will focus on individualists and cooperators. Some subjects are not classified because they do not make sufficient choices consistent with (any) value orientation. Table 4.4 provides more details of the value orientations measured in experiment 1.

All subjects who are classified have a consistency level of at least 33%. The overall level of consistency is 89%, which is relatively high. For example, Liebrand (1984) reports consistency levels of 76% and 80%. Thus, as in the preliminary experiment reported in section 3.2, the use of financial incentives seems to have yielded a high level of consistency.

Psychological hypotheses

Both the psychological *triangle hypothesis* and the *false consensus hypothesis* claim that cooperators will contribute more than individualists do. They also predict that cooperators expect more contributions by others than individualists do, especially in early rounds. The difference between the two hypotheses is that the triangle hypothesis predicts that behavior is determined by expectations, whereas the reverse is predicted by the false consensus hypothesis.

Here, the two common predictions of these models are considered. The first prediction is supported by the data: cooperators contribute significantly more than individualists do. For the analysis the data of all 5 treatments are pooled. In the strangers sessions, interaction exists between all subjects in a session, so the data are independent only at the level of sessions. For the partners sessions, subjects interact with their group-members, but not with subjects outside of their group. Here, the data are independent at the group level. Thus, the strangers treatments yield 10 truly independent pairs of contribution averages per orientation and the partners treatments yield 16 pairs of contribution averages. A Wilcoxon rank test rejects the hypothesis that the mean rank of individualists' contributions is equal to the mean rank of cooperators' contributions ($p=0.01$): cooperators contribute more than individualists.[4]

---

[4]The reported test result computes the average contribution level on the basis of all 20 periods. It could be argued that differences would especially be expected in the first periods, since after a while cooperators might adapt their behavior to individualistic behavior. Significant test results are also obtained if averages are computed on the basis of the first 5 periods only ($p=0.03$) and if averages are computed on period 6-20 ($p=0.01$). The test results are based on 25 pair-wise data only because one group in the partners mode does not contain any cooperator.

One may be concerned that this testing procedure puts too much weight on the data obtained

Figures 4.1 to 4.5 confirm the difference in behavior. In all treatments cooperators contribute more than individualists do. On the basis of the triangle hypothesis one might expect assimilation of behavior. This occurs if cooperators adapt to individualistic behavior because they do not want to be exploited. Assimilation does not seem to be a general force in public good games with a step-level production function.

Figures 4.1-4.5

Contributions per orientation

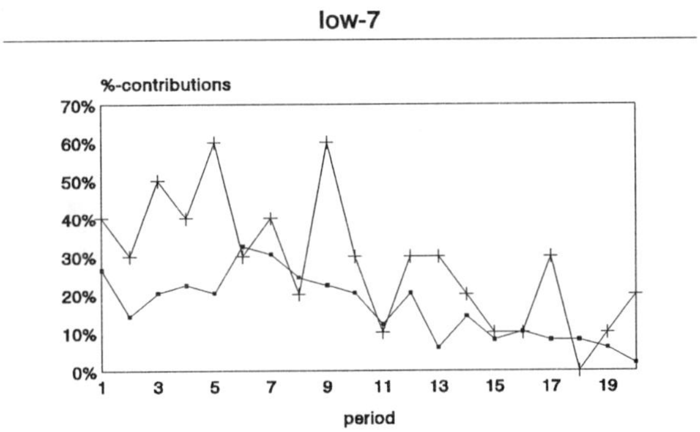

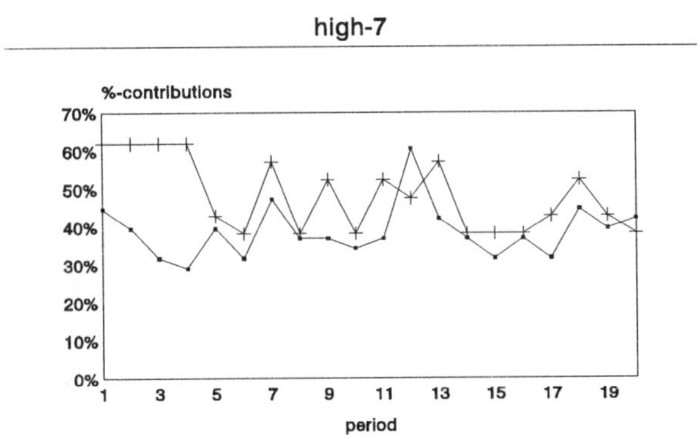

in the partners mode. 5 subjects in the partners mode yield one data-point, whereas in the strangers mode 15 subjects (high-5) or even 21 subjects (low-7, high-7) are needed for one data-point. If one focuses on the data obtained in each mode in isolation, similar results are obtained (Offerman, Sonnemans and Schram, 1996; Sonnemans, Schram and Offerman, 1996).

high-5

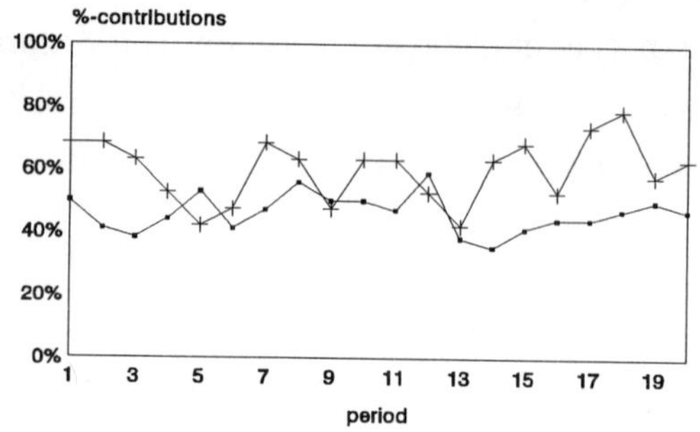

pubgood

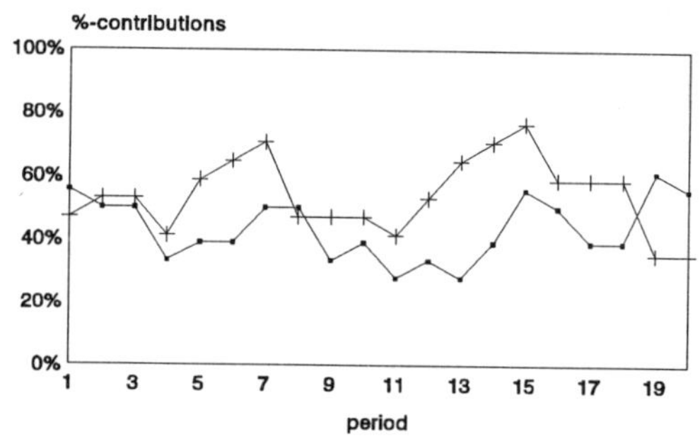

pubbad

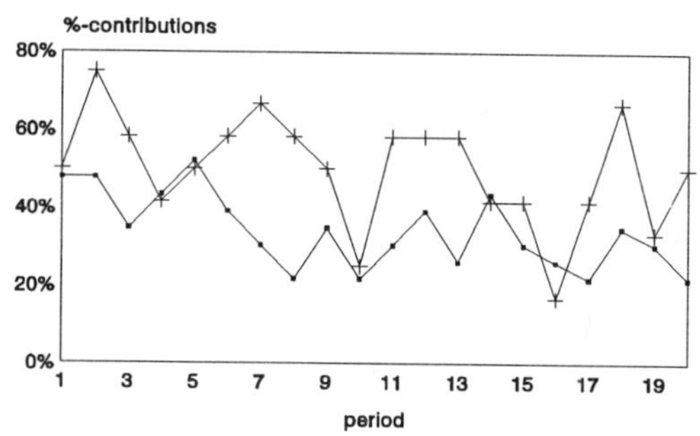

Note: The average contributions for individualists are represented by ⟷ and those for cooperators by ++.

One may argue that some assimilation is taking place in low-7 and high-7. But the difference in behavior seems persistent in the other treatments. The lack of assimilation is not so strange if average earnings on the public good decision are taken into account. Cooperators make as much money as individualists do on decision A (cf. table 4.4). Given that the environment does not give individualists the possibility to exploit cooperators, cooperators may feel less inclined to adapt their preferred behavior.

It might be conjectured that the behavioral difference between individualists and cooperators is an artifact resulting from differences in beliefs. The fact that cooperators contribute more than individualists do cannot be explained merely by a higher estimated probability of being critical for the provision of the good, however. In fact, cooperators do estimate this probability to be higher, but differences are small and insufficient to explain the observed differences in choices.

The second common prediction of the two psychological hypotheses concerns the difference in expectations between individualists and cooperators. Both hypotheses predict that (on average) cooperators expect more contributions by others than individualists do. The data do not provide strong support for this prediction. Table 4.5 presents measures of the estimated probabilities than another player cooperates by individualists and cooperators in the various treatments.

Table 4.5
Estimated probability that another player cooperates (full players only)

	period 1-5		period 6-20		period 1-20	
	individualists	cooperators	individualists	cooperators	individualists	cooperators
low-7	37.4%	41.8%	24.4%	28.0%	27.6%	31.4%
high-7	48.8%	48.9%	45.2%	44.0%	46.1%	45.2%
high-5	51.9%	52.9%	51.7%	52.3%	51.7%	52.4%
pubgood	65.2%	58.5%	61.5%	57.5%	62.4%	57.7%
pubbad	46.8%	51.5%	32.9%	40.5%	36.4%	43.2%
total	46.5%	50.5%	39.6%	45.5%	41.3%	46.8%

Note: The table shows the (average) means of the reported distributions divided by (group-size minus 1).

Treatments low-7 and pubbad yield results consistent with the hypotheses. But treatments high-7 and high-5 seem inconclusive, whereas the difference in expectations in pubgood is opposite to what is expected by the hypotheses. As already mentioned, it is in line with the triangle hypothesis to look at the first five periods only, because cooperators may adjust their expectations after having played against individualists for a while.[5] This does not alter the conclusions.[6]

The major difference between the triangle hypothesis and the false consensus hypothesis lies in the assumption about the causal relationship between expectations and behavior. This difference will be examined in section 4.3.2.

Economic hypotheses: expected value hypothesis

The economic hypotheses vary in degrees of freedom. The simplest of these hypotheses is that subjects maximize expected value. Degrees of freedom can be added to this hypothesis in various dimensions. The first dimension is to allow for utility transformations of the payoff matrix. The second dimension is to allow for differences between individuals (this is strongly suggested by the psychological work discussed). The third dimension is to allow individuals to make errors. The analysis will start with the simple hypothesis and add more freedom step by step.

The expected value hypothesis predicts that subjects will contribute if and only if the expected value of contributing is higher than the expected value of not contributing. In the experiments, subjects are endowed with an amount c, which they may contribute or not to obtain the value of the public good $f(s)-c$, where s contributors are needed in order to have the public good provided. It is easily derived that an expected value maximizer will contribute if and only if (s)he estimates $P(s-1) \geq c/(f(s)-c)$. In low-7 (s)he will contribute if and only if $P(2) \geq 0.5$ and in the other

[5] Instead of using the psychological classification in individualists and cooperators, one can also consider the relationship between the estimated probability that another contributes and (the angle of) the motivational vector itself. This yields similar results.

[6] Overall, the difference between individualists' and cooperators' estimated probability that another contributes is in the expected direction. However, on the truly independent level the difference is far from significant. Here, 10 pairs of averages per session in the strangers mode and 8 pairs of averages per group in the partners mode yield 18 independent pairs of observations. Wilcoxon rank tests miss the significant level for periods 1-5 ($p=0.78$), periods 6-20 ($p=0.37$) and periods 1-20 ($p=0.42$). On the other hand, if each reported distribution is supposed to yield an observation, test results are significant.

treatments if and only if $P(2) \geq 0.324$.

The data do not support this strong hypothesis: only 73% of the decisions not to contribute and 47% of the decisions to contribute are in line with the hypothesis. Because the decisions to contribute are especially inconsistent with reported expectations, it is examined whether the propensity to follow this rule is related to an individual's value orientation. It turns out that individualists behave more consistently with their reported probabilities than cooperators do. Table 4.6 shows the data aggregated over individuals in various treatment - orientation combinations. Underlined percentages are in line with the expected value hypothesis.

Note that cooperators contribute more often, when this is not justified on the basis of their reported expectations than individualists do. However, even though the behavior of individualists is more in line with the hypothesis than that of cooperators, there is still considerable discrepancy between their observed and predicted behavior. Sometimes it is argued that subjects need some time to understand the institutions of the game. To give such an idea a proper chance, percentages of behavior in line with the expected value hypothesis in periods 11-20 are also displayed. The conclusion that many choices are inconsistent with the expected value hypothesis does not change if only decisions in the last ten periods are considered.

Although the expected value hypothesis cannot be maintained in the light of this evidence, a natural question is whether a less demanding comparative statics result following from this hypothesis is supported. A straightforward prediction is that there should be a positive correlation between the estimated probability of being critical and the propensity to contribute. This hypothesis finds support in the data. Over all 20 periods, the reported probability of being critical is significantly higher when a subject chooses to contribute than when a subject chooses not to contribute.[7] As can be inferred from table 4.7, the difference is more pronounced in periods 11-20 than in periods 1-10. This may imply that subjects' comprehension of the situation increases with experience. This conjecture is corroborated by the estimation results for the naive Bayesian model reported in section 5.4.2.

---

[7]For this hypothesis a Wilcoxon rank test is used, $n=18$, $p=0.00$; 10 average session-pairs in the strangers mode and 8 average full players group-pairs in the partners mode are used. The test-results are also significant in each subject mode in isolation ($p=0.02$ in the strangers mode and $p=0.03$ in the partners mode).

Table 4.6

Observed percentage of behavior in line with expected value maximization

	according to expectations, should		does not contribute		contributes	
low-7						
individualists	not contribute:	n=905	85.6%	(90.9%)	14.4%	(9.1%)
	contribute:	n=75	57.3%	(82.1%)	42.7%	(17.9%)
cooperators	not contribute:	n=187	72.2%	(83.5%)	24.8%	(16.5%)
	contribute:	n=13	61.5%	(66.7%)	38.5%	(33.3%)
high-7						
individualists	not contribute:	n=549	73.2%	(64.2%)	26.8%	(35.8%)
	contribute:	n=211	56.9%	(50.8%)	43.1%	(49.2%)
cooperators	not contribute:	n=270	54.4%	(56.8%)	45.6%	(43.2%)
	contribute:	n=150	47.3%	(52.6%)	52.7%	(47.4%)
high-5						
individualists	not contribute:	n=252	65.9%	(72.2%)	34.1%	(27.8%)
	contribute:	n=428	46.7%	(46.6%)	53.3%	(53.4%)
cooperators	not contribute:	n=158	39.2%	(43.8%)	60.8%	(56.3%)
	contribute:	n=222	40.5%	(35.7%)	59.5%	(64.3%)
pubgood						
individualists	not contribute:	n=130	54.6%	(65.4%)	45.4%	(34.6%)
	contribute:	n=50	38.0%	(42.1%)	62.0%	(57.9%)
cooperators	not contribute:	n=72	54.2%	(75.0%)	45.8%	(25.0%)
	contribute:	n=108	29.6%	(28.8%)	70.4%	(71.2%)
pubbad						
individualists	not contribute:	n=121	77.7%	(82.5%)	22.3%	(17.5%)
	contribute:	n=79	50.6%	(56.8%)	49.4%	(43.2%)
cooperators	not contribute:	n=68	72.1%	(83.9%)	27.9%	(16.1%)
	contribute:	n=52	48.1%	(51.7%)	51.9%	(48.3%)
total						
individualists	not contribute:	n=1972	73.6%	(79.5%)	26.4%	(20.5%)
	contribute:	n=828	51.0%	(50.3%)	49.0%	(49.7%)
cooperators	not contribute:	n=759	56.9%	(65.5%)	43.1%	(34.5%)
	contribute:	n=541	41.8%	(40.4%)	58.2%	(59.6%)

Notes: The number of decisions *n* refers to the choices over all 20 periods. The numbers in parentheses are for periods 11-20 only. Underlined numbers are in line with the expected value hypothesis.

Table 4.7
(Mean) reported probabilities of being critical

		individualistic		cooperative	
	period	does not contribute	contributes	does not contribute	contributes
low-7	1-10	28.6%	32.4%	35.0%	27.5%
	11-20	20.8%	36.0%	20.4%	25.4%
	1-20	24.4%	33.4%	26.5%	26.8%
high-7	1-10	25.1%	24.4%	24.4%	30.8%
	11-20	25.4%	31.9%	27.7%	32.4%
	1-20	25.3%	28.3%	26.1%	31.6%
high-5	1-10	32.3%	37.8%	39.1%	34.2%
	11-20	33.5%	45.4%	39.0%	43.0%
	1-20	32.9%	41.5%	39.0%	38.7%
pubgood	1-10	19.9%	26.2%	32.0%	33.9%
	11-20	28.7%	41.0%	33.0%	51.8%
	1-20	24.8%	32.8%	32.5%	42.6%
pubbad	1-10	25.4%	42.6%	27.9%	30.4%
	11-20	21.3%	39.8%	26.3%	42.5%
	1-20	23.2%	41.4%	27.0%	35.4%
total	1-10	27.8%	32.0%	31.4%	32.0%
	11-20	24.7%	38.7%	28.7%	40.2%
	1-20	26.2%	35.1%	30.0%	35.8%

Expected utility hypotheses

Showing that people do not maximize expected value does not imply that they do not maximize expected utility. For example, warm-glow cooperators attach additional utility to the act of cooperation, implying that a lower probability of being critical is sufficient to induce them to contribute. The same implication follows for material cooperators adding extra utility to the value of the public good itself. In-group cooperators attach extra utility for being part of the sub-group providing the public good. Their inclination to contribute is not only positively correlated to the subjectively estimated probability of being critical (ceteris paribus), but also to the subjectively estimated probability of being redundant (ceteris paribus). The precise utility transformations for these different types were reported in table 2.2. According to expected utility theory, material cooperators should contribute if and only if they estimate $P(s\text{-}1) \geq c/(f(s)\text{-}c+x)$; warm-glow cooperators should contribute if and only if they estimate $P(s\text{-}1) \geq (c\text{-}y)/(f(s)\text{-}c)$ and in-group cooperators if and only if they estimate $P(s\text{-}1) \geq (c\text{-}zP(>s\text{-}1))/(f(s)\text{-}c+z)$ (cf. section 2.2.1).

The three expected utility hypotheses are given their best shot by allowing each subject to have a private subjective transformation of the payoff matrix. On the basis of her or his choices, for each individual the 'optimal' x, y, and z value can be determined. Optimality is defined such that the observed choices fit the expected utility hypothesis best. For the x and y transformation, each value of x or y yields a cut-off point in terms of the subjective probability that exactly two other individuals will contribute ($P(s\text{-}1)=P(2)$).[8] For in-group cooperators the decision whether or not to contribute should not only depend on $P(s\text{-}1)$, but also on $P(>s\text{-}1)$ (or $P(<s\text{-}1)$). When $z \geq (c\text{-}f(s)*P(s\text{-}1)+c*P(s\text{-}1))/(P(>s\text{-}1)+P(s\text{-}1))$, an in-group cooperator should contribute. For each individual the 'optimal' z can be computed by ordering her or his twenty realizations for $[c\text{-}f(s)*P(s\text{-}1)+c*P(s\text{-}1))/(P(>s\text{-}1)+P(s\text{-}1)]$ and subsequently choosing z such that (s)he makes the least possible errors against this bench-mark.

Only 19.5% of the players (n=226) make no mistake against their optimal x-y cut-off point. Of these 15% always or never contribute. These subjects act in line with the heterogeneous version of the expected utility hypothesis in a trivial sense. On average, subjects make 3.1 errors against their optimal x-y cut-off point. A considerable proportion of 30.1% of the players make 5 or more mistakes against their optimal x-y cut-off point (in 20 periods).

For the z transformation the results are even worse. The only subjects who make no mistakes against their optimal z cut-off point are those who always or never contribute (15%). On average subjects make 4.3 mistakes against their optimal z cut-off point. 49.9% of the subjects make 5 or more mistakes against their optimal z cut-off point.

---

[8]Note that if one computes the 'optimal' x or y as described, one is actually determining the value of $P(2)$ - the cut-off point - such, that the individual makes the least possible errors from an economic point of view. Therefore, the cut-off points in terms of $P(2)$ are the same for both transformations (though one value of $P(2)$ yields different values of x and y).

Strictly speaking, each expected utility hypothesis is a deterministic hypothesis, and should be rejected even if only one error is observed against it. That might be too strong a criterion. However, the best shot of the hypothesis, allowing each subject to have her or his own subjective cut-off point, does not survive even when weak criteria are used. On the basis of this analysis, it seems highly implausible that a deterministic model will do the trick. Therefore, the emphasis of the analysis will now shift to stochastic hypotheses allowing subjects to make genuine errors.

Expected value/utility with noise hypotheses
As discussed in section 2.2.1, a (logistic) quantal response is a noisy best response with the property that the probability of an error increases as the difference in expected value (utility) between the alternatives decreases. According to the expected value with noise hypothesis, subjects give a quantal response on the basis of the *expected values* of the alternatives. According to the expected utility with noise hypothesis, subjects give a quantal response on the basis of the *expected utilities* of the alternatives. Here, the three types of cooperators discussed above provide the operationalization of this hypothesis as well.

Under the expected value with noise hypothesis, given the assumption with respect to the distribution of the noise, the calculation of the likelihood of the data with maximum likelihood methods is straightforward (cf. equations 2.2, 2.3 and 2.4). The calculation of the likelihood for the expected utility with noise hypothesis with a heterogeneous population will be explained in detail. First, note that there are no compelling theoretical reasons to assume that the distribution of player types belongs to a particular parametric family. Heckman and Singer (1984) argue that it is risky to make an arbitrary choice for a particular parametric family of distributions in such a case, because the estimation results may vary considerably with the chosen distribution. They favor a non-parametric procedure to estimate the distribution of unobserved player types. This procedure is followed here.

For a start, assume that two internally homogeneous groups of a single type of cooperators exist. Given this assumption, it will be established which utility transformation has the highest probability of generating the data. In the material cooperators model, assume that a randomly drawn individual has the utility component $x=x_1$ with probability $Q(x_1)$ and utility component $x=x_2$ with probability $(1-Q(x_1))$. The probabilities reported by subjects are used to calculate the expected utility of an alternative given the subject's type. Let $P_j(i,t)$ denote the reported probability of outcome j by subject i in period t and $P_{>j}(i,t)$ the reported probability of an outcome greater than j by subject i in period t; $d_{i,t}$ denotes the decision, such that $d_{i,t}=0$ if subject i decides not to contribute in period t, and $d_{i,t}=1$ if (s)he does; $L_x(d_{i,t} \mid x_j)$ denotes the probability that i takes decision $d_{i,t}$, given that (s)he transforms the payoff matrix as a material cooperator with utility component $x=x_j$ (cf. equation 2.3). The notation for the warm-glow and in-group cooperators models is similar. Given the assumed extreme value error term, it holds that:

$$L_x\ (d_{i,t} \mid x_j) = \frac{d_{i,t}}{1+e^{\lambda*[c\ -\ (f(s)+x_j-c)*P_{s-1}\ (i,t)]}} + \frac{1\ -\ d_{i,t}}{1+e^{\lambda*[(f(s)+x_j-c)*P_{s-1}\ (i,t)\ -\ c]}} \qquad 4.1$$

$$L_y\ (d_{i,t} \mid y_j) = \frac{d_{i,t}}{1+e^{\lambda*[c\ -y_j\ -\ (f(s)-c)*P_{s-1}\ (i,t)]}} + \frac{1\ -\ d_{i,t}}{1+e^{\lambda*[(f(s)-c)*P_{s-1}\ (i,t)\ +\ y_j\ -\ c]}} \qquad 4.2$$

$$L_z(d_{i,t} \mid z_j) = \frac{d_{i,t}}{1+e^{\lambda*[c-(f(s)+z_j-c)*P_{s-1}(i,t)-z_j*P_{>s-1}(i,t)]}} + \frac{1-d_{i,t}}{1+e^{\lambda*[(f(s)+z_j-c)*P_{s-1}(i,t)+z_j*P_{>s-1}(i,t)-c]}}\ . \qquad 4.3$$

The unconditional probability that subject i takes decisions $d_{i,1},..,d_{i,20}$ according to model u (with $u \in \{x,y,z\}$) is denoted by $L_u(d_{i,1},..,d_{i,20})$:

$$L_u\ (d_{i,1},..,d_{i,20}) = Q(u_1)*\prod_{t=1}^{20} L_u\ (d_{i,t} \mid u_1) + (1-Q(u_1))*\prod_{t=1}^{20} L_u\ (d_{i,t} \mid u_2). \qquad 4.4$$

The results of the estimations for the model without utility transformations and the results for two-groups models are summarized in table 4.8.[9]

The two-groups expected utility with noise hypotheses explain the data better than the expected value with noise hypothesis. The addition of 3 parameters u_1, u_2 and $Q(u_1)$ to the basic model for expected value increases the likelihood of the data significantly in each treatment (Likelihood Ratio test).

---

[9]For the maximum likelihood estimations and the logit regressions reported in this study the data are assumed to be independent at the choice level. This is not a completely innocent assumption, as was discussed in chapter 1.

Table 4.8

Maximum likelihood estimations for expected value/utility with noise hypotheses

		low-7	high-7	high-5	pubgood	pubbad
Expected value with noise	λ	0.0362**	0.0106**	0.0079**	0.0126**	0.0145**
	-logL	674.7	856.2	820.4	267.4	261.7
Expected utility with noise: Material cooperators	λ	0.0319**	0.0156**	0.0114**	0.0085*	0.0269**
	x_1	-139.83**	-162.60**	-306.89**	-856.33*	-140.97**
	x_2	17.59	275.24**	103.34**	193.86*	-50.19**
	$Q(x_1)$	0.62**	0.71**	0.31**	0.15*	0.24
	-logL	575.8	777.4	756.6	241.9	241.7
Expected utility with noise: Warm-glow cooperators	λ	0.0144**	0.0083**	0.0093**	0.0129**	0.0132**
	y_1	-154.68**	-202.33**	-155.15**	-190.49**	-126.11**
	y_2	-16.98	61.44**	61.32**	44.05**	-16.87
	$Q(y_1)$	0.54**	0.43**	0.34**	0.15*	0.35**
	-logL	569.3	739.9	740.0	239.6	237.9
Expected utility with noise: In-group cooperators	λ	0.0334**	0.0084**	0.0103**	0.0176**	0.0197**
	z_1	-100.13**	-231.48**	-155.87**	-39.19**	-106.11**
	z_2	9.43*	71.73**	88.10**	87.64**	-9.57
	$Q(z_1)$	0.41**	0.41**	0.37**	0.52**	0.29*
	-logL	603.2	737.7	745.0	240.2	251.5

Notes: Estimation of utility parameters in two-groups quantal response function. * indicates significance at the 5%-level; ** at the 1%-level (t-tests). The log-likelihood displayed is the log-likelihood of all choices in a treatment.

The comparison *between* the three two-groups models is obscured by the fact that none is nested in any other. Nevertheless, the structure of the models is very similar: all three models assume that people give quantal responses to subjective expectations and all three models have an equal number of degrees of freedom. Furthermore, the same basic expected value with noise model is nested in each of the three general models. If the 3 parameters u_1, u_2 and $Q(u_1)$ are set equal to 0 in any of the general models, the basic model is obtained. Comparing the likelihood of the three two-groups models gives an idea which utility transformation is most likely, given that subjects make quantal responses. The transformation for warm-glow cooperators scores better in this respect than the transformation for material cooperators in all treatments, and it works better than the transformation for in-group cooperators in all treatments except high-7.[10] For the remainder of the estimations, the focus will therefore be on the warm-glow cooperators model.[11]

Of course, there is no a priori reason to restrict the number of internally homogeneous groups of warm-glow cooperators to two. Starting with two groups, the number of internally homogeneous groups can be allowed to increase for each treatment as long as the likelihood of the data increases significantly according to a likelihood ratio test (at the 5%-level). With k groups of internally homogeneous warm-glow cooperators, the unconditional likelihood of an individual's choices can be adapted straightforwardly:

$$L_y\,(d_{i,1},..,d_{i,20}) = Q(y_1) * \prod_{t=1}^{20} L_y(d_{i,t} \mid y_1) + Q(y_2) * \prod_{t=1}^{20} L_y(d_{i,t} \mid y_2) \\ + \ldots + (1-\sum_{i=1}^{k-1} Q(y_i)) * \prod_{t=1}^{20} L_y(d_{i,t} \mid y_k)\ , \qquad 4.5$$

where $Q(y_i)$ denotes the probability that a randomly selected individual has utility component y_i. The estimation results for this model are summarized in table 4.9.

A comparison of the estimation results reported in table 4.8 and 4.9 reveals that the heterogeneity of the subjects is not yet sufficiently captured by the two-groups hypotheses with the exception of treatment pubbad. Four types of players are even selected by the estimation procedure in treatments high-7 and high-5.

The estimates for the utility components vary considerably within a treatment. Some of the subjects contribute always or never. If a subject always contributes, the

[10]As already indicated in the analyses of the deterministic hypotheses, subjects make a considerable number of errors. Nevertheless, the low estimates for λ may be misleading in the sense that they suggest an even lower level of rationality than actually present. For example, if λ would be equal to 0.1 and if the difference in expected value between the alternatives would be equal to 30 cents, an individual would make an error with a probability of less than 5%.

[11]Note also that the estimates of the utility transformation parameters x, y, and z vary between treatments. For example, pubbad seems to elicit more competitive rules than pubgood. This issue is elaborated in detail in section 4.3.4.

Table 4.9

Maximum likelihood estimations for heterogeneous warm-glow cooperators

	low-7	high-7	high-5	pubgood	pubbad
λ	0.0150**	0.0121**	0.0083**	0.0169**	0.0132**
y_1	-264.85**	-328.88**	-622.61	-226.04**	-126.11**
y_2	-66.08**	-54.81**	-140.77**	-3.35	-16.87
y_3	36.73**	58.21**	57.49**	94.76**	XX
y_4	XX	1573.45	415.51**	XX	XX
$Q(y_1)$	0.27**	0.17**	0.05	0.10	0.35**
$Q(y_2)$	0.59**	0.45**	0.29**	0.54**	XX
$Q(y_3)$	XX	0.32**	0.62**	XX	XX
-logL	558.4	689.2	724.6	228.5	237.9

Notes: * indicates significance at the 5%-level; ** at the 1%-level (t-tests). The log-likelihood displayed is the log-likelihood of all choices in a treatment. XX indicates that the introduction of the parameter concerned does not increase the likelihood of the data significantly (Likelihood Ratio test).

model's maximum likelihood estimate for this subject's utility component will approach infinity, because that maximizes the probability that the subject will contribute. The opposite effect results if a subject never contributes. Therefore, from a mathematical point of view one might have expected more extreme estimates than those reported in table 4.9.

However, for a meaningful interpretation the estimates for some of the utility components are already very extreme.[12] The presence of never or always contributing subjects in the experiments apparently renders some of the estimates implausibly low or high. One should be cautious not to attach too much value to the exact value of the estimates.

Nevertheless, the estimates can be used for two purposes. First, the estimates

[12]An alternative procedure would be to bound the utility components from below and from above. For example it might be assumed that utility components are such that subjects do not have a dominant strategy to choose either of the alternatives in a one-shot game. Of course, the choice of such a criterion would be rather arbitrary.

of unobserved utility components can be compared to the observed scores on the decomposed game technique. If the results of the economic approach of estimating unobserved utility components correspond to the results of the psychological approach to measuring value orientations, further credence is lent to the approach of differing value orientations. Second, the estimation results can be used for simulations. Even with these quite extreme estimates, the general picture of the experimental results can be simulated reasonably well, as will be seen in chapter 5.

For the comparison with the results of the decomposed game technique, the posterior probability is calculated that an individual is of the y_1, y_2, y_3 or y_4 type, on the basis of the estimation results. For example, in high-7 the posterior probability $P(y[i] = y_3 \mid d_{i,1},\ldots,d_{i,20})$ that a subject has utility component y_3 is equal to:

$$P(y[i]=y_3 \mid d_{i,1},..,d_{i,20}) = \frac{Q(y_3) * \prod_{t=1}^{20} L_y(d_{i,t} \mid y_3)}{\sum_{i=1}^{4} [Q(y_i)) * \prod_{t=1}^{20} L_y(d_{i,t} \mid y_i)]} . \qquad 4.6$$

Using these probabilities, one can determine the mean value of y per individual. One would expect that individuals classified as cooperators on the basis of the decomposed game technique would have higher means on the posterior probability distribution over types than individuals classified as individualists. One would also expect a positive correlation between the ranks of the means of the posterior probability distributions and the ranks of the angles observed with the decomposed game technique.

Table 4.10 shows that the relationship between the estimated probability distribution and the score on the decomposed game technique is positive as expected: the mean (posterior) value of y is smaller for individualists than for cooperators. However, the Spearman rank correlation coefficients only differ significantly from 0 in high-5 and for the pooled data. The decomposed game technique may be a noisy measurement instrument. The extremity of the estimates of the warm-glow cooperator types should not bias the correlation coefficients too much in this analysis, since the correlation coefficient reported takes only the ranks into consideration, and not the absolute magnitudes.

The estimation results favor the hypothesis that people transform the payoff matrix as warm-glow cooperators. However, there is another aspect which allows one

Table 4.10
Mean of the estimated posterior distribution

	low-7	high-7	high-5	pubgood	pubbad	total
individualists	-117.84 (n=49)	-20.12 (n=38)	-54.11 (n=34)	6.34 (n=9)	-59.69 (n=10)	-63.70 (n=140)
cooperators	-65.39 (n=10)	180.41 (n=21)	45.83 (n=19)	5.01 (n=9)	-46.98 (n=6)	57.98 (n=65)
Spearman rank correlation	0.20 (n=59)	0.07 (n=59)	0.42** (n=53)	0.15 (n=18)	0.40 (n=16)	0.27** (n=205)

Notes: Between parentheses the number of subjects is displayed. * indicates significance at the 1%-level, ** at the 0.1%-level. Only consistent individualists and consistent cooperators are included.

to distinguish between the three utility transformations. The model of in-group cooperators predicts that a negative correlation will exist between the subjectively estimated probability of one's contribution being futile and the inclination to contribute. Such a correlation is not predicted by the models based on warm-glow or material cooperators. The actual correlation may thus serve as additional, more direct evidence for which model organizes the data best.[13]

Table 4.11 reports the average reported probability of being futile when a contribution is made and this probability when no contribution is made. The evidence supports the in-group cooperators model. Over all 20 periods, the reported probability of being futile when a contribution is made is significantly smaller than the reported probability for being futile when no contribution is made.[14] Both cooperators and individualists expect a higher probability of being futile when they do not contribute,

---

[13]In the notation of section 2.2.1, in-group cooperators contribute if they estimate the probability of being critical $P(s\text{-}1) \geq (c\text{-}zP(>s\text{-}1))/(f(s)\text{-}c+z)$, or, equivalently, if they estimate $P(s\text{-}1) \geq (c\text{-}z+zP(<s\text{-}1))/(f(s)\text{-}c)$. Therefore, if $z>0$, they will sooner contribute if they estimate the probability of being redundant higher, or, equivalently, if they estimate the probability of being futile smaller (given the probability of being critical).

[14] Wilcoxon rank test with average values per session in the strangers mode and average values per group in the partners mode as data-points (n=18; p=0.00). Again, the hypothesis is significant in the strangers mode (n=10; p=0.05) as well as in the partners mode (n=8; p=0.04).

Table 4.11
(Mean) reported probabilities of being futile

	period	individualists: does not contribute	individualists: contributes	cooperators: does not contribute	cooperators: contributes
low-7	1-10	37.0%	25.1%	25.4%	21.7%
	11-20	64.9%	28.1%	61.5%	40.6%
	1-20	52.1%	26.0%	46.4%	27.4%
high-7	1-10	14.0%	11.4%	14.8%	11.4%
	11-20	9.9%	13.6%	14.2%	10.5%
	1-20	12.0%	12.5%	14.4%	11.0%
high-5	1-10	30.4%	28.2%	28.6%	23.7%
	11-20	28.5%	26.0%	25.3%	26.6%
	1-20	29.4%	27.1%	27.0%	25.2%
pubgood	1-10	24.1%	12.2%	25.6%	13.5%
	11-20	17.9%	12.4%	21.1%	14.4%
	1-20	20.6%	12.3%	23.3%	13.9%
pubbad	1-10	53.8%	29.6%	51.8%	29.0%
	11-20	71.6%	37.8%	49.6%	39.1%
	1-20	63.5%	33.0%	50.6%	33.2%
total	1-10	30.1%	21.3%	25.6%	18.3%
	11-20	43.3%	21.2%	32.6%	21.0%
	1-20	37.0%	21.3%	29.3%	19.6%

and this effect is found in the first ten periods of the game as well as for the second ten periods.

These results are not consistent with the results of the maximum likelihood estimations. This may indicate that a part of the population transforms the payoff matrix as a warm-glow cooperator, whereas another part transforms it as an in-group cooperator.

4.3.2 The relationship between expectations and behavior

The causal relationship between expectations and behavior can be assessed using the distinction in players and spectators introduced in the high-5 treatment. According to the false consensus hypothesis, expectations are determined by behavior. Players have a narrow view of the world around them, because they tend to expect that others make the same choice they do. Spectators do not fall prey to such projection, because they do not make a choice. As a result one would expect the variance of the player's expectations to be smaller than the variance of the (paired) spectator's expectations. In the triangle hypothesis and the hypotheses abstracted from the expected utility approach, behavior is assumed to be determined by expectations. Players' expectations are not affected by their choice. As a result one would expect that there are no systematic differences between the variances of players and of spectators.

As discussed above, 31 spectators were added to the public good game in the high-5 treatment, implying that 31 players were paired to an anonymous spectator, and 29 were not.[15] Comparing the distributions reported by spectators and players, there is no systematic difference between the means of their reported distributions.[16] There is a slight difference in the variance of the reported distributions, however. It turns out that 20 spectators report distributions with a smaller variance and 11 spectators report distributions with a greater variance than the corresponding players do. Dawes, McTavish and Shaklee (1977) report similar results. On the basis of this comparison, the triangle hypothesis does better than the false consensus hypothesis: if anything, players report distributions with variances *greater* than those of spectators. Of course, it is impossible to conclude from this evidence that choices do not affect expectations in any way. But the evidence is more consistent with hypotheses based on the assumption that expectations determine behavior than with the hypothesis assuming that behavior determines expectations.

One may also search for more complicated ways in which choices affect expectations. For example, players may consider the decision whether or not to contribute and the decision to report expectations as a super-decision, so that they insure themselves for a bad outcome on one (sub-)decision by the choice for the other

---

[15]There does not seem to be a difference in the decisions of players that have spectators paired to them and players that do not.

[16]A Wilcoxon rank test does not reject the hypothesis that the average mean of a player is equal in rank to the average mean of the corresponding spectator ($n=31$, $p=0.23$). There are not enough sessions (4) to use average data per session as observations for this hypothesis.

(sub-)decision. Or they may neglect valuable information about others' choices in order to rationalize their expectations on the basis of their own choice. These are all factors causing a gap between 'true' original expectations and 'biased' reported expectations. In all these cases, one would expect players with biased expectations to earn less money from their predictions than spectators with true expectations. This is not the case. If anything, spectators make *less* money from the reported distributions than players do (although the difference is small, f 14.00 versus f 14.33).

A related question is whether the mere elicitation of beliefs affects decisions. To investigate this question, one session in the pubgood treatment and one session in the pubbad treatment are carried out without the elicitation of beliefs. Simple players only make the decision to contribute, and full players both make the decision to contribute and report their beliefs. On average, 40 simple players contribute as much as 40 full players (45.6% contributions versus 45.4% contributions). Nevertheless, simple players earn somewhat more money than full players from the decision whether or not to contribute to the public good (f22.25 versus f21.25). A Mann-Whitney rank test does not reject the null-hypothesis that the mean rank decision A earnings for simple players are equal to those for full players (m=40, n=40, p=0.26).[17]

Although one can never be sure that the elicitation of expectations does not affect the choices made, or that the decision whether or not to contribute does not affect the beliefs reported, this analysis indicates that at least some obvious effects do not exist. The data favor the hypotheses based on the assumption that expectations determine behavior more than the hypothesis based on the opposite relationship.

4.3.3 Group-size, value of the public good and subject mode

In this section the effects of three different changes in the institutions on the individual propensity to contribute are investigated experimentally. The effects of changing group-size or the value of the public good are investigated for the strangers treatments only, and the effect of changing the subjects mode (the variability of the group-composition) is investigated for high payoff and small group-size only. The impact of a change in group-size on individual contribution behavior is assessed by a comparison

---

[17]For this test the true independent averages on group level could have been used as data points (n=16), but it was feared that such a test would be too conservative in order to conclude that no differences exist.

of the treatments high-5 and high-7 (with 5 and 7 subjects in a group, respectively). The impact of a change in the value of the public good is assessed by comparing the number of contributions in low-7 with the number in high-7 (with a public payoff *f(s)* equal to 180 and 245, respectively). The impact of a change in subject mode is assessed by comparing treatments high-5 and pubgood (with changing versus constant groups).

The effects of a change in the value of the public good and a change in group-size are intuitive and as expected by various models discussed in chapter 2. The average contribution levels are given in table 4.12. Increasing the value of the public good from low-7 to high-7 increases the individual propensity to contribute. This effect is significant: subjects in high-7 contribute more than subjects in low-7 (Mann-Whitney test at the independent session level: m=3, n=3, p=0.05). Increasing group-size from high-5 to high-7 decreases the individual propensity to contribute. This difference is significant as well: subjects in high-5 contribute more than subjects in high-7 (similar Mann-Whitney test: m=4, n=3, p=0.03). Figure 4.6 presents the contribution rates over periods for these three strangers treatments.

Table 4.12
Mean contribution percentage per treatment

% contributions	low-7	high-7	high-5	pubgood
individualists	16.5% (n=49)	38.7% (n=38)	46.2% (n=34)	43.3% (n=18)
cooperators	28.5% (n=10)	48.1% (n=21)	60.0% (n=19)	54.1% (n=17)
all	19.8% (n=63)	41.0% (n=63)	50.4% (n=60)	51.1% (n=40)
% threshold reached	18.3%	61.7%	51.3%	50.6%

Note: Between parentheses the number of individuals is depicted.

The effect of a change in subject mode is negligible. Individuals contribute as much when groups remain constant as when groups change all the time. The difference in contributions between pubgood (constant groups) and high-5 (changing groups) is far from significant (Mann-Whitney test with averages per group in pubgood and averages per session in high-5 as observations, m=8, n=4, p=0.73). This result can be rationalized by belief learning models, assuming that players do not think strategically, although it is formally not inconsistent with game theoretic models either.[18] The repeated play of an equilibrium in the one-shot game is an equilibrium of the repeated game, so it is possible that players focus on the same equilibrium in both treatments. Figure 4.7 presents the contributions per period in pubgood and high-5.

One may be concerned that the behavioral differences found as a result of a change in the value of the public good are actually caused by a different mixture of types of individuals in treatments low-7 and high-7. In low-7 the relative number of individualists is higher than in high-7. However, this difference does not explain the differences in contributions observed. In fact, this treatment effect carries over to both individualists and cooperators in low-7 and high-7 (see table 4.12). Both orientations contribute more in high-7 than in low-7. A similar observation can be made for the effect of group-size. Both individualists and cooperators contribute more in high-5 than in high-7. The conclusion for the effect of subject mode is not affected by a different mixture of types of individuals either. Overall, subjects contribute a little more in pubgood than in high-5, but this effect seems to be mainly due to the fact that relatively more cooperators are present in pubgood. In fact, both orientations contribute *less* in pubgood than high-5, but differences are quite small (table 4.12).[19]

The treatment effects may be the result of either differences in decision rules or differences in beliefs. Subjects may be more inclined to contribute in a particular

---

[18]One might fear that the test at the truly independent level is too conservative to conclude that the null-hypothesis is not rejected. In order to include more of the variation in group contributions, the group data per period can be pooled by treatment to test the coincidence of the distributions of group contributions between two treatments using a Mann-Whitney test. The difference between pubgood and high-5 remains far from significant with such a test (m=160, n=240, p=0.76). The difference between low-7 and high-7 is more significant with such a test (m=180, n=180, p=0.00). The same test can be used to test the coincidence of the distributions of the *percent* of total potential markers purchased in high-7 and high-5 (percentages because these treatments differ in group-size). The difference between high-7 and high-5 is also more significant with such a test (m=180, n=240, p=0.00).This test was suggested by an anonymous referee of the Economic Journal.

[19]Note that the decline in contributions with repetition often reported for public good games with a dominant strategy to contribute is only found for low-7 (cf. Ledyard, 1995). Given the declining contributions in the last two rounds in high-5 and high-7, it might be argued that there is a general final round effect. However, the fact that there is an increase in the contributions in these treatments just before these last two rounds renders such a conclusion less straightforward.

Figure 4.6
Contributions per period in the strangers treatments

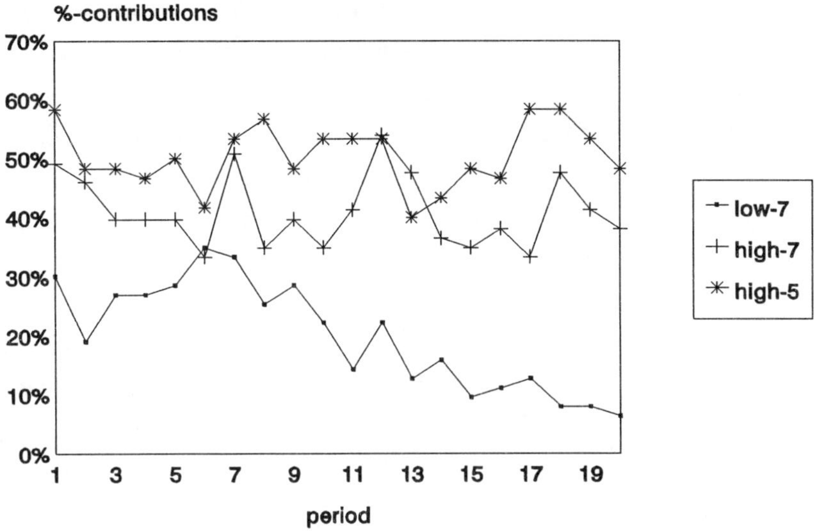

Figure 4.7
Contributions per period: high-5 versus pubgood

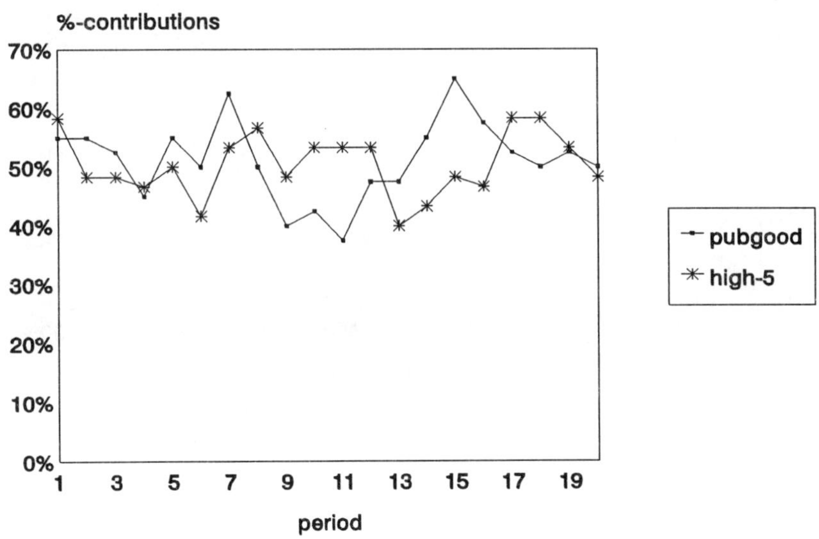

treatment because they value contribution more or because they estimate the probability of being critical higher than in another treatment. This is analyzed in figure 4.8 by considering the results of some logit regressions. In these regressions the choice whether or not to contribute is explained by the estimated probability of being critical. Consider the effect of a change in the value of the public good from low-7 to high-7. The logit regressions strongly suggest that there is a difference in decision rules between these treatments. Given any estimated probability of being critical, subjects are more inclined to contribute in high-7 than in low-7. At the same time, there is no substantial difference in the estimated probability of being critical in these treatments. In low-7, the average estimated probability of being critical is 26.4%, whereas this probability is 26.8% in high-7. Therefore, the effect of a change in the value of the public good is mainly attributed to a difference in decision rules.

Figure 4.8
Logit regressions for low-7, high-7, high-5 and pubgood

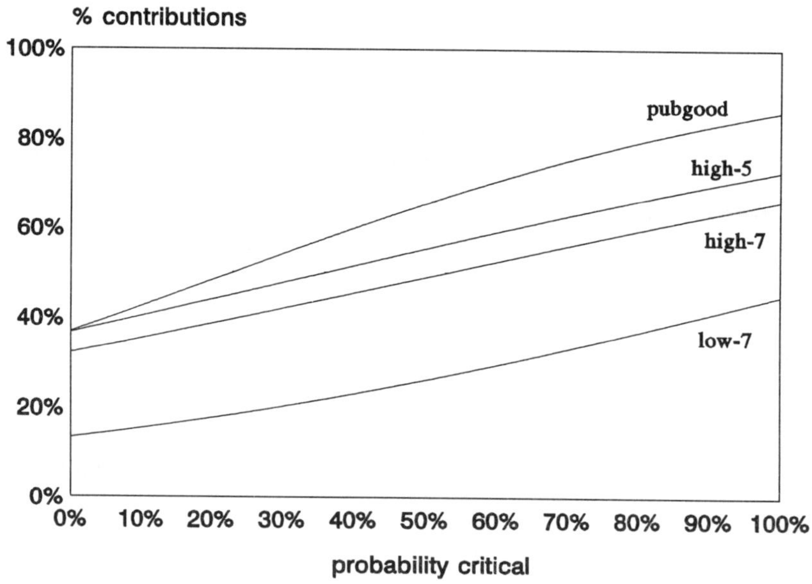

Notes: The results for the logit regression are for low-7: constant=-1.8684, B=0.0167, n=1260; for high-7: constant=-0.7462, B=0.0142, n=1260; for high-5: constant=-0.5453, B=0.0153, n=1200; for pubgood: constant=-0.5372, B=0.0236, n=400. All coefficients are significant at the 1% level (t-tests).

The picture is different for the effect of group-size. The logit regressions indicate that the effect may partly be explained by a difference in decision rules: given any probability of being critical, subjects are more inclined to contribute in high-5 than in high-7. However, the difference is rather small. In fact, this treatment effect may be better explained by a difference in beliefs. In high-5 subjects estimate the probability of being critical substantially higher than in high-7 (36.9% versus 26.8%).

The result that a change in the subject mode does not affect the inclination to contribute seems to be due to the interplay of two opposing forces. The logit regressions suggest that given a probability of being critical, subjects are more inclined to contribute when groups remain constant (pubgood) than when they change (high-5). On the other hand, subjects estimate the probability of being critical to be higher when groups change (36.9% in high-5 versus 33.4% in pubgood). However, both the difference in decision rules and the difference in beliefs are rather small.

The treatment effects are in line with both the predictions of various game theoretic models and the predictions of different belief learning models. For the effect of a change in the value of the public good, theorem 2.2 and corollary 2.1 (but not corollary 2.2) provide game theoretic predictions consistent with the evidence and theorem 2.12 provides belief learning predictions consistent with the evidence. For the effect of a change in group-size, theorems 2.3 and 2.13 provide a game theoretic and a belief learning prediction, both consistent with the evidence. A sharper analysis to distinguish between these different models will be provided in the next chapter.

4.3.4 Effect of framing: public good provision versus public bad prevention

In this section an experimental analysis is provided for subjects' behavior in strategically equivalent public good and public bad games. In the public good game subjects choose whether or not to contribute to the public good, and if enough contributions are made, the public good is provided. In the public bad game, subjects choose whether or not to withdraw an amount from a common pool, and if too many withdrawals are made, the public bad occurs, i.e., the public good is not provided. For both frames the partners mode is used: groups remain constant over periods. Uncontrolled empirical research suggests that an interesting behavioral difference exists between the two frames: in public good games often more cooperative actions are observed than in public bad games (cf. section 2.2.3).

As already mentioned, to avoid confusion a subject's decision not to withdraw the amount from the common pool in the public bad game will be referred to as the cooperative action, or simply a contribution. Table 4.13 shows that subjects indeed make more cooperative choices in the public good frame than in the public bad frame. The difference is significant using a Mann-Whitney test (at the independent group level: m=8, n=8, p=0.04).[20] As a consequence, subjects earn more money (table 4.4) and reach the threshold more often in the public good treatment than in the public bad treatment.

Table 4.13

Mean contribution percentage per partners treatment

	treatment	public good	public bad
% contributions	individualists	43.3% (n=18)	33.9% (n=23)
	cooperators	54.1% (n=17)	50.0% (n=12)
	all	51.1% (n=40)	39.9% (n=40)
	% threshold reached	50.6%	31.3%

Note: Between parentheses the number of individuals is depicted.

Figure 4.9 displays the percentage of cooperative choices per period for both treatments. The difference appears to grow over periods: while the level of cooperation starts off approximately equal in both cases, in the public good treatment the number of cooperative choices stays stable, whereas the public bad treatment shows a decrease. In the first 5 periods there is almost no difference, in periods 6-15 the difference is roughly 10%-points and in the last 5 periods the difference is 20%-points. There may be an end-period effect in the public bad game, but not in the related public good game.

There is a difference in behavior observed in the two strategically equivalent frames. The question is how this behavioral difference is best explained. A first possibility is

[20]The same test as described in footnote 16 can be applied here to include more of the variation in group contributions. Again, the Mann-Whitney test is more significant at this level (m=160, n=160, p=0.00).

Figure 4.9
The percentage of contributions in the public good and the public bad treatment

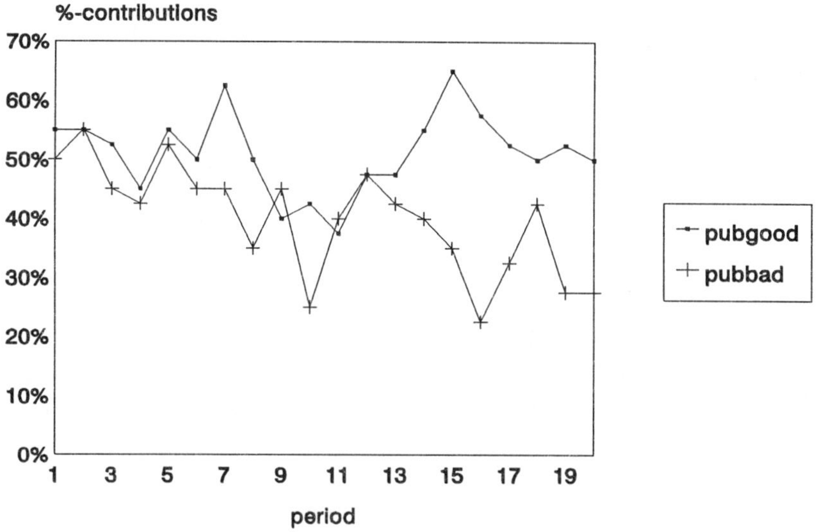

that the effect is 'coincidentally' caused by the presence of a relatively high number of cooperators in the public good treatment and a relatively low number of cooperators in the public bad treatment. In table 4.13 it can be seen that the treatment effect carries over across value orientations: both orientations make more cooperative choices in the public good game. The framing effect cannot be attributed to a difference in the mixture of types of subjects.

Another potential explanation is that the difference between both treatments is caused by a difference in expectations. Subjects may act less cooperatively in the public bad treatment because they think it is less likely that their contribution is critical. The data show that this is not the case. In fact, subjects estimate the probability of being critical higher in the public good treatment than in the public bad treatment, but the difference is small (33.4% versus 31.0%). Figure 4.10 presents a scatter-gram and the results of a simple logistic regression where the probability of acting cooperatively is a function of the probability of being critical. The estimated regression line for the public bad frame is below the line for the public good frame, implying that for any subjective probability of being critical, subjects are less likely to cooperate in preventing public bads than in providing public goods.

Figure 4.10
Decision to contribute by probability of being critical in partners treatments

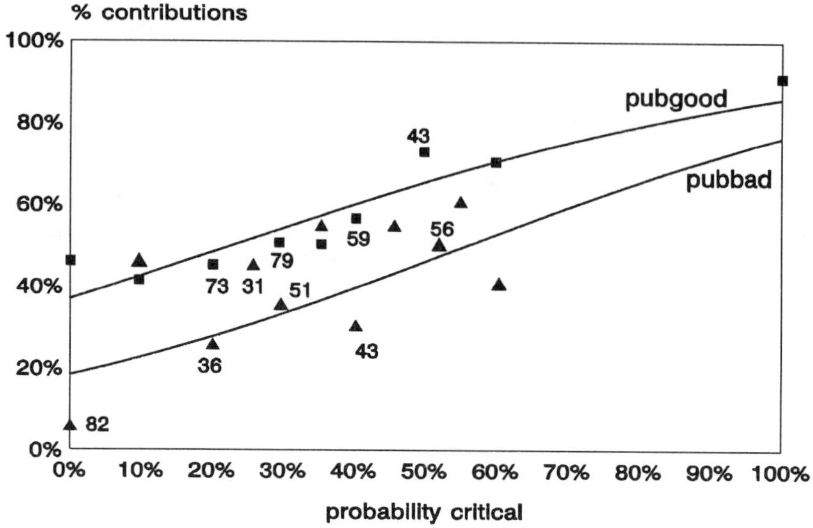

Notes: Only cases are displayed with 10 or more observations and their number is indicated if it exceeds 30. Squares represent public good cases and triangles represent public bad cases. The logit regressions are for pubgood: constant=-0.5372, B=0.0236 (n=400) and for pubbad: constant=-1.4961, B=0.0268 (n=400). All coefficients are significant at the 1% level (t-tests).

Given that the difference in behavior between the frames cannot be accounted for by either a difference in the relative number of cooperators present or a difference in beliefs, one is tempted to conclude that there must be a difference in decision rules used in the different frames. Two potential explanations why decision rules might differ are offered in the literature: prospect theory and Pruitt's hypothesis.

Prospect theory suggests that people handle problems framed in terms of losses differently than problems framed in terms of gains. Prospect theory has been successfully used in the area of individual decision making, where the point of reference is relatively well defined. It is less straightforward to apply prospect theory to a complex social situation. Using prospect theory and the auxiliary assumption that subjects regard money contributed to the public good as a loss, and money taken from a common pool as a gain, it was predicted in section 2.2.3 that fewer cooperative decisions would be made in the public good frame than in the public bad frame. This prediction is rejected by the data.

However, there is no objective way of determining the reference points a priori. Maybe reference points change in a repeated game when experience changes aspiration levels. A handicap for the application of prospect theory to social situations is that prospect theory tries to explain behavior from (differences in) risk attitudes without any reference to the social aspect of the situation. This obviously causes problems. For example, prospect theory cannot explain the positive contribution levels observed in one-shot prisoners' dilemmas, where subjects have a dominant strategy not to contribute (cf. Ledyard, 1995). Therefore, prospect theory is discarded as an explanation of the framing effect.

A prediction in line with Pruitt's hypothesis would be that subjects perceive a higher interdependence between themselves and other group-members in the public good game than in the public bad game, value mutual cooperation higher in the public good game than in the public bad game and therefore cooperate more often in the public good game than in the public bad game. The last part of this prediction is clearly true, but the supposed role of subjective interdependency is not observed: the questionnaire revealed no significant differences in subjective interdependency between the public good and the public bad game.[21]

On the other hand, the related explanation that the public good frame triggers a warm-glow, whereas the public bad frame triggers a cold-prickle cannot be discarded so easily. The estimation results reported in tables 4.8 and 4.9 suggest that an expected utility approach might be able to explain the difference in behavior observed. The mean of the estimated distribution of utility components is smaller in the public bad game than in the public good game. However, this analysis treats the expectations as exogenously given. A complete explanation takes account of the process via which expectations are formed. Such a theory could explain differences

[21] A seven-point scale was used for the five following questions: (1) how much influence do you think you have on your own payoffs; (2) how much influence do you think you have on the earnings of other members; (3) how much influence do you think you have on the decisions of others; (4) how much influence do you think the others have on your earnings; and (5) to what degree do you agree with the statement "In this experiment I and the other groups members depend on each other for good results". The difference between the treatments in the answers of each of the five questions is far from significant using Mann-Whitney tests.

in behavior over time. Game theory and belief learning provide potential underpinning of this hypothesis drawn from the expected utility approach. In chapter 5 these more complete explanations are considered.

A completely different explanation, in the spirit of the reinforcement learning model discussed in section 2.4.2, is suggested by the answers given in the questionnaire administered after the last round. The basic idea of the reinforcement learning approach is that individuals are inclined to repeat successful actions but abandon unsuccessful actions. Subjects were asked to grade their satisfaction with their decision after the outcome was announced for each of six possible situations (cf. section 4.2). Table 4.14 presents the mean answers to the questions. In both frames there appear to be 'satisfactory' and 'unsatisfactory' outcomes. Subjects are most satisfied when their decision proves to be right: a decision is right when a subject cooperates, while exactly two others do (the subject makes a critical contribution), or when (s)he does not cooperate, while fewer or more than two others do (the subject does not make a futile or redundant contribution). Note that subjects report a different pattern in satisfaction scores between the treatments: the worst case scenario for subjects in the public good game appears to be that they do not contribute in a situation where they are critical; in the public bad game the worst case occurs when they provide a futile contribution (i.e. they do not take 60 cents from the common pool, but find out that 3 or more group-members do).

Table 4.14

Mean satisfaction with the decision after the outcome was announced

satisfaction public good	not contributing	contributing	satisfaction public bad	not contributing	contributing
futile	5.03	2.71	futile	5.00	2.14
critical	2.22	5.86	critical	3.13	5.60
redundant	6.38	3.84	redundant	6.33	4.54

Note: Subjects answered the questions on a 7-point scale.

These results from the questionnaire are supported by observed behavior. Subjects who are less satisfied with their decision are more inclined to change their decision in the next period. The mean satisfaction for decisions that are repeated next period is 4.56 in the public good game and 4.98 in the public bad game and for decisions that are not repeated 2.99 in the public good game and 3.16 in the public bad game.

Table 4.15 shows the percentage of individual decisions that were repeated in the next period, for the six possible outcome combinations. In the public good game, the order corresponds to the order of satisfaction as presented in table 4.14, in the sense that a choice is repeated more often if the satisfaction with the result of the choice in the former round is higher. There are slight differences with the order in the public bad game. In line with the results in table 4.14 however, a subject is most likely to change behavior in the public good game when (s)he fails to make the critical contribution and in the public bad game when (s)he makes a futile contribution.

Table 4.15
Percentages of repeated decisions in next period

public good treatment:	not contributing	contributing	public bad treatment:	not contributing	contributing
futile	74% (n=93)	66% (n=125)	futile	75% (n=208)	52%(n=140)
critical	63% (n=162)	81% (n=135)	critical	70% (n=162)	71% (n=105)
redundant	84% (n=116)	71% (n=129)	redundant	83% (n=82)	57% (n=63)
all	72% (n=371)	73% (n=389)	all	75% (n=452)	60% (n=308)

Note: The numbers of occurrences are given in parentheses.

The main difference between the games does not seem to be how often subjects switch from not contributing to contributing (28% in the public good frame and 25% in the public bad frame), but how often cooperative choices are repeated (73% in the public good frame and 60% in the public bad frame). The effect of this is reflected at the group level: if a group reaches the threshold, it will reach the threshold the next period in 63% of the cases in the public good game, and only in 46% of the cases in the public bad game.

The next chapter will present a sharper view on the dynamics of a utility based explanation and a reinforcement learning based explanation for the behavioral difference between the public good and the public bad frame (section 5.5). There, the focus will be explicitly on the interaction between the individuals, and the impact of this interaction on the evolution of play.

4.4 Conclusions

A key observation from former experiments in public good environments used as the basis for the experiments described here is that individual propensities to contribute vary substantially. The decomposed game technique provides a way to acquire an independent measure of these different attitudes. Individuals classified as individualists contribute less in the public good game than individuals classified as cooperators. If value orientations are not taken into account in the analysis explicitly, then it seems difficult to capture what is really going on in the public good game.

The independent measurement of beliefs via a scoring rule allows for a direct assessment of the intermediating role of beliefs in the determination of behavior in public good games. The experimental results positively support the existence of a relationship between expectations and behavior. Subjects are more inclined to contribute to the public good if they estimate the probability that their contribution is critical for the provision of the public good to be higher. But there is not only a role for the probability of being critical in the determination of behavior. Subjects seem to dislike the possibility that their contribution is futile more than the possibility that their contribution is redundant. Ceteris paribus they are more inclined to contribute when they estimate the probability that their contribution is futile to be smaller.

These independent measures on the social aspect of preferences and beliefs provide useful tools to analyze psychological and economic theories about behavior in public good games. Consistent with the psychological triangle hypothesis and false consensus hypothesis is the finding that cooperators contribute more than individualists do. The triangle hypothesis fares better than the false consensus hypothesis, because expectations do not seem to be affected systematically by behavior. Inconsistent with both hypotheses is that cooperators do not seem to expect (substantially) more contributions of the others than individualists do. But it could be argued that this is caused by the production function of the public good studied here, which differs from the production function for which these hypotheses were originally developed. In the present game the Pareto optimum coincides with one of the Nash equilibria, allowing for the possibility that both types of individuals focus on the same point: the threshold. This may have happened specifically in the high-7 and high-5 treatments of the strangers mode and in the pubgood treatment of the partners mode. In these treatments the play focuses on the threshold.

As for the economic theories on individual behavior, the deterministic hypotheses that people maximize expected value or expected utility (after transforming the payoff matrix as if they are material, warm-glow or in-group cooperators) cannot be maintained. Even if each individual is allowed to have a subjective transformation of the payoff matrix, many choices cannot be rationalized. The assumption that subjects do not err has to be rejected. For stochastic versions of the hypotheses, most support was obtained for the hypotheses that subjects transform the payoff matrix as warm-glow cooperators or as in-group cooperators. Maximum likelihood estimations favor the hypothesis based on warm glow. On the other hand, subjects' choices show a negative correlation with their estimated probability of being futile. This fact is consistent with the hypothesis based on in-group cooperators but not with the others. The psychological idea that subjects differ in the goals pursued can be translated successfully to these economic hypotheses. Maximum likelihood estimations show that it is likely that the population is heterogeneous. Estimated utility components correlate with subjects' choices in the decomposed game technique.

Various treatment effects were investigated. Increasing the payoff for getting the public good provided yields more contributions. This treatment effect carries over to the two most observed orientations: cooperators and individualists. It is caused by a difference in decision rules and not by a difference in beliefs. Decreasing group-size also yields more contributions of both individualists and cooperators. This treatment effect can better be attributed to a difference in beliefs than to a difference in decision rules. Contribution levels are not systematically affected by the subject mode. People contribute as much when groups remain constant as when they change.

Perhaps the most intriguing treatment effect is the framing effect. Strategically equivalent versions of the game elicit different levels of cooperation. The framing effect seems to be the hardest to take account of. In the public good frame both individualists and cooperators cooperate more than in the public bad frame. The difference cannot be attributed to a difference in beliefs between the frames. Two theories potentially explain why decision rules might differ between the frames. This effect may either be due to different utility components elicited by the different frames (e.g., warm-glow versus cold prickle), or to differences in satisfaction level with the former outcome elicited by the different frames. In the public good game subjects especially dislike the situation where they did not contribute in the former period, but where their contribution would have been critical to provide the public good. In the public bad game, they especially dislike the situation where their contribution in the former period was futile in preventing the public bad. In order to evaluate these different explanations, one needs a theory describing the interaction between the subjects. Therefore, the evaluation is postponed until the next chapter.

The analyses of the factors affecting a subject's choice whether or not to contribute have a rather partial character. One may wonder what the relative strength of the various determinants of behavior is in an overall analysis. This chapter concludes with the results of a logit regression including all determinants. The results are summarized in table 4.16.

The model with the nine independent variables reported in table 4.16 describes the choices significantly better than the model with only a constant term (Likelihood Ratio test, p=0.00). All variables with significant coefficients have the expected sign. Consistency does not affect choices directly. However, if the regression is run with the choices of only those individuals who have a consistency measure greater than 33% and who have an individualistic or cooperative value orientation, the coefficients for angle and for the probability of being critical increase. This may indicate that the decomposed game technique does not do a good job in assessing subjects with extreme value orientations (extreme in the sense that only few choices consistent with any orientation are made, or in the sense that a rare orientation is pursued).

The hypotheses investigated in this chapter abstract from the interaction between subjects. If one wants to have a complete picture of human behavior in public good games, one should also address the question whether beliefs about others' behavior are completely determined by the structure of the game, or whether they are adapted contingent on the history of the game. Or one should investigate how the outcome of a game in the former period affects behavior in the current period directly. These types of questions are the subject of the next chapter.

Table 4.16
Logit regression for the determinants of behavior

	coefficient	standard error
P(s-1)	0.0132	0.0019
P(<s-1)	-0.0128	0.0015
angle	0.0074	0.0014
consistency	-0.0015	0.0018
period	-0.0239	0.0058
dummy group-size	-0.4866	0.0900
dummy payoff	0.6858	0.1014
dummy frame	0.4655	0.1559
dummy mode	-0.0895	0.1205
constant	-0.8673	0.2390

Notes: The regression is run for the choices of the twelve sessions for which subjects reported beliefs (n=4520). P(s-1) and P(<s-1) refer to the reported probability of being critical and futile respectively. The angle and the consistency are determined by the motivational vector measured by the decomposed game technique ($-90° \leq$ angle $\leq 90°$; $0\% \leq$ consistency $\leq 100\%$). The dummy for group-size equals 0 if the groups consist of 5 players and 1 otherwise. The dummy for payoff equals 0 if the public payoff equals 180 and 1 otherwise. The dummy for frame equals 0 if the framing of the game is the public bad frame and 1 otherwise. Finally, the dummy for mode equals 0 in the partners mode and 1 in the strangers mode. All coefficients are significant at the 1% level, except those for consistency and the dummy for strangers which are far from significant (t-tests).

5. Beliefs and learning

5.1 Introduction

After having discussed the evidence on decision rules in the former chapter, this chapter focuses on the beliefs individuals have about other players' behavior in experimental (public good) games, and the potential development of these beliefs in the course of the game. One main objective is to find out whether players' expectations in public good games are history-dependent, and if so, whether this history-dependence is in accordance with belief learning models. Another objective is to provide a complete model taking account of the interaction and the decision rule simultaneously and to confront such a model with the experimental data. Simulations will be used to see to what extent this model can describe the general patterns in the data.

By and large, two views exist about how players form expectations in games. One view assumes that players are sophisticated strategists who believe that everyone will behave fully rational in every period. Game theoretic models elaborate this view rigorously. The alternative view assumes that players are naive in the sense that they think that there is an essentially constant element in others' behavior. According to this view, players assume that the probability distribution generating the choices of other players does not change. Belief learning models capture this idea mathematically.

The essential difference between game theoretic models and belief learning models is not that they expect players to use different decision rules. In fact, both models usually assume that decision rules are distilled from the expected utility approach. The essential difference lies in the characterization of the expectation formation process. Therefore, a large part of this chapter will concentrate on the expectations reported by subjects. The use of *reported* expectations contrasts with former experimental work on expectation formation which focused on subjects' choices. In former work (untested) auxiliary assumptions about the relationship between expectations and choices were used, such that *indirect* evidence on beliefs could be inferred from choice data. Usually the auxiliary assumption was that players give a best response. There is an important advantage to using *direct* evidence on expectations, because subjects do not always behave optimally given their expectations (cf. chapter 4). Before the evidence on expectations is presented, the main features of the two different views and the resulting predictions are summarized.

Traditional game theoretic models assume that the common knowledge assumption and the rules of the game are sufficient to induce people to play a (Bayesian) Nash equilibrium.[1] Players are assumed to appreciate the strategic nature of the game. They assume that other players are rational individuals who reason like themselves. If a player thinks it is worthwhile to adapt her or his expectations and behavior, (s)he will not exclude the possibility that other group-members expect her or him to do so and adapt their expectations and behavior in turn.

A common feature of game theoretic models is that in equilibrium expectations about other group-members' behavior are accurate. In an experiment where subjects possess only limited computational abilities, one cannot expect subjects to have completely accurate expectations, so one must allow for some (random) error in expectations within a period.

Furthermore, game theory does not predict expectations to be constant across periods in a repeated game (as in the partners treatments) or in subsequent plays of a one-shot game (as in the strangers treatments). For example, even in a static analysis there are multiple equilibria and it may be that one equilibrium is played in one period and another in the next. As a consequence, a player's expectations may shift between periods. However, static game theoretic models do not positively predict any specific pattern in expectations, only that expectations are accurate in each period.

According to adaptive belief learning models, people abstract from the strategic nature of a game. Players assume others' behavior to be constant (in a probabilistic sense) and independent of the experience of these others. They disregard the possibility that other people may adapt their expectations and behavior on the basis of their own experience. Basically, this implies that individuals' perception of the game is not different from the perception they would have if they played a similar game against nature.

A representative of the class of belief learning models is the naive Bayesian

---

[1]In fact, common knowledge is a stronger assumption than needed to characterize a Nash equilibrium. For a theoretical discussion of this issue, see Aumann and Brandenburger, 1995.

model. According to this model, players do update beliefs in a Bayesian manner, but do not think strategically in the sense that they realize that others may do the same. They assume that the behavior of the others can be learned by carefully observing these others' past behavior. This model is not consistent in a game theoretic sense, since others' behavior is assumed to be constant while these others, if the model is correct, also adapt their expectations and behavior on the basis of past observations. In the present public good game, expectations about other group-members will be accurate if the process has hit on an equilibrium for some periods. But if the empirical frequency distribution of (the sum of) others' choices is not constant, the model predicts that players' expectations will be overtaken by events. If the empirical frequency distribution shifts upwards, players will be too pessimistic about others' behavior, whereas the opposite is predicted if the frequency distribution shifts downwards.

The naive Bayesian model is less complex than a sophisticated game theoretic model, but the computational capabilities required are still enormous. It may be unreasonable to expect that individuals update expectations precisely according to this process. Nevertheless, as discussed in chapter 2, a naive Bayesian abstracting from strategic considerations can be expected to comply to the so-called belief learning pattern in the public good game (cf. section 2.4.1). This pattern describes how the predictive distribution shifts as a consequence of the last event. Specifically, shifts in the mean, the variance and the probability of the former outcome are described by this pattern.

Without a standard for comparison it might be difficult to distinguish whether people do or do not incorporate strategic considerations in their expectations in public good games. Since both assumptions lead to models which require very much of the computational abilities of subjects, noise may be expected whichever assumption is true. To get an estimate of the natural amount of noise in the naive Bayesian model, a base-line treatment is carried out where people really do play a game against nature and know that they do. In this game the behavior of 'others' is replaced by a truly binomially $(n\text{-}1,\theta)$ distributed variable, such that any possible strategic considerations are eliminated. If the naive Bayesian model gives the better description of the expectation formation in the public good games, one would expect approximately the same pattern emerging in the public good game as the pattern emerging in the base-line treatment without interaction, with similar levels of noise. If the sophisticated game theoretic model gives the better description, one would expect approximately accurate expectations in the public good treatments and approximately the Bayesian learning process in the base-line treatment.[2] In that case, a distinct pattern in expectations will emerge.

The assumption that players neglect strategic considerations seems most plausible in settings where individuals are matched with different group-members each period. The partners treatments form a stronger test-case for the naive Bayesian model, since players may be more encouraged to reason strategically. Therefore, it may be expected that the naive Bayesian model performs less effectively in the partners mode than in the strangers mode. Table 5.1 summarizes the predictions of the two models for the various treatments.

Table 5.1
Predictions about patterns in beliefs

	naive Bayesian model	game theoretic model
nature	belief learning pattern ++	belief learning pattern ++
strangers mode	belief learning pattern ++	no specific pattern
partners mode	belief learning pattern +	unknown

Note: ++ indicates 'strongly predicted'; + 'weakly predicted'.

The evidence on reported expectations favoring either model is stronger if it is corroborated by the evidence on the choices actually made. The concept of quantal response allows for a computation of the (maximum) likelihood that choice data arise from either model. Therefore, for both types of models it will be assumed that players give noisy best responses. This assumption is not very accurate, because the results on decision rules reported in chapter 4 indicate that it is likely that subjects transform the payoff matrix according to utility transformations. However, there is no a priori reason why the assumption should harm either model more than the other. This procedure

[2]Note that the Bayesian updating process without strategic considerations is not naive in the game against nature.

provides additional *indirect* evidence for the predictive power of the models.

The combination of the results on expectation formation and decision rules gives a full picture of the interaction between players in public good games. Simulations of this interaction process will be presented that should be able to replicate the patterns observed in various treatments. In particular, it is interesting to investigate whether simulations can capture the behavioral differences observed between the strategically equivalent public good and public bad treatment. An alternative reinforcement learning model based on the different satisfaction scores obtained in the public good and public bad treatment will be presented as well. This model takes a short-cut by neglecting the mediating role of expectations. It will be discussed to what extent simulations based on the models can reproduce the general patterns observed in the experiments.

The remainder of this chapter is organized as follows: in section 5.2 the design of the treatment where subjects play the related game against nature will be discussed. The public good treatments have been discussed in section 4.2. Section 5.3 discusses the experimental results on expectation formation by focusing on reported beliefs. In section 5.4 models will be evaluated with respect to their ability to predict actual choices whether or not to contribute. Section 5.5 will present the simulation results.

5.2 Experimental design and procedures

The treatment where subjects play the game against nature (*'nature'*) resembles treatment high-5 as much as possible, and therefore has close resemblance to the treatments pubgood and pubbad as well. All rules of the game were carefully communicated to the subjects. Subjects had to answer some questions testing understanding before the start of the experiment. Subjects played 20 periods. Subjects made choices simultaneously and communication was prohibited. The description of the rules and possible actions was neutral: words like 'investment' were avoided. The experiment was completely computerized.

In nature subjects were informed that their payoffs depended on their decision whether or not to invest and on the number of red balls in a cage. The decision to invest in the game against nature corresponds to the decision to contribute in the public good games, and the number of red balls in a cage in nature corresponds to the number of other contributors in the public good games. At the beginning of each period the cage was 'emptied' and four new balls were drawn at random by the computer and 'put in the cage'. Subjects knew that, for each ball, there was an equal probability p of being red. Thus, the number of red balls was binomially *(4,p)* distributed. At the start of the first period subjects did not know anything about the value of p, but they did know that p would remain constant during the experiment. To make nature and high-5 as comparable as possible, p was chosen to be equal to the observed average contribution level in high-5 (0.50). Different individuals observed different and independent realizations of the binomial (4,0.50) process. In this way, subjects in nature observed different outcomes from the (same) binomial process, just like subjects in high-5 observed different aggregate contribution levels because they were in different groups. Table 5.2 shows that the same payoff structure underlay the treatments nature and high-5, which in turn had the same payoff structure as pubgood and pubbad. The investment was economically sound if and only if the favorable state of the world occurred, i.e., if and only if two of the balls in the cage were red (the favorable state of the world in the investment game corresponds to the critical state of the world in the public good game).

After a subject had made the decision whether or not to invest, her or his expectations about the number of red balls in the cage were elicited. Subjects were asked to report in percentages their subjectively estimated probabilities that the outcomes 0,1,2,3 and 4 would occur. The same incentive compatible quadratic scoring

Table 5.2
The payoff schemes of high-5 and nature

game: high-5			game: nature		
# others cooperating	own decision		# red balls in cage	own decision	
	non-cooperative	cooperative		non-investing	investing
0,1	60	0	0,1	60	0
2	60	185	2	60	185
3,4	245	185	3,4	245	185

rule as in the public good treatments was used (cf. section 4.2). As before, it was given to the subjects in a handout and it was emphasized that no mathematical understanding of the equation was needed. It was explained to the subjects that it was in their own best interest to report probabilities truthfully.

At the end of a period, each subject was informed about the number of red balls in her or his cage, and the resulting payoffs for the investment decision and for the reported probabilities. Then the game proceeded to the next period. A more elaborate description of the instructions is provided in appendix B.

In nature, 24 subjects participated in one session. The subject pool was the undergraduate population of the University of Amsterdam. A majority of 71% of the subjects was male; 50% of the subjects majored in economics or econometrics. On average subjects were 22 years old. As in the public good treatments, there was a show-up fee of 5 guilders. In addition, in somewhat less than 3 hours an average of 39.75 guilders (= ± 26.1 US-dollar) was earned by the subjects.[3]

5.3 Experimental results: spotlight on expectations

Experimental results on expectation formation are relevant for the study of human behavior in public good games, because expectations affect behavior in systematic ways. In chapter 4 it was found that subjects are more inclined to contribute to the public good if they estimate the probability that their contribution is critical to be higher. Similarly, in nature subjects are more inclined to invest if they estimate the probability of the favorable state of the world to be higher. In fact, a logistic regression in nature provides results quite similar to the logistic regressions for the public good treatments reported in chapter 4 (figures 4.8 and 4.10).[4] On aggregate, the investment level in nature (51%) is similar to the contribution levels in high-5 and

---

[3]The session was run in September 1994. Because there was no interaction between subjects, no observer was appointed to check procedures.

[4]The coefficient for constant is -0.6148 and the coefficient for reported probability of the favorable state of the world is 0.0227 (n=480). Both coefficients are significant at the 1%-level (t-tests). For comparison, in treatment high-5 the coefficient for constant was -0.5453 and the coefficient for reported probability of being critical was 0.0153 (section 4.3.3).

pubgood (50%; 51%), and higher than in pubbad (40%). Quite some choices whether or not to invest are inconsistent with the hypothesis that subjects maximize expected value (40%). Hence, choices in the public good games are similar to choices in nature even in this respect.

Section 5.3.1 will discuss the experimental results in a qualitative way. It will be assessed whether subjects' expectations are accurate and whether or not the belief learning pattern emerges in subjects' expectations. The analysis presented in section 5.3.2 is more quantitatively orientated. There, it will be assessed which model of a general class fits the data on expectations best.

5.3.1 Qualitative analysis of expectation formation

Whether expectations are expected to be unbiased in the public good treatments depends on the model studied: according to the static game theoretic models, expectations are supposed to be unbiased; according to the naive Bayesian model, one would expect unbiased expectations if the probability that a randomly chosen group-member contributes remains constant over a number of periods. However, contribution level falls over periods in some of the treatments reported in chapter 4. In fact, the regression covering all relevant factors affecting choices reported at the end of that chapter reveals a significant negative effect for the period number. In such cases the naive Bayesian model predicts that players will be too optimistic about the contribution level of other players.

For any observed pattern of contributions, one can determine what a naive Bayesian would do (given an uninformative prior distribution). In the data, the hypothesis that the mean of the distribution of such an ideal naive Bayesian observer is equal to the actual contribution level of others is rejected in favor of the hypothesis that the former is greater. Like the ideal naive Bayesian observer, subjects appear to be too optimistic about the behavior of others. The means of the actually reported distributions tend to be systematically greater than the actual number of other contributors.[5] This effect is obtained for the first ten periods as well as for the last ten periods for individualists as well as for cooperators, as can be inferred from table 5.3. The

---

[5]For both hypotheses (observed choices versus ideal naive Bayesian and reported expectations, respectively) the Wilcoxon rank test are used. The data are pooled across all public good treatments. Averages per session in the strangers mode and averages per group in the partners treatments serve as observations (p=0.00 and n=18 for both hypotheses).

bias in the distributions reported by subjects appears to be stronger if the bias for the ideal naive Bayesian observer is stronger. This is confirmed by closer analysis. The Spearman rank correlation coefficient between the difference between the reported mean and the realized outcome of others' contributions on the one hand, and the difference between the (ideal) naive Bayesian's mean and the realized outcome on the other hand is equal to 0.62.[6] This evidence is consistent with the result reported by Palfrey and Rosenthal (1991), who infer from their data on subjects' choices that their subjects were too optimistic about other players' behavior.

A similar bias is not expected in the nature treatment, where the distribution of states of the world is stable. In fact, the realizations of the binomial distribution are (by chance) such that an ideal naive Bayesian observer would make slightly pessimistic predictions about the future state of the world (similar Wilcoxon rank test as in the previous paragraph, with averages per individual as data-points: p=0.53, n=24). In accordance with the expectations of a naive Bayesian observer, subjects are slightly pessimistic about the realized state of the world, although not significantly so (Wilcoxon rank test, p=0.32, n=24).

The biases observed in subjects' expectations in the public good games as well as in the game against nature can be explained by the naive Bayesian model. A different question is whether the belief learning pattern emerges in all treatments as expected by this model, or only in the game against nature as expected by static game theoretic models (cf. table 5.2). The naive Bayesian pattern consists of three hypotheses: the first (H1) states that the mean of the reported distribution in any period will be smaller (equal/greater) than the mean in the previous period if the outcome was smaller (equal/greater) than the reported mean in that period. The second hypothesis (H2) states that the reported probability of a particular outcome will not decrease if that outcome is observed. The third hypothesis (H3) states that the variance of the reported distribution will decrease on average, as more information is revealed. Since some people may follow Bayes' rule (qualitatively) and others may not, and since some individuals may abstract from strategic considerations while others may not, the

[6]Again, averages per session in strangers mode and averages per group in partners mode are used as observations: p=0.01, n=18. The spearman rank correlation is greater if all reported and Bayesian distributions and realizations of others' play are used as observations.

Table 5.3
Biases in the means of the expectations

	all subjects			individualists			cooperators		
	Bayes	report	real	Bayes	report	real	Bayes	report	real
low-7									
p 1-10	1.88	2.16	1.66	1.86	2.07	1.62	1.97	2.36	1.77
p 10-20	1.47	1.33	0.72	1.44	1.24	0.71	1.53	1.41	0.67
p 1-20	1.68	1.74	1.19	1.65	1.66	1.17	1.75	1.88	1.22
high-7									
p 1-10	2.69	2.82	2.45	2.73	2.83	2.47	2.56	2.75	2.36
p 11-20	2.49	2.71	2.48	2.49	2.70	2.42	2.48	2.68	2.58
p 1-20	2.59	2.76	2.46	2.61	2.76	2.45	2.52	2.71	2.47
high-5									
p 1-10	2.04	2.09	2.02	2.07	2.06	2.05	2.05	2.14	2.02
p 11-20	2.01	2.08	2.01	2.04	2.07	2.06	1.97	2.05	1.89
p 1-20	2.02	2.09	2.02	2.05	2.07	2.05	2.01	2.10	1.96
pubgood									
p 1-10	2.35	2.46	2.34	2.43	2.55	2.49	2.38	2.36	2.32
p 11-20	2.23	2.32	2.12	2.38	2.45	2.24	2.19	2.26	2.10
p 1-20	2.29	2.39	2.23	2.40	2.50	2.37	2.29	2.31	2.21
pubbad									
p 1-10	1.96	1.83	1.68	1.91	1.73	1.65	2.11	1.87	1.80
p 11-20	1.57	1.32	1.12	1.53	1.18	1.06	1.69	1.59	1.28
p 1-20	1.77	1.57	1.40	1.72	1.46	1.36	1.90	1.73	1.54
nature									
p 1-10	2.07	2.03	2.05						
p 11-20	2.09	2.00	2.14	X	X	X	X	X	X
p 1-20	2.08	2.01	2.09						

Notes: The column 'Bayes' displays the means of the distributions which would have been reported by an ideal naive Bayesian observer; the column 'report' displays the means of the distributions reported by subjects; the column 'real' displays the realizations or the sum of others' contributions in the public good treatments and the observed states of the world in the game against nature; 'p' denotes period; 'X' indicates that no value orientations are measured.

analysis is carried out at the individual level.[7]

To test H1, for each individual the number of times is counted that the mean

[7]For the derivation of the third hypothesis, it is formally required that the underlying probability θ remains constant, which may not be true in the actual public good game. However, in the experiments the outcomes subjects observed were such, that a naive Bayesian would conform to the hypothesis.

of the reported distribution shifts in the 'wrong' direction and the number of times that it shifts in the 'right' direction, given the naive Bayesian model. An individual's mean shifts in the wrong direction if in the previous period a greater (smaller) outcome was observed than the reported mean and the mean in this period is smaller (greater) than the mean in the former period. An individual's mean shifts in the right direction if in the previous period a greater (equal/smaller) outcome was observed than the reported mean and the mean in this period is greater (equal/smaller) than the mean in the former period.[8] A Wilcoxon rank test is then used to find out whether the ranks of the number of right shifts are systematically greater than the ranks of the number of wrong shifts.

H2 and H3 are tested in similar ways. For H2 the number of times is counted that an individual shifts the estimated probability of the previous outcome in the wrong direction, and the number that (s)he shifts it in the right direction. The probability of the previous outcome shifts in the right direction if it increases and it shifts in the wrong direction if it decreases. If it remains constant, it is assumed to be inconclusive. For H3 for each individual it is counted how often the variance of the reported distribution shifts in the right and how often it shifts in the wrong direction. The variance of a reported distribution shifts in the right direction if it decreases and in the wrong direction if it increases. If it remains constant, it is assumed to be inconclusive. The results are presented in table 5.4.

For all treatments, the evidence on all hypotheses is in the direction predicted by belief learning models. Furthermore, 16 of the 18 test results are significant at the 1%-level.[9] Remarkably, the naive Bayesian pattern emerges *even more pronounced*

[8]This definition of wrong and right shifts leaves some cases undefined. The reason for doing this is that some cases seem inconclusive. For example, consider the case that in the former period a higher outcome than expected is observed but that the individual's reported mean in the new period is the same as the one in the former. Strictly speaking, this might be seen as a mistake against the naive Bayesian model. On the other hand, it may be that the already accumulated evidence is so massive that a true Bayesian would imperceptibly update the mean in the light of the new observation. This may induce even true Bayesians to report the same distribution in both periods.

[9]Note that the tests reported differ from former test results since they are not at the truly independent level. There are not sufficient data to perform the tests with independent data *within* treatments, because a Wilcoxon rank test cannot obtain a significance level of 5% with 4 pair-wise data only. However, when data are pooled *across* public good treatments, and averages per session in the strangers mode and averages per group in the partners mode serve as data points, significant results are also obtained at the 1% level for Wilcoxon rank tests on all three hypotheses: H1, H2, H3:

Table 5.4
Belief learning pattern

		low-7	high-7	high-5	pubgood	pubbad	nature
H1	# right	12.7	11.0	11.7	11.7	12.1	9.1
	# wrong	3.1	4.6	4.8	4.1	4.3	4.9
	Z	-6.89**	-6.51**	-6.48**	-3.71**	-3.70**	-3.31**
H2	# right	10.9	8.9	9.8	9.2	8.4	6.3
	# wrong	2.5	3.9	4.1	3.5	4.8	4.8
	Z	-6.82**	-5.62**	-5.89**	-3.68**	-3.29**	-1.72
H3	# right	9.5	9.1	9.4	8.4	8.7	7.5
	# wrong	6.8	7.3	7.4	7.4	6.5	6.2
	Z	-5.05**	-4.31**	-4.62**	-1.89	-3.03**	-2.79**

Notes: '# Wrong' indicates the average number of wrong shifts ($0 \leq$ # wrong ≤ 19), '# right' indicates the average number of right shifts ($0 \leq$ # right ≤ 19). * indicates significance at the 5%-level and ** at the 1%-level with respect to the Wilcoxon rank test. H1, H2 and H3 are explained in the text.

in the public good treatments than in nature. This justifies the conclusion that individuals play these public good games as if they play a game against nature. Moreover, the relatively moderate results for nature suggest that noise observed against the belief learning pattern in the public good treatments can be attributed to imperfect Bayesian updating.

The noise in the data may partially be due to the fact that some of the subjects use a simplifying casino-heuristic which yields opposite predictions compared to Bayesian updating. In roulette, it is often observed that people place bets on red after black has been observed in a few subsequent trials. Although the trials are independent, some people tend to think that it is not likely that black will emerge again. In a post-experimental questionnaire, one of the subjects commented on her choices as follows:

Z=-3.72, n=18 (3x).

'It was logically sound to buy a red ball if there were already two in the cage. If that had happened only a few times in former periods, I gambled that it would occur again' (subject b1, nature).

If the noise against the belief learning pattern results from the use of such a casino-heuristic by some participants, it must be concluded that the heuristic is used at least as much in nature as in the public good games. Subjects may consider the game against nature as more difficult than public good games, and therefore be more inclined to resort to simplifying heuristics.

Both the bias in subjects' expectations and the support for the belief learning pattern favor belief learning models over static game theoretic models in the public good games. Nevertheless, there are two anomalies which are not satisfactorily explained by either type of model. First, subjects sometimes report distributions with more than one mode. Second, subjects report distributions with a smaller variance than expected by either of the models. These anomalies will be dealt with subsequently.

Both the game theoretic models and the naive Bayesian model yield uni-modal distributions. Nevertheless, 3% of the reported distributions in the public good treatments and 18% of the reported distributions in the nature treatment have more than one mode.[10] Distributions with more than one mode may occur if subjects use a different belief learning model than the naive Bayesian model. According to fictitious play, for example, subjects assign probabilities in correspondence with observed frequencies in the past. The assumption about prior distributions for this model is that subjects assign equal weight to each possible outcome before the start of the experiment (similar to the assumption of a non-informative prior distribution in the naive Bayesian model). In this case, if a subject has observed outcome 1 in 30%, outcome 2 in 20% and outcome 3 in 50% of former periods, (s)he reports a distribution with a mode at 1 and a mode at 3. Thus, according to fictitious play, subjects will report multi-modal distributions if the observed frequency-distribution of the former outcomes is multi-modal. This can explain 1%-point of the multi-modal

[10] This anomaly does not occur frequently in the public good treatments. Those mainly interested in a theory explaining expectations and behavior in public good games may not be bothered by it.

distributions in the public good treatments and 5.5%-point of the multi-modal distributions in the nature treatment, still leaving 12.5% of the distributions in nature unexplained. More seriously, fictitious play cannot explain that subjects quite often report distributions with one mode only, while their observed frequency-distribution is multi-modal. Furthermore, the difference in occurrence of this anomaly between public good treatments and the nature treatment suggests that multi-modal distributions may be the result of a difference in the perceived difficulty of the task. A difference in perceived difficulty is also suggested by the fact that subjects use considerably more time to make their decisions in the nature treatment than in the public good treatments.

The second anomaly is that subjects are overconfident in the public good treatments. Overconfidence occurs if subjects report distributions with a variance smaller than the variance predicted by the model (overconfidence has been reported before in different contexts by Dunning *et al.*, 1990; Griffin and Tversky, 1992; Schmalensee, 1976; and Vallone *et al.*, 1990).[11] In the public good treatments the variance predicted depends on whether the naive Bayesian model or the game theoretic model serves as the bench-mark. The variance predicted by the naive Bayesian model is described explicitly in theorem 2.8 in chapter 2. The variance predicted by the game theoretic model depends on what particular assumption is made. If it is assumed that all subjects in a group play a symmetric mixed strategy (cf. the model reported in section 2.3.1), the variance reported is to be compared to the variance of the binomial distribution based on the true probability of contributing p. Because this true probability of contributing is not known in any period, it is approximated by the mean of a subject's reported distribution μ divided by $(n-1)$. Thus, given that the mean of the binomial distribution is equal to $(n-1)*p$, and its variance equal to $(n-1)*p*(1-p)$, the variance predicted by the game theoretic model is equal to $(n-1)*[\mu/(n-1)]*[1-\mu/(n-1)]$.

In the public good treatment subjects appear to be overconfident in comparison

---

[11]Whether subjects are overconfident is usually assessed in a different way in social psychological work. There, subjects' confidence of having selected the right answer to for example the question 'Is Istanbul or Ankara the capital of Turkey?' is compared to the empirical distribution of right and wrong answers. So, if subjects' average assessment of the probability that they selected the right answer is higher than the actual proportion of right answers, subjects are assumed to be overconfident. In this study, subjects' predictions are not compared to an empirical distribution, but to the distribution an 'ideal' observer (with the same history as the subject) would have. The advantage of this approach is that the extent of overconfidence can be assessed individually for each subject, whereas in the other approach overconfidence is a characteristic of a group of subjects.

to both models. Wilcoxon rank tests show that the variance of reported distributions is significantly smaller than both the variance based on the naive Bayesian model and the variance based on the game theoretic model.[12] This is not an artifact of subjects confused in early periods: similar results are obtained if the analysis is restricted to distributions reported in period 20. In the game against nature, the appropriate model to compare the reported variance to is the naive Bayesian model. Here the reported variance is slightly *greater* in rank than the naive Bayesian variance, though not significantly so (averages per individual serving as data-points: p=0.14, n=24). So subjects are overconfident in various public good games, but not in a related game against nature. This gives further support to the idea that subjects perceive the game against nature as a more difficult game than the public good games.

5.3.2 Quantitative analysis of expectation formation

Given that the evidence reported in the former section favors the interpretation that people tend to perceive various public good games as decision theoretic problems instead of as strategic games, one may question what particular decision theory describes the data best. Various models in the spirit of the naive Bayesian model are considered here and assessed with respect to their ability to reproduce the (means of the) reported distributions. The class of models considered is given by equations 5.1-5.4:

$$y_{i,t} = x_{i,t} + \epsilon_{i,t} \qquad 5.1$$

$$\epsilon_{i,1} = \nu_{i,1}\ ;\ \ \epsilon_{i,t} = \rho_i \epsilon_{i,t-1} + \nu_{i,t};$$
$$\forall t{\neq}s:\ E[\nu_{i,t}\nu_{i,s}]=0;\ \ \forall i{\neq}j:\ E[\nu_{i,t}\nu_{j,s}]=0;\ \ \nu_{i,t}{\sim}N[a,\sigma_i^2] \qquad 5.2$$

$$x_{i,t} = \frac{(n-1)(s_{i,t-1}+1)}{(n-1)(t-1)+2} \qquad 5.3$$

[12]For the two tests averages per session in the strangers treatments and averages per group in the partners treatments serve as data-points: p=0.00 and n=18 (2x).

$$s_{i,t-1} = \frac{(t-1)\sum_{j=1}^{t-1} z_{i,j}\, j^{c_i}}{\sum_{j=1}^{t-1} j^{c_i}}, \qquad 5.4$$

where:

i and t refer to individuals and periods, respectively;

n denotes group-size;

y denotes the mean of the reported distribution;

x denotes the mean predicted by the model;

ε, ν are error terms;

a, ρ, σ are parameters of the stochastic structure;

z denotes the actually observed number of contributions/red balls;

s is a weighted sum of former observations;

c is a parameter determining the weights in s.

Equation 5.1 states that subjects make errors when reporting their expectations. The error structure is given by equation 5.2. The parameter a allows for a systematic bias in the reported expectations; the parameters ρ_i and σ_i allow for auto-correlation and heteroscedasticity. Equation 5.3 describes how the aggregate previous observations are used to predict a new mean (cf. theorem 2.8 in chapter 2). Finally, equation 5.4 describes how the t-1 previous observations are weighted to arrive at an aggregate.

The parameter c in equation 5.4 allows for a wide range of aggregation processes. To be more precise, it allows for varying speeds in the updating process. For example, $c=0$ yields the case where all previous observations receive equal weight. This is what a true (naive) Bayesian would do. Varying c allows for different relative weights for early and recent periods.

As noted in section 2.4.1, both updating too slow (referred to as conservatism, or primacy) and too fast (representativeness, or recency) have been observed in previous research. Note that if $c_i>0$, the weighted naive Bayesian model attributes relatively high value to recent observations, implying recency. If $c_i<0$, the model attributes relatively low value to recent observations, implying primacy. As mentioned above, if $c_i=0$ the model describes pure (naive) Bayesian updating. This latter case is referred to as the 'base model'. In the extreme case where $c \rightarrow \infty$, equation 5.4 reduces to: $s_{i,t-1}=(t-1)*z_{i,t-1}$, so extreme value is placed on the most recent observation. However, it is more common to consider extreme primacy of the form $s_{i,t-1}=z_{i,t-1}$. In the spirit of Milgrom and Roberts (1991) this will be referred to as the 'Cournot model', because it assumes that players only remember the most recent observation. Even though it is not completely nested in equation 5.3, estimates of this model will be reported as well. For the Cournot model, equation 5.3 needs to be adapted to $x_{i,t}=(z_{i,t-1}+1)*(n-1)/(n+1)$.[13]

In the model, the variance σ_i and correlation ρ_i are allowed to vary over individuals, as is the parameter c_i. When estimating the parameters of the model, it turns out that all variation across individuals in ρ compensates the variation in σ such, that the covariance between ε_t and ε_{t-1} (denoted by cov) remains more or less constant. This can be captured by either estimating the variation in σ or the variation in ρ across individuals, while keeping cov constant.[14] Therefore, cov is kept constant over i: $cov_i=cov, \forall i$, but σ_i is allowed to vary over i. The parameter ρ_i automatically varies with σ_i to keep cov constant. The likelihood of the data does not improve when this is replaced by an estimation procedure in which both ρ_i and σ_i vary freely. Finally, people are allowed to use different updating speeds, by allowing c to vary over i.

The following estimation procedure is used. It turns out that adding different parameters σ_i increases the likelihood of the data relatively more than adding different parameters c_i. Therefore, it is first assessed how many different error parameters are used, by iteratively adding σ_i's until the likelihood of the data is not increased significantly. If more than one σ_i is estimated in the general model, the proportion p_i of the population using each σ_i is estimated as well. Second, given the number of errors observed in each treatment, different updating strategies c_i are iteratively added to the model in a similar way.

Table 5.5 presents the results of this exercise. The first two sets of results concern the base model and the Cournot model, respectively. The parameters of the

---

[13]Formally, theorem 2.8, underlying equation 5.3, is only derived for the base model in appendix A. It can be shown, however, that it also holds for the more general aggregation function 5.4. For the Cournot model, the adaptation presented is needed.

[14]The relationship between cov, ρ and σ is given by $cov = \rho\sigma^2/(1-\rho^2)$.

Table 5.5
Maximum likelihood estimations for the expectations (belief learning models)

treatment		low-7	high-7	high-5	pubgood	pubbad	nature
Base model	σ_1	0.49**	0.47**	0.48**	0.46**	0.56**	0.48**
	cov	0.55**	0.24**	0.13**	0.17**	0.16**	0.18**
	a	-0.10*	0.17**	0.07**	0.12**	-0.19**	-0.05
	-logL	901.7	840.1	830.3	259.0	335.0	331.4
Cournot model	σ_1	0.78**	0.94**	0.67**	0.63**	0.71**	0.82**
	cov	0.36**	0.15**	0.09**	0.18**	0.18**	0.14**
	a	-0.02	0.14**	0.07**	0.24**	-0.06	-0.04
	-logL	1480.8	1716.0	1226.1	380.9	428.0	585.0
General model	c	X	-0.35**	X	X	X	-1.43**
	σ_1	0.24**	0.20**	0.16**	0.16**	0.17**	0.09**
	σ_2	0.46**	0.35**	0.37**	0.36**	0.43**	0.32**
	σ_3	0.72**	0.50**	0.64**	0.62**	0.74**	0.76**
	σ_4	X	0.88**	X	X	X	X
	cov	0.59**	0.25**	0.14**	0.17**	0.17**	0.27**
	p_1	0.20**	0.08*	0.07*	0.05	0.05	0.13*
	p_2	0.62**	0.51**	0.59**	0.62**	0.60**	0.63**
	p_3	X	0.32**	X	X	X	X
	a	-0.07	0.15**	0.06**	0.15**	-0.16**	-0.07*
	-logL	809.8	698.1	722.1	226.5	301.7	184.9

Notes: LogL denotes the loglikelihood for a model per treatment. * denotes statistical significance at the 5% level; ** at the 1% level (t-tests). An 'X' denotes that the addition of the parameter concerned does not improve the likelihood of the data significantly at the 1% level according to the likelihood ratio test. For the general model of low-7 and for the general model of nature one parameter c is added in the estimation procedure (the whole population updates with the same c according to the estimations).

models (σ, *cov*, a) are presented, as well as the loglikelihood. The other results concern the procedure described above, allowing for multiple σ's and c's in the population. The parameters p describe the fractions of the population using various parameters.

A first thing to note from these results is that the base model seems to do better than the Cournot model in all treatments. Though the models are not nested, the difference in likelihood for two models estimated with the same data-set and using the same number of parameters is clearly suggestive. Furthermore, the error rate (as witnessed by σ) is much smaller for the base model. This suggests that it is likely that when adapting expectations subjects take all previous observations into account, and not the most recent observation only.

A remarkable result is the difference in rate of updating between the treatment without interaction (nature) and the treatments with interaction (the public good treatments). In nature, primacy is observed in the updating of subjects ($c<0$). In the other treatments no systematic deviations from (true) naive Bayesian updating are observed (hence, $c=0$), except in treatment high-7, where primacy is observed ($c<0$). Neither in nature, nor in high-7, does systematic variation exist in c amongst individuals (only one c is selected by the estimation procedure). In fact, for the public good games, the main deviation from naive Bayesian updating as described in the base model is given by a varying degree of errors across individuals. Apparently, subjects differ in the extent to which they err against the model. Differences in the error structure explain the results better than (differences in) order effects in the public good games.

5.4 Experimental results: spotlight on choices

The analysis of the data on expectations favors the belief learning approach. However, if subjects really update their beliefs under the assumption that the distribution of others' behavior is stationary, one would also expect this to be reflected in the choices subjects make. The evidence for belief learning models is enhanced if it is also supported by an analysis of the choices subjects make in public good games.

Given the lack of support for deterministic decision rules reported in chapter 4, it is not very likely that the game theoretic models based on such rules will receive much support. For completeness, a test for deterministic game theoretic predictions that does not make use of the data obtained on expectations is provided in section 5.4.1. This analysis shows the need for stochastic equilibrium models. In section 5.4.2 the stochastic quantal response equilibrium is applied to the specific treatments used in this study. The predictive power of this equilibrium concept will be compared to the predictive power of the naive Bayesian model.

5.4.1 Results for deterministic game theoretic models

First, the evidence for the game theoretic model assuming homogeneous (expected value maximizing) players is discussed (cf. section 2.3.1). Then the evidence for heterogeneous (expected utility maximizing) players is presented (cf. section 2.3.2). The analysis will give the theory its best shot by focusing on the strangers treatments. These treatments resemble the starting point of the static models most closely. For homogeneous individuals, the focus will be on symmetric Nash Equilibria. In low-7, the only symmetric equilibrium is obtained if nobody contributes (the condition described in equation 2.7 of chapter 2 is not fulfilled). In 52 of the 180 groups nobody contributes. If the second half of each session is considered (periods 11-20), in 43 of the 90 groups no contribution is made.

In high-7, three symmetric equilibria exist: one consisting of pure strategies, where nobody contributes, and two consisting of mixed strategies such that all individuals contribute with a probability of 30.1% or 36.7%. The mixed strategies equilibrium with contribution probability 36.7% is the payoff dominant symmetric equilibrium (cf. theorem 2.1). No support for any symmetric strategies equilibrium can be found: in only 5 of the 180 groups no contribution is made. Using a Kolmogorov-Smirnov one-sample test the hypotheses can be tested that all subjects use a mixed strategy with a contribution probability of 30.1% or 36.7%. If they do, the number of contributions per subject should be (approximately) normally distributed with mean 6.02 and standard deviation 2.05 or with mean 7.34 and standard deviation 2.15. Both hypotheses are rejected (for these tests the sum of contributions per subject serves as a data-point, $p=0.00$, $n=63$ (2x)). Not only the number of contributions is too high (8.20), the standard deviation is much too high (5.66).

In high-5 the same kind of results are found. Again, three symmetric equilibria exist: one consisting of pure strategies, where nobody contributes, and two consisting of mixed strategies such that all individuals contribute with a probability of 36.8% or 63.2%. If all group-members contribute with probability 63.2%, the payoff dominant symmetric equilibrium is obtained. No support for any symmetric strategies equilibrium can be found, however: only in 5 of the 240 groups no contribution is made. Using a Kolmogorov-Smirnov one-sample test the hypotheses can be tested that all subjects use a mixed strategy with a contribution probability of 36.8% or 63.2%. The number of contributions per subject should be (approximately) normally distributed with mean 7.36 and standard deviation 2.16 or with mean 12.64 and standard deviation 2.16. Both hypotheses are rejected (p=0.00, n=60 (2x)). The standard deviation is much too high (5.09).[15] This suggests that the assumption of homogeneity may not be correct.[16] Nevertheless, this model's comparative statics results are not rejected. An increase in the value of the public good and a decrease in group-size both increase the inclination to contribute (theorems 2.2 and 2.3).

Theorem 2.6, as reported in chapter 2 and the scores for the value orientations obtained in the decomposed games will be used to evaluate the deterministic game theoretic model for heterogeneous players. According to theorem 2.6, assimilation of behavior will result, such that only one type of player randomizes with positive probability. Those types of players obtaining less social utility than this type should not contribute at all, whereas those acquiring more social utility should always contribute.

The motivational vectors obtained via the decomposed game technique are used to rank subjects in ascending order, such that they can be divided into three groups in a session, with probabilities of contributing equal to p_1, p_2, and p_3. The groups are numbered such, that they represent an increasing angle of the motivational vector. According to theorem 2.6, p_1 should be equal to 0% and p_3 should be equal to 100%. With a Kolmogorov-Smirnov test it can be tested whether individuals not fulfilling one of these two criteria contribute in accordance with the same mixed strategy p_2, where p_2 is the maximum likelihood estimate obtained from the data. Since the decomposed

---

[15]It could be argued that since there are multiple equilibria, the appropriate test is at the level of sessions: maybe one session one equilibrium is played and in another session the other. This does not change the results. In fact, in high-7 the payoff dominant symmetric equilibrium p=0.367 fits best in each session, so the result is the same. In high-5 the equilibrium p=0.368 fits best in session 10, but is rejected by a K/S test (p=0.05, n=15). The payoff dominant symmetric equilibrium p=0.632 fits best in the remaining sessions 7, 8 and 9, but is also rejected (p=0.00).

[16]The most obvious asymmetric equilibrium is in pure strategies and results if s of the n group-members contribute. In 24 of the 180 groups of low-7, 58 of the 180 groups of high-7 and 84 of the 240 groups in high-5 exactly s of the n group-members contribute.

game technique appears to be a noisy method on the basis of the analysis presented in chapter 4, these predictions are relaxed somewhat. Group 1 contains as many subjects with the lowest scores on the value orientation as possible such that the maximum likelihood estimate for p_I is smaller than 5%. Group 3 contains as many subjects with the highest scores on the value orientation as possible such that the maximum likelihood estimate for p_I is greater than 95%. Thus, groups 1 and 3 are chosen as large as possible to give the hypothesis its best shot.

The results are not in line with the hypothesis. In 7 of the 10 sessions of the strangers treatments, group 1 and group 3 are completely empty and the analysis degenerates to the (homogeneous) groups analysis presented above. In session 2, group 1 consists of 10 individuals and group 3 is empty; in session 3, group 1 consists of 1 individual and group 3 is empty; and in session 6, group 3 consists of 1 individual and group 1 is empty. Although the inclination to contribute varies substantially between individuals, it does not vary as specifically as could be expected on the basis of the game theoretic model for heterogeneous individuals.[17] It seems that the game theoretic model for heterogeneous individuals provides an improvement compared to the model for homogeneous individuals, because of its more realistic assumption about the differences in individuals' preferences. However, the deterministic character of the model makes it unrealistic. It appears necessary to consider stochastic equilibrium concepts.

5.4.2 Quantal Response Equilibria and Quantal Response Belief Learning

The concept of Quantal Response Equilibrium (QRE) developed by McKelvey and Palfrey (1995) and discussed at more length in section 2.3.3 is applied here to public good games with a step-level production function to obtain stochastic game theoretic predictions which can be used for more straightforward testing. The predictive power of this equilibrium model is compared to the predictive power of a contestant from the class of belief learning models, the Quantal Response Naive Bayesian model (QRNB). According to this model, players adapt their expectations like naive Bayesians, as discussed in section 2.4.1. Both models assume that players use the same decision rule. Players are supposed to give noisy best responses. More specifically, players try to

[17]In this analysis individuals with a consistency level below 30% are excluded. The conclusion remains the same if individuals with consistency levels lower than 70% are excluded.

maximize expected value but fall prey to extreme value errors. The experimental analysis of decision rules in chapter 4 has indicated that this decision rule is too simple to capture subjects' choices, since subjects' choices are affected by social utility components not incorporated in the expected value approach. However, the goal of the analysis presented here is to discriminate between the QRE model and the QRNB model, and not to give a full realistic picture of subjects' interaction in these games. This is postponed to the next section. Of course, there is no a priori reason why this partially wrong assumption about decision rules would favor either of the two models.

The Quantal Response Equilibrium model shares the problem of many equilibrium concepts that it potentially gives rise to multiple equilibria. This is certainly the case in the type of public good games studied here. One way to select between the equilibria is to focus on symmetric equilibria only. In a symmetric QRE each individual contributes with probability p_c, and expects each other individual in the group to contribute with the same probability p_c. Given that subjects in the public good treatments only receive information about the aggregate contribution level of the other group-members, such that they cannot keep track of individual differences, the assumption of symmetry does not seem to be unreasonable. As indicated in section 2.3.3, these symmetric equilibrium probabilities are determined by the following equation:

$$p_c = \frac{1}{1 + e^{\lambda \left[c - (f(s)-c) \binom{n-1}{s-1} p_c^{s-1} (1-p_c)^{n-s} \right]}} . \qquad 5.5$$

The solution of this equation can be obtained numerically for each λ. The equation yields one, two or three solutions, dependent on the treatment and the value of λ. The equilibrium paths are shown in figures 5.1-5.3 for the different public good treatments. Each path in each treatment converges to one of the symmetric mixed strategies Nash equilibria of the public good game as λ approaches ∞. Note that the symmetric equilibria of the treatments low-7, high-5, pubgood and pubbad reported in the former section are already approximated for λ=0.2.

According to the Quantal Response Naive Bayesian model, subjects give quantal responses to the expectations a naive Bayesian observer would have formed. As explained in section 2.4.1, a subject expects each other group-member to contribute with probability θ. Individuals' prior distribution on θ is assumed to be the uniform distribution. The sum of the k observations on other group-members' former play $x_1,\ldots,x_k$ is denoted by s_k. Then, the posterior distribution on θ is a beta distribution,

Figure 5.1

The Quantal Response Equilibrium paths for treatment low-7

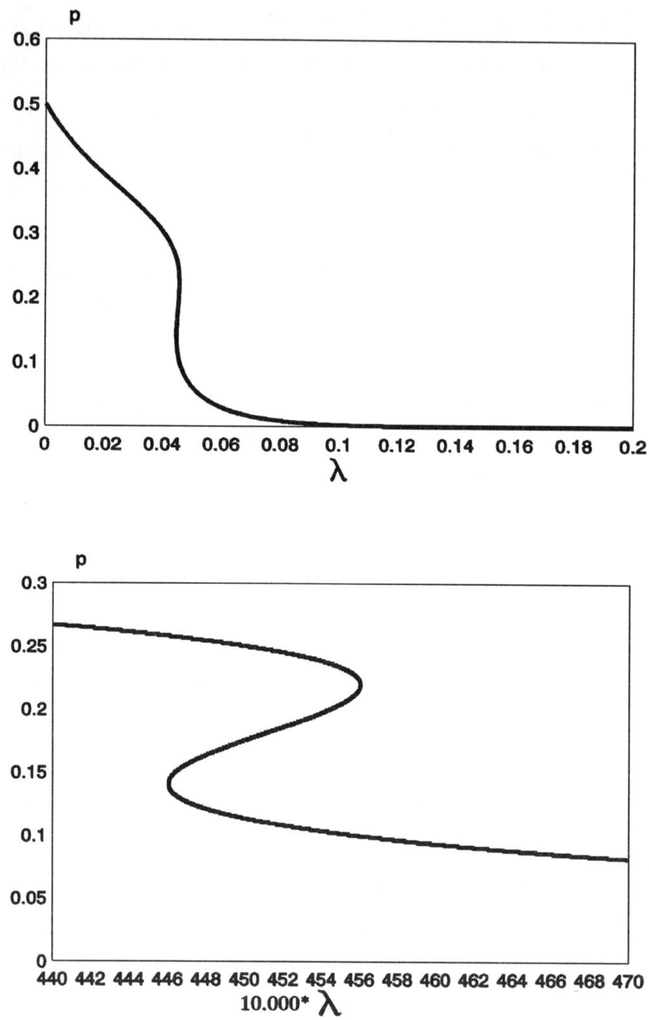

Notes: The upper part provides an overview. The lower part provides a detail.

Figure 5.2
Quantal Response Equilibrium paths for treatment high-7

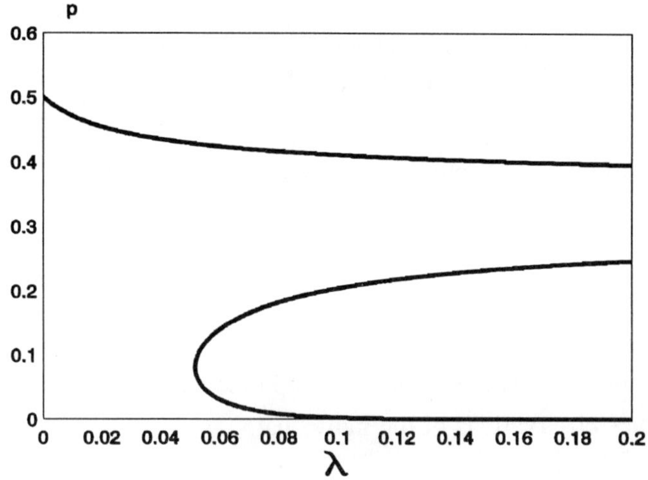

Figure 5.3
Quantal Response Equilibrium paths for treatments high-5, pubgood and pubbad

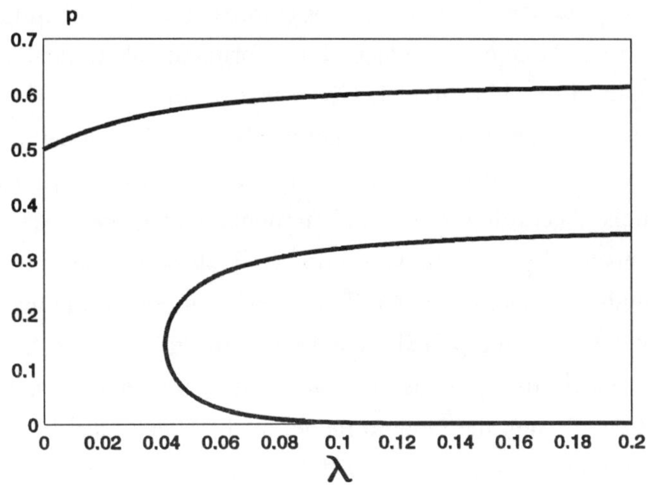

and the density of the predictive distribution $g(y \mid s_k)$ for a new observation y is given by the following equation (cf. theorem 2.8 in section 2.4.1):

$$g(y|s_k) = \frac{k\ (n-1)+1}{(n-1)\ (k+1)+1} \binom{k\ (n-1)}{s_k} \frac{\binom{n-1}{y}}{\binom{(n-1)\ (k+1)}{s_k+y}} . \qquad 5.6$$

Thus, according to the QRNB model an individual will contribute with probability p_c equal to:

$$p_c = \frac{1}{1 + e^{\lambda * [c - (f(s)-c) * g(s-1|s_k)]}} . \qquad 5.7$$

The dynamic element in this theory is apparent in the term $g(s\text{-}1 \mid s_k)$ which is contingent on the former observations of the individual.

For each model, the likelihood of the observed *choices* is used as the criterion to assess its empirical strength. Reported *expectations* are not used in this analysis. An obvious difficulty in a direct comparison of the QRNB model and the QRE model is that neither model is nested in the other. However, two aspects of the models seem to imply that some comparisons can be made. First, the structure of the models is very similar. Both models assume the same decision rule: individuals are supposed to give a quantal response given their expectations. A comparison of the likelihood of the data under both models can be interpreted as giving information about the likelihood of the expectations predicted by either model. Given that people give quantal responses, is it more likely that their expectations are generated by the QRE model or by the QRNB model? Second, it is useful to recognize that the *random* model is nested in a similar way in both models. According to the random model a decision-maker chooses either alternative with probability ½. The restriction $\lambda=0$ in either the QRE model or the QRNB model yields this random model. The exercise of comparing the likelihoods of the models may thus be interpreted as a search for the answer to the following question: under which model does the rationality-parameter λ add most to the likelihood of the data, using the random model as the bench-mark?

There is another difficulty. The QRNB model makes a unique prediction for each individual given the history of the game, but the QRE model does not, as a result of the presence of multiple equilibria. In fact, one can view the QRE model in the present public good game as a model with three separate predictions: the higher part path, the middle part path and the lower part path (cf. figures 5.1-5.3). For low-7, the higher part path is defined by the higher (or unique) values for p on the interval $\lambda \in [0, 0.0456]$, the middle part path by the middle values for p on the interval $\lambda \in [0.0446, 0.0456]$ and the lower part path by the lower (or unique) values for p on the interval $\lambda \in [0.0446, \infty\rangle$. For the other treatments, the higher part path is defined by the higher (or unique) values for p on the interval $\lambda \in [0, \infty\rangle$. The middle part path is defined by the upper part of the parabola and the lower part path by the lower part of the parabola. For each of these three paths the maximum likelihood estimate of λ is determined, and the path with the highest likelihood for generating the data serves as the prediction of the QRE model. This procedure obviously biases the comparison of the models in favor of the QRE model. This model gets its best shot.[18]

As can be inferred from table 5.6, the estimation results favor the QRNB model

Table 5.6

Maximum likelihood estimations for the QRNB and the QRE model

	QRNB model		QRE model			Random model
Treat-ment	λ	-logL	best shot	λ	-logL	-logL
low-7	0.0476	622.3**	middle	0.0454	627.7**	873.4
high-7	0.0353	834.0**	high	0.1033	853.0**	873.4
high-5	0.0054	831.4	high	0.0018	831.7	831.8
pubgood	0.0128	551.7*	high	0.0048	554.3	554.5
pubbad	0.0176	549.3**	middle	104.871	539.6**	554.5

Notes: logL denotes the likelihood of all choices in a treatment. * denotes statistical significance of the likelihood ratio test at the 5% level; ** at the 1% level. 'Best shot' indicates which of the three QRE paths yields the highest likelihood of the data. For pubgood and pubbad all subjects are used, including those that do not report expectations.

[18]Another possibility is to select between the three symmetric paths on the basis of a refinement. For example, one may choose the path with the highest expected payoff. However, as will become clear in footnote 21, this may increase the econometric problems when estimating the parameters of the QRE.

over the QRE model, even if the QRE model is evaluated at its best shot. The likelihood of the data is greater under the QRNB model in all treatments, except in pubbad. With the exception of treatment high-5, the QRNB model describes the data significantly better than the random model in all treatments.[19]

The differences in the likelihoods are informative: if a more general model would be constructed that contained the QRE and QRNB model as special cases, then the QRE model would certainly be rejected in treatments low-7, high-7 and pubgood using the likelihood ratio test at the 5% level. On the other hand, the QRNB model would be rejected in pubbad. Offerman, Sonnemans and Schram (1996) estimate such a model for the strangers treatments.

The estimation results per 5 periods are presented in table 5.7 for the QRE model. As subjects obtain more experience with the game, their understanding may increase. Behavior in later periods may be more rational than behavior in early periods. In fact, this is suggested by the finding reported in section 4.3.1 that there is a stronger relationship between subjects' estimated probability of being critical and their propensity to contribute in the second ten periods than in the first ten periods. If the level of precision or rationality increases throughout the experiment, one would expect the estimates for λ to increase within a treatment.[20] This does not happen in the estimation results for the QRE model, however. Especially in treatments high-7 and pubbad, the estimates for λ jump up and down over time. It seems impossible to give a meaningful interpretation for this phenomenon.[21]

---

[19]It may be noted that both the QRE and the QRNB models were originally developed with the strangers treatments of public good games in mind. Static game theoretic models (like QRE) assume that players are involved in one-shot games, which is approximately the case in the strangers treatments but not in the partners treatments. The QRNB model's assumption that players do not think strategically is more likely to be fulfilled in the strangers than in the partners treatments.

[20]Again, despite the fact that subjects make a considerable number of errors, the low numbers for λ may be misleading in the sense that they suggest an even lower level of rationality than actually present. The low numbers can partially be explained by the unit of the payoffs used (cents).

[21]The QRE model has problems organizing the data in some treatments. The maximum likelihood procedure selects a point on one of the (λ,p) paths. For an average observed contribution level of p^* the corresponding λ^* on a graph is selected. If the aggregate contribution level lies within certain regions, no corresponding optimal λ exists. These regions are for low-7: $\langle 0.5;1]$; for high-7 $\langle 0.301; 0.367\rangle$ and $\langle 0.5; 1]$; for high-5, pubgood and pubbad $\langle 0.368; 0.5\rangle$ and $\langle 0.632; 1]$ (cf. figures 5.1-5.3). For contribution levels within these regions the estimation procedure selects an extreme value for λ, i.e., $\lambda=0$ or $\lambda\rightarrow\infty$. The GAUSS program used for the estimations typically

Table 5.7
Maximum likelihood estimations for the QRE model per 5 periods

treatment + best shot	period 1-5		period 6-10		period 11-15		period 16-20	
	λ	-logL	λ	-logL	λ	-logL	λ	-logL
low-7	0.0443	181.7**	0.0417	189.4**	0.0446	132.7**	0.0461	96.8**
path	high		high		middle		low	
high-7	0.0509	215.1*	0.3419	210.3**	0.0509	215.1*	0.1938	211.6**
path	high		high		high		high	
high-5	0.0014	207.9	0.0029	207.9	0.0000	207.9	0.0135	207.4
path	high		high		high		high	
pubgood	0.0111	138.4	0.0000	138.6	0.0021	138.6	0.0111	138.4
path	high		high		high		high	
pubbad	0.0000	138.6	174.593	134.0**	297.640	136.1*	0.0814	123.0**
path	high		middle		middle		middle	

Notes: logL denotes the likelihood of the choices of 5 periods in a treatment. * denotes statistical significance of the likelihood ratio test at the 5% level; ** at the 1% level. 'Best shot' indicates which of the three QRE models yields the highest likelihood of the data. For pubgood and pubbad all subjects are used, including those that do not report expectations. The estimations allow for different paths to be selected each 5 periods.

Table 5.8 presents similar results for the QRNB model. For this model, moderately increasing estimates for λ are obtained. These results corroborate the evidence obtained for reported expectations in the former section and suggest that subjects are learning to play according to the naive Bayesian model. In doing so, their error rate decreases (λ increases).

The purpose of this section is to discriminate between the QRNB model and the QRE model in a basic frame-work. A comparison of tables 5.7 and 5.8 indicates that the QRNB model does a better job in explaining the data than the QRE model. However, it is clear from the estimation results reported in chapter 4 that either of the models can be improved by allowing for utility transformations of the payoff matrix. In the next section simulations will be presented which take these estimations of utility

---

reports that the covariance matrix fails to invert in these cases.

Table 5.8
Maximum likelihood estimations for the QRNB model per 5 periods

treatment	period 1-5		period 6-10		period 11-15		period 16-20	
	λ	-logL	λ	-logL	λ	-logL	λ	-logL
low-7	0.0301	182.0**	0.0338	189.2**	0.0664	127.1**	0.0811	90.6**
high-7	0.0165	212.1**	0.0743	192.7**	0.0664	205.0**	0.0945	201.2**
high-5	0.0000	207.9	0.0322	207.0	0.0023	207.9	0.0432	205.6*
pubgood	0.0061	138.2	0.0188	137.4	0.0203	137.8	0.0394	136.7*
pubbad	0.0000	138.6	0.0080	138.5	0.0569	131.8**	0.0322	134.0**

Notes: logL denotes the likelihood of the choices of 5 periods in a treatment. * denotes statistical significance of the likelihood ratio test at the 5% level; ** at the 1% level. For pubgood and pubbad all subjects are used, including those that do not report expectations.

functions into account.

5.5 Simulations of the interaction between players

Simulations may serve two purposes here. First, they may reveal to what extent a theory can reproduce the general picture observed in the experiments. Second, one may wonder whether the processes described by a dis-equilibrium theory would converge to an equilibrium (or a stationary distribution of outcomes) in the long run, and if so, whether the equilibrium selected varies over treatments.

Given that both the experimental analysis of the expectations reported and the analysis of choices made by subjects favor the naive Bayesian model over game theoretic models, the naive Bayesian model is used in section 5.5.1 to model the interaction in the simulations. Subjects update their expectations about other players' behavior as a result of the previous outcome of the game. For these simulations the estimation results on utility functions will be used as well.

In addition, in section 5.5.2 the simulations based on a simple reinforcement learning model will be reported. This model is suggested by the results on differing satisfaction scores obtained for subjects in the public good and the public bad treatment. The reinforcement learning model takes account of the interaction differently than the naive Bayesian model. Subjects update their propensity to contribute as a result of their satisfaction with the previous outcome of the game.

5.5.1 Simulations based on a belief learning model

The simulations reported here assume that players update their beliefs as naive Bayesians, and subsequently give a quantal response contingent on these expectations when choosing whether or not to contribute. Given that the estimation results favor the interpretation that subjects choose as warm-glow cooperators, the estimates of this particular transformation are used in the simulations.

The characteristics of the sessions of the experiments are replicated carefully in the simulations. For example, to simulate low-7, the simulation-program randomly and independently draws 21 types of the estimated types distribution (cf. table 4.9, chapter 4):

$$P(y=-264.85)=0.27; \quad P(y=-66.08)=0.59; \quad P(y=36.73) = 0.14. \qquad 5.8$$

The 21 types drawn are scrambled in each period and allocated to one of the three groups (see table 4.1 in chapter 4 for details of the sessions). This procedure is replicated for 500 periods. Each period a simulated group-member contributes with probability p_c:

$$p_c = \frac{1}{1 + e^{\lambda * [c - y - (f(s)-c) * g(s-1|s_k)]}} \qquad 5.9$$

The term $g(s\text{-}1 \mid s_k)$ is described explicitly in theorem 2.8 (chapter 2). In one type of simulations the maximum likelihood estimate is used for λ (chapter 4, table 4.9). In a second type of simulations artificially (more) rational agents are used. In these sessions λ is set equal to 0.1. Maybe the choices of 'experts' with similar preferences as the 'naive subjects' yield different patterns of outcomes. In each type of simulations, the choices of the simulated group-members determine the group outcome, which each member uses to update her or his expectations ($g(s\text{-}1 \mid s_k)$). Each simulated subject has a private record keeping track of her or his history. For each treatment 30 sessions are run. Figures 5.4-5.8 summarize the results of the simulations.

Figure 5.4 - 5.8
Results for the simulations

low-7

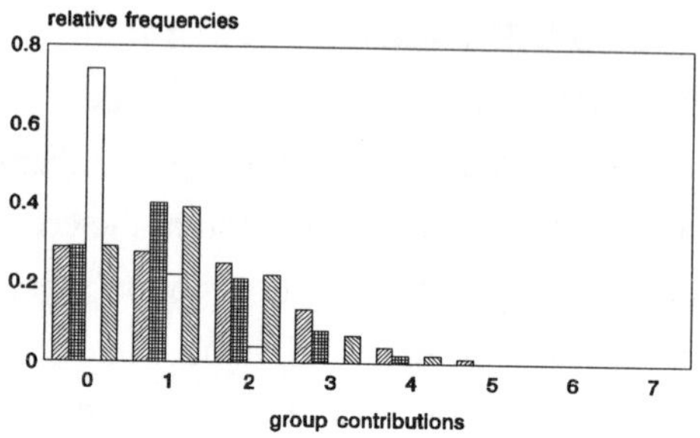

high-7

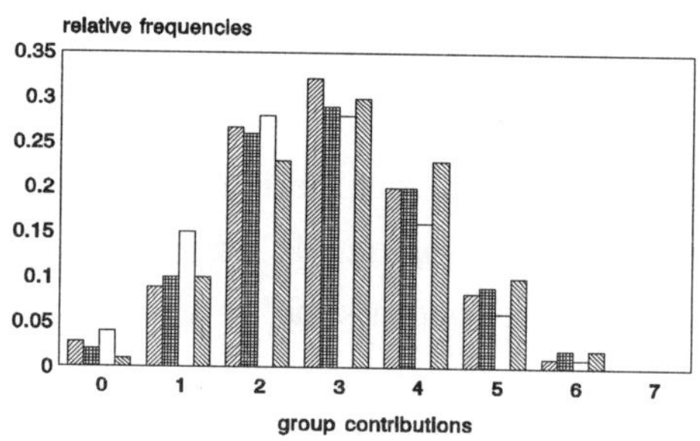

high-5

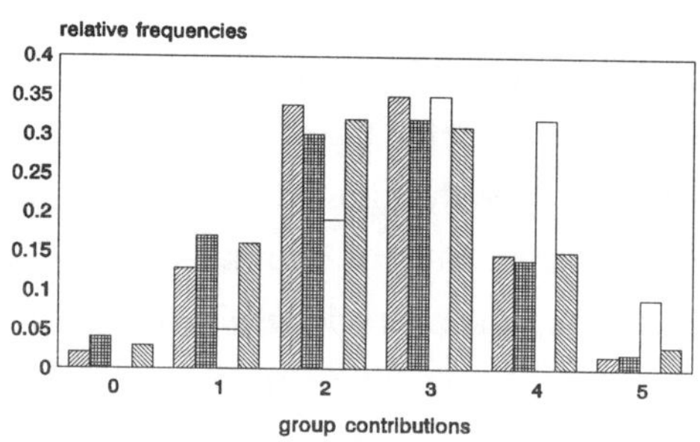

pubgood

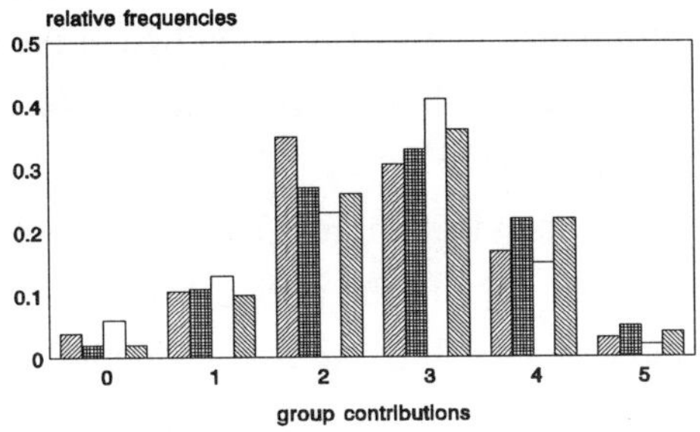

pubbad

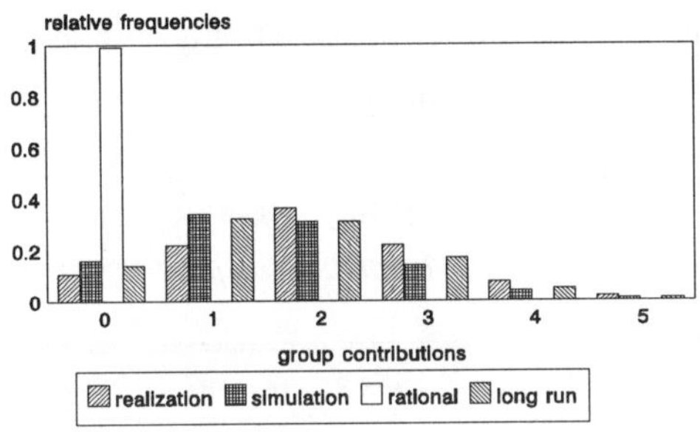

Notes figures 5.4-5.8: 'Realization' shows the frequencies of the group contributions in the experiments (period 1-20); 'simulation' shows the frequencies in the simulations with the maximum likelihood estimate for λ (period 1-20); 'rational' shows the frequencies in the simulations with 'rationality parameter' $\lambda=0.1$ (period 1-20); 'long run' shows the long term frequencies in the simulations with the maximum likelihood estimate for λ (period 450-500).

Visual inspection of the figures yields the following conclusions:

(1) The simulated period 1-20 data with the maximum likelihood parameter for λ resemble the observed data in the experiment fairly well in all treatments.

(2) The distributions of group contributions seem stationary: the simulated period 1-20 distributions resemble the simulated period 450-500 distributions. The process does not converge to pure strategies equilibria (which is not surprising given the fact that players make an error with considerable positive probability).

(3) The distributions of artificial experts seem to be more concentrated around the pure strategies equilibrium outcomes 0 and 3 (except in high-7).

A comparison of figures 5.7 and 5.8 reveals that the QRNB combined with warm-glow utility transformation model gives a potential explanation for the difference of subjects' behavior in public good and public bad games. In pubgood the frequency distribution of the simulated model ('simulation') has a higher mean than in pubbad. However, a difference between the patterns observed in the simulations and the patterns in the experiment is that the simulations yield approximately stable contribution levels over time, whereas the experimental data in the public bad game show a decline in the contribution level (cf. table 5.9). The stable contribution levels obtained in the simulations may be due to the rather extreme estimates obtained for the utility functions (cf. section 4.3.1). However, at present it is not so clear whether the decline in contribution level observed in the public bad experiments is a general phenomenon. Andreoni (1995a) obtains the same difference between a public bad frame and a public good frame in a quite similar experiment, but his public bad treatment shows an approximately stable level of contributions.

Table 5.9

Group outcome per 4 periods in partners treatments

	periods 1-4	periods 5-8	periods 9-12	periods 13-16	periods 17-20
pubgood experiments	2.59	2.72	2.09	2.81	2.56
Pubgood simulations	2.58	2.77	2.83	2.82	2.73
Pubbad experiment	2.41	2.22	1.97	1.75	1.63
Pubbad simulations	1.52	1.62	1.47	1.58	1.76

Note: The simulations reported use the maximum likelihood estimate for λ.

5.5.2 Simulations based on a reinforcement learning model

An alternative explanation for the difference in behavior in the public good and public bad treatment is provided by a dynamic reinforcement learning model. This model assumes that the satisfaction with the outcome of the former period affects the propensity to contribute. The difference in predicted behavior is driven by a difference in satisfaction scores elicited by the different frames, just like it is driven by a difference in utility components in the belief learning model. The major conceptual difference with the model proposed here is that in the belief learning model learning takes place at the level of beliefs, while it takes place at the level of the decision rule in the reinforcement learning model. In this model beliefs do not play a role at all. The structure of the reinforcement learning model differs a lot from the structure of the belief learning model, so no serious comparison of the explanatory power of the models will be made. The two models are simply considered to be alternative explanations of the same phenomenon.

According to this reinforcement learning model, a subject is supposed to update her or his propensity to play one of the two available actions as a result of the satisfaction with the outcome in the previous period. Let $prop(i,t) \in \langle -\infty, \infty \rangle$ denote the 'propensity for cooperation' by subject i in period t. Furthermore, $p_c(i,t) = exp[prop(i,t)]/(1+exp[prop(i,t)])$ denotes the probability of a cooperative choice by subject i in period t. The propensity $prop(i,t)$ depends on the subject-specific history, and is adjusted after each period. The direction in which the propensity is adjusted depends on the satisfaction $s(i,t\text{-}1)$ subject i experienced with the previous decision:

$$prop\ (i,\ t) = prop\ (i,\ t-1) + \alpha * s(i,\ t-1) * d(i,\ t-1)\ . \qquad 5.10$$

Here $d(i,t\text{-}1)=1$ if subject i cooperates in $t\text{-}1$ and $d(i,t\text{-}1)=-1$ if subject i does not cooperate in $t\text{-}1$. α denotes a learning parameter (to be estimated); a higher α coincides with faster learning. The equation implies that a positive satisfaction enhances the probability that the choice will be repeated by the subject. Note that this specification, unlike the specification in section 2.4.2 (equation 2.30), has the attractive property that it guarantees that the probability of a choice lies between 0 and 1.

The estimated α is used as input for simulations of this simple model. The satisfaction $s(i,t\text{-}1)$ depends on the choice of i in $t\text{-}1$, the outcome of that period and the treatment. As already noted in section 4.3.4, satisfaction scores measured in a questionnaire differ between the public good and public bad treatment. Satisfaction scores are not elicited in the other treatments, so the simulations will be limited to the partners treatments. For the simulations the mean satisfaction scores are used. They are obtained by subtracting 4 from the numbers in table 4.14 in chapter 4. Thus a score less/more than 4 (the midpoint of the seven-point scale) yields a negative/positive satisfaction score. The starting values for $prop(i,1)$ are set equal to 0.3 for all i, which corresponds with $p_c(i,1)=0.5075$ (the proportion of cooperative choices observed in the first 5 periods). The maximum likelihood estimate of α=0.08.

With these parameters 1000 simulations of 20 periods each are run. Note that the different values for $s(.,.)$ are the only differences between the (input of the) simulations of the public good and the public bad treatment.

The results of the simulations replicate the general pattern in the experimental data quite well: the proportion of cooperative choices in the public good treatment stays at roughly the same level throughout the 20 periods, and decreases in the public bad treatment. However, the percentages of decisions repeated are lower in the simulation than in the experimental data. This suggests that subjects do not randomize (with changing probabilities) in the experiment as much as the reinforcement learning model suggests. Therefore inertia in choices is introduced in a more general model.

The idea behind the modelling of inertia is that subjects may not reconsider their strategy every period; they may stick to a strategy for several periods. The inertia parameter $r \in [0,1]$ is assumed constant across periods and players. With probability r players are inert: they do not randomize but repeat their former decision. With probability $1-r$ they randomize. In that case they choose to contribute with probability $p_c(i,t)$. The propensities $prop(i,t)$ are adjusted every period in the same way as described above. Thus, after a contribution in $t-1$ a subject i will choose to contribute again in t with probability $r+(1-r)*p_c(i,t)$ and choose not to contribute with probability $(1-r)*(1-p_c(i,t))$. After a choice not to contribute subject i will choose to contribute with probability $(1-r)*p_c(i,t)$ and not to contribute with probability $r+(1-r)*(1-p_c(i,t))$.

For this model, the maximum likelihood estimates of α and r are 0.08 and 0.37 respectively. The addition of the parameter r to the model significantly increases its likelihood (likelihood ratio test, p=0.00). If α and r are estimated separately for the public good and the public bad treatment, the likelihood of the data does not increase significantly. This suggests that the learning process is the same in both treatments and that the difference in behavior can be accounted for by differences in satisfaction scores.

Similar to the experimental data, the simulations of the reinforcement learning model with inertia show a decrease in the number of contributions in the public bad treatment while the number of contributions in the public good treatment remains stable. The proportion of periods in which the threshold is reached, tends to be larger than in the experiment in the public bad treatment, however. The percentages of repeated decisions are close to the experimental percentages, as can be seen in table 5.10.

Table 5.10
Simulations of the reinforcement learning model

	Experimental data	Simulations without inertia	Simulations with inertia
Cooperative choices			
Public Good period 1-10	50.8%	49.9%	50.4%
period 11-20	51.5%	48.8%	49.0%
all periods	51.1%	49.4%	49.7%
Public Bad period 1-10	44.0%	48.3%	48.6%
period 11-20	35.8%	41.8%	41.9%
all periods	39.9%	45.1%	45.2%
Threshold reached			
Public Good all periods	50.6%	48.8%	50.0%
Public Bad all periods	31.3%	40.9%	42.0%
Repeated choices			
Public Good all periods	72.5%	53.0%	70.6%
Public Bad all periods	68.9%	52.9%	70.7%

A remarkable result is obtained if the number of periods in the simulation is increased. All groups end up in a pure strategies Nash equilibrium: after 250 periods 63% of the public good groups are in an equilibrium in which the same 3 players contribute every period and 37% of the groups are in the equilibrium where nobody contributes. For the public bad game these numbers are 3% and 97% respectively. Thus it appears that differences in satisfaction provide a mechanism for equilibrium selection.

Although these simple reinforcement learning models describe the data rather well, they fall short on one account. The efficiency is higher in the simulations than in the public bad experiment (with roughly the same number of contributions the threshold is reached more often). Possibly the models can be improved by including individual differences (value orientations), for example by setting the starting value of *prop* equal to the realization of a random variable. Nevertheless, this does not affect the observed differences in behavior between the public good and the public bad game. These differences appear to be captured by the models.

5.6 Conclusions

This chapter focuses on the expectation formation process and interaction in various public good games. Two elements in the design allow for a sharp analysis. First, information about individual expectations is gathered explicitly in an incentive compatible way. Second, a treatment is run in which subjects play a game against nature that corresponds to the treatments high-5, pubgood and pubbad.

The experimental results on expectations favor the belief learning approach. In particular, they favor the naive Bayesian model over static game theoretic models. Subjects' expectations about other group-members' behavior are systematically biased. The naive Bayesian model predicts that subjects will be too optimistic when the contribution level falls as it does in (some of) the public good games. The bias in subjects' expectations is in accordance with this prediction, and the bias is larger when the model predicts it to be larger. A similar bias is neither predicted by the naive Bayesian model nor observed in the related game against nature.

Furthermore, subjects tend to update their expectations in the direction predicted by belief learning models. The belief learning pattern emerges in all treatments. A remarkable result is that the noise observed against this pattern is not greater in the public good games than in the true game against nature. This suggests that deviations from the naive Bayesian model may be caused by imperfect Bayesian updating, as opposed to sophisticated strategic reasoning. The naive Bayesian model even yields a good description of expectations in the partners treatments, where the possibility of strategic reasoning is larger.

In the game against nature, a notable difference between the actual updating process and the ideal Bayesian updating process is that people tend to underweight the impact of new evidence. A similar difference is observed in the public good treatment high-7. Primacy in the judgments is only found in these treatments, however. In the other public good games the introduction of a recency/primacy parameter in the model does not increase the likelihood of the data significantly. The actual rate of updating is approximately equal to the rate of an ideal naive Bayesian observer in these public good treatments. Although there is not much variation in recency/primacy in updating, there is considerable variation across individuals in the errors against ideal updating. Finally, when subjects update, they seem to take all former observations into account, and not just the most recent one as suggested by the Cournot model.

The conclusion drawn on the basis of reported expectations that the data are better organized by belief learning models than by static game theoretic models is corroborated by an analysis of the choices made by subjects. Assuming the decision rule that subjects give noisy best responses to their expectations, maximum likelihood estimations indicate that the probability is greater that the choices are generated by a model assuming that subjects adapt their expectations as naive Bayesians than by a model assuming that subjects' expectations are in equilibrium. Furthermore, according to the estimations of the naive Bayesian model, subjects' precision when they make choices increases moderately throughout the experiment. As McKelvey and Palfrey (1995) argue, this could intuitively be expected as subjects gain experience in playing a particular game. A similar increase in subjects' precision is not observed in the estimations for the equilibrium model.

A striking anomaly for all models considered here is that people tend to be overconfident in the public good games, but not in the game against nature. In addition, it takes subjects considerably more time to make decisions in the game against nature than in the public good games. From a rational point of view these differences are puzzling. The decisions in the public good games are more difficult, because of the strategic interaction between the subjects. The interaction between subjects should stimulate them to consider the possibility that others' behavior changes over time. In that case other group-members do not contribute with a constant probability, which makes the prediction-task more difficult than in the game against nature, where a constant probability is used. The experimental results suggest that subjects in the public good games neglect such strategic considerations, but that does not explain why subjects seem to perceive the game against nature as the *more difficult* game. Maybe the social interaction in the public good games increases the confidence in people's judgments and the speed of decision-making, because it reminds them of similar situations in daily life. The task in the game against nature may be perceived as more abstract and difficult, because the resemblance with daily life is more remote.

Note that the conclusion that the process of expectation formation is captured better by the naive Bayesian model does not in itself make the concept of Nash equilibrium useless. In combination with a decision rule, the development of expectations yields a dynamic pattern of choices. Simulations show that the decisions often converge to a Nash equilibrium. For example, simulations based on the naive Bayesian model, taking into account that when making a decision people differ in their attitudes towards others in public good games, show that the interaction is drawn to the inefficient equilibrium where nobody contributes in the pubbad treatment, while the interaction centers around one of the efficient interior equilibria in the pubgood treatment. Similarly, in low-7 the interaction focuses more on the zero-contribution equilibrium, while the interaction in high-7 and high-5 is more attracted by the interior equilibria (figures 5.4-5.8). This suggests that the naive Bayesian model may successfully be used as a model for equilibrium selection.

However, a simpler reinforcement learning model is also capable of tracing the dynamics observed in the pubgood and the pubbad treatment. This model neglects the intermediating role of expectations in the determination of subjects' choices. Simulations based on this model show a 'cleaner' convergence to one of the (pure strategies) Nash equilibria. A straight comparison of the empirical performance of the reinforcement learning model and the belief learning model is not possible given the rather large differences in structure.

Of course, it cannot be excluded that new dynamic game theoretic models will be developed which take account of the pattern in the expectations and the choices observed in the experiments. El-Gamal, McKelvey and Palfrey (1994) propose an algorithm to solve the history dependent Bayesian Nash equilibria in a *2*-periods centipede game. Even in their relatively simple game the algorithm is computationally very intensive, and not particularly intuitive. The naive Bayesian model, and perhaps also the reinforcement learning model, can be seen as powerful alternative models based on very simple assumptions.

An interesting question for future research is whether the assumption that subjects play strategic games as games against nature can be generalized successfully to other games. In principle the naive Bayesian model can be extended to any game where a discrete number of players form expectations about other players' choices from a discrete number of options. The naive Bayesian model can be expected to perform better in strategically complicated games than in strategically transparent games.

PART III: Evaluation of the results

This final part provides a summary and interpretation of some of the results discussed in the previous chapters. It sketches the potential contribution of this study to the development of a positive theory of games.

6. Towards a positive theory of public good games

6.1 Introduction

A positive theory is concerned with the description and explanation of real world phenomena. Wong (1987) describes the purpose of positive economic theorizing as follows: "The goal of positive economics is said to be the formulation of empirical hypotheses that are testable or refutable. It is no longer acceptable to consider the premises from which these hypotheses are derived to be self-evident truths about human nature." In line with this view, it is argued here that a positive theory of behavior in games should be constructed as much as possible on empirically supported elements.

The general structure of the theories on public good games considered in this study consists of two cornerstones: expectations and decision rules (cf. figure 6.1). The decision rule describes how a player chooses given her or his beliefs. Internal and external factors may affect both players' beliefs and their decision rules. The internal

Figure 6.1
General structure of positive theories

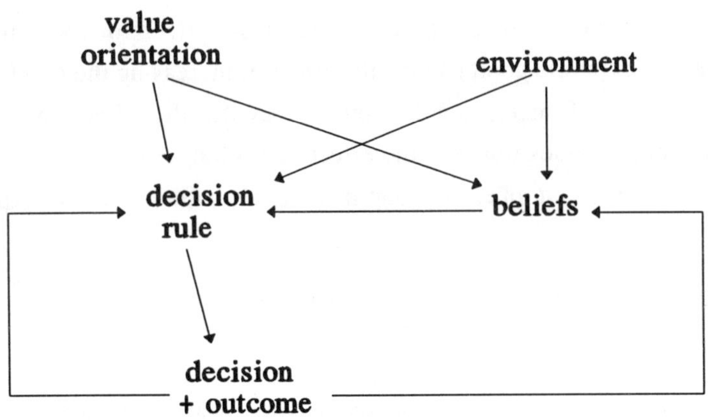

factor considered in this study is a player's preferences regarding the outcomes for others, or simply her or his value orientation. The external factor considered is the environment of the game.[1] Group-size is an example of an environmental factor affecting beliefs. Some environments induce more cooperative decision rules than others. The framing of the public good and the value of the public payoff are two environmental factors affecting decision rules. Given their beliefs, value orientation and environment, players decide whether to contribute or not to the public good. The outcome of the game may lead to an adjustment of beliefs in the next play.[2]

The various elements of this general structure of a positive theory are addressed in turn in this final chapter: section 6.2 provides the summary and evaluation of environmental effects on the provision of public goods. Section 6.3 draws the attention to the merits and limits of the concept of value orientation and the method to measure it, the decomposed game technique. It also provides some discussion on the question whether players with a cooperative value orientation can survive the eliminating forces of evolution. In section 6.4 the focus shifts to the evidence obtained on decision rules used by people when choosing whether or not to contribute in public good games. Section 6.5 provides a discussion of some conceptual issues concerning expectation formation about other players' behavior and the interaction between players. Section 6.6 concludes with a sketch of a positive theory in public good games.

6.2 Environmental effects

Changes in the environment may affect both players' decision rule and their beliefs (figure 6.1). This section contains a discussion of the effects of four environmental changes in step-level public good games: the effect of increasing the number of group-members, the effect of increasing the public payoff, the effect of changing the variability of group-composition and the effect of framing.

An increase in the number of group-members has the intuitively expected effect

---

[1]Note that the false consensus hypothesis does not fit in the structure described in figure 6.1. The reason is that this hypothesis finds relatively little support in the data (cf. chapter 4).

[2]The outcome of a game may also affect the propensity to contribute directly, as assumed by reinforcement learning models. In that case the outcome does not affect beliefs but the decision rule.

on individual choices to contribute. In big groups players are less inclined to contribute than in small groups. The effect can mainly be attributed to a difference in beliefs: individuals feel that the probability that their contribution is going to be critical is smaller in large groups than in small groups. However, in this study the effect on the individual contribution level was not so great that it affected the provision of the public good. On the contrary, the public good was provided more often in the large group than in the small group. In a large group a lower average contribution level suffices to provide the public good.

The effect of an increase in the value of the public good is both intuitive and clear cut. A higher value of the public good induces individuals to make more contributions. This seems to be mainly due to a difference in decision rules. Given their expectations, individuals are more inclined to contribute when the value of the public good is high than when it is low. At the same time the public good is more often provided when its value is high.

These first two effects can be rationalized by different theories and can thus not be used to discriminate between them. Both effects can be explained by the naive Bayesian model, and they do not contradict game theoretic predictions either. Often the empirical validity of a game theoretic model is assessed merely by its ability to predict the effects of changes in the environment. This study indicates that this might be a risky procedure, since there is a systematic possibility that different models of individual behavior in games generate similar comparative statics results.

A change in the variability of group-composition does not affect the inclination to contribute or the frequency that the public good is actually provided. Players' decision rules seem to be somewhat more cooperative when groups remain constant than when they change all the time. On the other hand, subjects estimate the probability of being critical to be higher when groups are changing. Both differences are small and work in opposite directions, so that the overall effect is negligible. This result is easier rationalized by belief learning models than by game theoretic models.

The most remarkable effect is that there is a difference between behavior in an environment with positive externalities and behavior in an environment with negative externalities. Individuals are more inclined to contribute in a public good game than in a strategically equivalent public bad game. As a consequence, the provision of the public good is easier than the prevention of the public bad. If the organizer of the voluntary provision of a public good may choose to frame it either as a public good or a public bad, (s)he should choose the public good frame. People are more inclined to contribute if they are told about the positive consequences of their contribution than if they are told about the negative consequences of their refusal to contribute. Fundraisers may grasp this asymmetry intuitively, since in advertisements of charitable organizations comments about the positive effect of a contribution seem more common than comments about the negative effect of a refusal to contribute.

The effect cannot be attributed to a difference in beliefs. There seems to be a difference in decision rules, however. This difference can be incorporated both by a belief learning model and by a reinforcement learning model. According to the belief learning model there is a difference in utility when contributing to the public good or to the public bad. Specifically, contributing in the public good game elicits a 'warm glow', whereas contributing in the public bad game elicits a 'cold prickle'. According to the reinforcement learning model the difference in behavior between the frames is driven by a difference in the level of satisfaction with the former outcome of the game. Players in the public good game seem to especially dislike the situation where they did not contribute while their contribution would have been critical for the provision of the public good, whereas players in a public bad game seem to especially dislike the situation where their contribution was in vain. This study has not addressed the question where such differences in utility or satisfaction come from. One may conjecture that evolution causes players to associate the public bad game with scarcity and potential shortage of basic commodities. In that case, this frame may emphasize the possibility that a cooperative action will put them in the position of the loser. In times of war many people seem to display greedy behavior and hoard commodities. Evolution may have caused the public good game to be associated with times of abundance of commodities, times where a loss of some wealth does not have very negative effects.

6.3 Value orientations

The previous section discussed (among others) the effects of changes in the environment on a player's decision rule in the public good game. This section focuses on an internal factor determining a player's decision rule: her or his value orientation.

Section 6.3.1 describes some of the merits and limits of the concept of value orientation and the method used to measure it, the decomposed game technique. Section 6.3.2 provides a discussion of the question whether differences in value orientation can be explained from an evolutionary perspective.

6.3.1 Merits and limits of value orientations and decomposed game technique

An individual's value orientation has been interpreted here as a personality variable, as a person's attitude towards an unknown other. This interpretation does not exclude the possibility that an individual's orientation is affected by situational factors. For example, if a cooperator is paired to an individualist in a repeated prisoners' dilemma, (s)he will probably adapt her or his attitude towards this other. But that does not necessarily imply that her or his attitude towards a new unknown other would change. There are some indications that value orientations are quite stable over time (Dehue *et al.*, 1993; Kuhlman *et al.*, 1986). Dehue, McClintock and Liebrand (1993) find that for the majority of subjects, the decomposed game technique measures the same orientation in two measurements with a time period of two months in between. Instability in measured orientations can by and large be attributed to shifts to adjacent orientations, rather than to arbitrary shifts. They also provide evidence indicating that the method for measuring value orientations is quite robust in the sense that similar outcomes result if a slightly different way of measurement is used.[3]

Usually the decomposed game technique is applied without incentives. In this study subjects are actually paid for their choices. The main effect of the use of incentives is that subjects choose more consistently. A smaller, albeit not significant effect is that subjects are somewhat less pro-social if they play for real money (cf. section 3.2). Moreover, the experiments in the present study contains relatively more subjects majoring in economics or econometrics than previous studies. The average angle of the motivational vector measured is 9.5 degrees for economists versus 14.0 for non-economists. Although this difference is not statistically significant (Mann-Whitney test for players, 154 economists versus 90 non-economists, $p=0.17$), it adds to the difference caused by the use of incentives. These two factors taken together may

---

[3]Social psychological studies also support the ecological validity of value orientations. A value orientation is a helpful factor to explain or predict social behavior outside the laboratory (for references to this work, cf. Van Lange, 1995).

explain why relatively more individualists are observed in the population of this study than in previous (social psychological) studies. Here, 61% of the subjects are classified as individualists and 30% as cooperators, whereas in social psychological studies usually 25%-30% of the subjects are classified as individualists and 50%-60% as cooperators (Van Lange, 1995).

The scores for value orientations generated by the decomposed game technique can be used to predict behavior in the public good game with *n* persons and a step-level production function. Subjects with a cooperative value orientation contribute more to the public good than subjects with an individualistic value orientation. The results for value orientations have been linked to the indirect results of the maximum likelihood estimates for the distribution of warm-glow cooperators. These estimates are based on the choices and reported probabilities in the public good game. They can be used to calculate the posterior probability that a subject is of a particular type, or similarly, that (s)he has a particular social utility component for the warm-glow transformation (cf. section 4.3.1). Subjects who are classified as cooperator on the basis of the decomposed game technique have a higher mean on this posterior probability distribution than subjects classified as individualists. The Spearman rank correlation between the angle measured by the decomposed game technique and the mean of the estimated posterior distribution is significantly positive, but not very high (0.27 for the pooled sample). This indicates that the decomposed game technique provides a meaningful measurement, but that it may be quite a noisy method. Of course, a measure of personality characteristics can hardly be expected to measure as precisely as say a thermometer measures temperature.

6.3.2 Value orientations and evolutionary forces

Experimental evidence has shown the existence of distinct social value orientations in this study. A legitimate question is where such differences in orientations come from, and whether they can survive the evolutionary forces of competition. Especially, it might be questioned whether individuals of the cooperative type can survive. Sociobiology uses the metaphor of the ultimately selfish gene. According to this metaphor, genes 'act as if' they maximize the probability of survival by reproduction of the own genes or of copies of the own genes possessed by relatives. Genes which do not maximize inclusive fitness cannot probabilistically survive the eliminating forces of natural selection.

If a link is made between the selfish gene and the selfishness of human behavior, it must not be overlooked that the concept of the selfish gene leaves some scope for basic forms of altruism. A possible form of altruism which can survive the eliminating forces of natural selection is kin altruism (Alexander, 1987). Cooperative behavior may evolve as the result of self-sacrifice of an individual such that the benefits of the self-sacrifice accrue to a genetic relative of the individual.

Another form of altruism compatible with evolutionary theory is reciprocal altruism (Trivers, 1971). An individual may act altruistically if the beneficiaries of the act reciprocate the favor. It is generally believed that reciprocity can only be realized in relatively small groups, because in small groups an individual may have strong indications that her or his act is going to be reciprocated. In large groups an individual may not be able to discriminate between potential cooperators and defectors and in the long run (s)he will be exploited by defectors, whom (s)he unintentionally favored. Some economists have used the concept of reciprocal altruism to model the interaction between players. For example, Sugden (1984) explains contributions to public goods as the result of reciprocity. Fehr, Kirchsteiger and Riedl (1993) use reciprocity to explain that employers pay higher than market clearing wages and that workers provide higher than minimally necessary efforts. Brandts and Schram (1996) explain experimental data in public good games as the result of the interaction of individualists and 'cooperative gain seekers'. A cooperative gain seeker contributes if and only if (s)he expects that the level of contributions by other subjects (of this type) is high enough to make earnings higher than if none of them contributed anything.

Güth and Nitzan (1993) investigate whether a moral objection against free riding is evolutionary stable in the specific step-level public good environment studied here. They provide a rigorous analysis of the setting where a population consisting of two types of players interacts repeatedly in the same game. The more successful type is better able to reproduce in the population. Güth and Nitzan find that the type with a moral objection against free riding does not survive the evolutionary selection process, except in some border cases (two-player and unanimity games).

However, Güth and Nitzan propose a different transformation of the utility matrix than the transformations considered in this study. The type with a moral objection against free riding has a strict preference for contribution not only in the case that the contribution is critical, but also in the case that the contribution is redundant. Therefore, the consequences of their analysis for the survival possibilities of the warm-glow, in-group and material cooperators of this study are not clear.

These results suggest that other-regarding behavior is only viable in a very limited sense. This view is attacked by Caporael, Dawes, Orbell and van de Kragt (1989), who argue in favor of the opposite view. They obtain experimental results on the provision of public goods with a step-level production function indicating that voluntary cooperative actions occur frequently even in the absence of direct economic incentives or indirect selfish incentives as reciprocal altruism or kin altruism. They favor the hypothesis that people cooperate as a result of an in-group biasing effect. According to this hypothesis, individuals in a group tend to redefine the 'self' in terms of shared group-membership or social identity. As a consequence, individuals may behave as exemplars of their group rather than as differentiated individuals, so that group identification becomes a basis for cooperative behavior. Data obtained in experiments support the hypothesis of an in-group biasing effect (for overviews of social identity theory, see Tajfel and Turner, 1986; Taylor and Moghaddam, 1994).

Caporael and others argue that in-group biasing fits in the sociobiological model of cooperative behavior. In early evolution, group behavior was favored because individuals living in isolation would be more vulnerable to predation than individuals living in a group and because the environment was such that the optimal foraging strategy was to search collectively for resources and share them. On this point of view Caporael and others base their sociality hypothesis. According to this hypothesis, individuals who are better adapted to group living are more successful, because groups of individuals cooperating to exploit the habitat are more successful in surviving than individuals operating in isolation. Critical for the argument seems to be that cooperation based on in-group biasing will not be eroded by competition within the group. Caporael and others note that 'cheaters' may be detected and excommunicated. But this supports the existence of reciprocal altruism and not the existence of in-group biasing altruism.

However, Caporael *et al.* (1989, p.694) extend their sociality hypothesis by arguing that "mechanisms evolved for sociality may be accessed by other adaptive specializations (most notably language) and generalized to problems in domains for which they were not adapted - including interactions with nonsocial objects and large scale organizations". People are involved in many types of games, and the lack of success of a strategy in one type of environment may be compensated by its success in other environments. The present study indicates that even in one game it may not be so easy for individualists to exploit cooperators. In the public good game reported here subjects classified as cooperators made as much money as subjects classified as individualists (cf. table 4.4 in chapter 4).

One problem with a direct application of evolutionary arguments to the interaction of human beings is that it seldom leads to sharp predictions. Even if it would be possible to prove that cooperative types cannot survive the evolution and that their presence must be interpreted as a random error of evolution, it might take nature a couple of hundreds or even thousands of years to 'correct its mistake' and to get rid of this aberration. In the mean time, it might be more fruitful to simply accept their presence, and to construct theories which do not neglect them.

6.4 Decision rules

The previous sections discussed internal (value orientations) and external (environment) factors affecting decision rules of players in public good games. This section focuses directly on decision rules. In particular, a comparison is made between evidence on decision rules in games and evidence on decision rules in decision theoretic tasks.

Many experiments have been designed to test theories describing behavior in decision theoretic tasks without interaction between the decision-makers. Systematic violations of the predictions of the hypothesis that people maximize expected value and even of the hypothesis that people maximize expected utility have been recorded. More general theories have been proposed to take account of various violations. Unfortunately, an increase in the fit of the data is accompanied by a decrease of the parsimony of the proposed theory. There is no single theory that outperforms all other theories on all criteria. However, one conclusion that does seem to emerge is that the answer will not be found in a deterministic theory. There is no single rule describing human behavior for 100%. The time has come to develop stochastic models allowing subjects to make errors (Harless and Camerer, 1994; Hey and Orme, 1994).

This study suggests that there is no difference in this respect between behavior in decision tasks and behavior in games. Various deterministic rules describing behavior in public good games have been considered and none of these rules could adequately take account of observed decisions. The quantal response function was used to model the stochastic component of players' decision rules. This function has the appealing property that it allows players to make an error with increasing probability, as the difference in expected value (utility) between the options decreases. This property is reflected in the data. Players are more likely to err if they estimate the probability that their contribution is critical to be in the neighborhood of $c/(f(s)-c)$ than if they estimate this probability to be far away from this cut-point $c/(f(s)-c)$ (cf. figures 4.8 and 4.10 in chapter 4).

A difference between decision rules in decision tasks and in games suggested by this study is that decision rules in games need to take account of the social aspect of the game.[4] Two routes both point in the direction that an error component alone in the decision rule is not sufficient to capture behavior in public good games. For convenience, one route is labelled the psychological route and the other the economic route. On the psychological route independent measures on individuals' social attitudes towards others are obtained in a game preceding the actual public good game. These independent measures provide meaningful predictions about subjects' behavior in the subsequent public good game. On the economic route assumptions are made about unobserved social components in subjects' utility functions. Maximum likelihood estimations indicate that the addition of social components to a utility function allows for a considerably and significantly better fit of the choice-data. Both routes lead to the conclusion that not only confusion but also kindness plays a role in behavior of public good games. This conclusion is also reached by Andreoni (1995b).

On the other hand, it is certainly not concluded that *all* players have cooperative or altruistic feelings towards others. On the contrary, a majority of the subjects in this study pursue their direct self interest, and a small minority even appears to have negative feelings towards others. The number of players with a positive attitude towards others seems too large to neglect, however.

This study is less conclusive about which particular model incorporates the social utility component of these players best. Three utility transformations of the payoff matrix have been considered: the hypothesis that players transform the payoff

---

[4]Of course, it cannot formally be concluded from this study that value orientations do not affect decision rules *in decision tasks*. However, no researcher argues that value orientations matter in decision tasks.

matrix as material cooperators who generate additional utility from the provision of the public good itself receives least support. Maximum likelihood estimations favor the interpretation that players feel a warm glow (or cold prickle) for the act of contributing. However, the warm-glow transformation does not explain why subjects are relatively more inclined to contribute when they estimate the ratio of the probability that their contribution will be redundant to the probability that it will be futile to be greater. This is actually predicted by the hypothesis that subjects transform the payoff matrix as in-group cooperators who acquire extra utility for being part of the sub-group of individuals responsible for the provision of the public good.

This study did not consider the potential explanatory power of other possibilities to explain pro-social behavior. Players may be driven by fairness, for example. Fairness may be operationalized in several ways. People may try to match the average contribution level of others, such that the probability that they contribute increases in the expected number of other contributors. Alternatively, people may try to achieve a situation where differences in group-members' earning are minimized. In the symmetric games considered in this study these different interpretations of fairness yield the same predictions. Consider the following extreme situation. Suppose that a player knows that $n-2$ of the $n-1$ others contribute, whereas only s $(<n-2)$ contributors are needed to provide the public good. In such a situation a subject driven by fairness should contribute to the public good even knowing that the contribution does not make anyone better off. Maybe some subjects will contribute as a matter of principle, but it does not seem unlikely that some pro-social subjects will refrain from contributing for utilitarian reasons. In fact, the outcome where all or almost all players contribute in a public good game with step-level production function is rarely observed in the experiments, and it does not seem to attract aggregate behavior. It seems very unlikely that fairness can explain *all* behavior.

On the other hand, fairness may play *some* role in explaining pro-social behavior, as well as warm-glow considerations and in-group arguments. It may be interesting to design experiments to determine the relative strength of each of these explanations for pro-social behavior.[5] The experiments reported here are not

---

[5]The decomposed game technique detects one notion of fairness. A subject plays the 'equity strategy' if (s)he selects in each of the 24 choices the alternative which minimizes the difference between the payoff for the outcome of one-self and the payoff for the outcome of the other. A person who pursues this strategy precisely will end up with a motivation vector with length 0. Players with

specifically designed for this goal, and do not help very much to solve the question.

Sometimes it is suggested that individual differences result from the background of subjects. Some studies report less pro-social behavior by students of economics than by students of other departments. For example, Marwell and Ames (1981) report that subjects from economics departments free ride more often than subjects from other departments. In a bargaining experiment, Carter and Irons (1991) find the result that economists keep more money for themselves if they are in a position to give and that they are satisfied with less in the position to receive (where the alternative is that they receive nothing at all). Carter and Irons attribute their results to a selection mechanism, and not to a learning principle: economists are already more selfish at the start of their study. In an experiment on voter turnout, Schram and Sonnemans (1995) find that students from economics cast fewer votes than students from other disciplines. Nevertheless, such differences are not found in every study. For example, Isaac, McCue and Plott (1985) find no significant difference in free-riding behavior in a public good game. In the experiments reported here students from economics contribute less than students from other departments (36% contributions for economists versus 46% for non-economists). Whether the difference is significant depends on the level of the test. A Mann-Whitney test using the contribution level per individual as data points yields a significant result (154 economists versus 90 non-economists, $p=0.01$). A Wilcoxon rank test using truly independent pair-wise averages per session in the strangers treatment and pair-wise averages per group in the partners treatment is not significant ($n=23$, $p=0.12$). The difference found in this study may not be impressive, but it is striking that the bias always seems to be in the same direction. There do not seem to be studies that report the opposite effect.[6]

---

a consistency less than 33% are classified to pursue the equity strategy if they make 18 or more of the 24 choices in accordance with the equity strategy. None of the subjects actually pursued this equity strategy.

[6]There are no (clear) gender effects in the experiments reported here. Neither on the angle measured by the decomposed game technique nor on the contribution level in the subsequent public good game are systematic differences found between the sexes.

6.5 Expectation formation and learning

Here, several conceptual issues concerning beliefs and learning will be addressed. Section 6.2 discussed the role of environmental factors on beliefs. Beliefs are an essential input for the decision rules discussed in section 6.4. Players choose given their beliefs, and the outcome of the game may affect the beliefs and the decision rule in the next play of the game (cf. figure 6.1).

Section 6.5.1 makes a comparison between two different ways to endogenize beliefs: game theoretic models and belief learning models. Section 6.5.2 discusses the close connection between the psychological triangle hypothesis and belief learning models. In section 6.5.3 a comparison is made between belief learning and reinforcement learning. Section 6.5.4 discusses the matter of convergence to equilibrium. It also argues that the level of strategic reasoning is a function of the perceived difficulty of the game and it suggests that experimental economics may help to distinguish different games in this respect.

6.5.1 Game theoretic modelling and belief learning

From a game theoretic point of view one would sooner expect a difference in the process of expectation formation than a difference in decision rules between games and decision theoretic tasks. This study suggests the opposite effect for the public good game with a step-level production function and the related game against nature. The social aspect distinguishes the decision rule used in the public good game from the decision rule in the game against nature. Players' negative or positive attitudes towards others affect their decisions in the public good game. But the process of expectation formation in the public good game is quite similar to that in the game against nature. It is as if players neglect the strategic aspect of the public good game when they form their beliefs.

Both (static) equilibrium models and (dynamic) learning or dis-equilibrium models have been considered with respect to their ability to organize the data. For equilibrium models the best results are obtained for the Quantal Response Equilibrium. This concept allows players to make errors. However, this (static) model does not allow players to adapt their beliefs on the basis of the development of the game. Therefore, it cannot take account of the historical pattern observed in players' beliefs.

An outcome of others' play turns out to have a systematic impact on a player's beliefs. A player who observes an outcome smaller (greater) than the mean of her or his reported probability distribution tends to shift the distribution to the left (right). A player tends to increase the probability of the latest observed event. And a player tends to become more confident as more events are observed (the variance of the reported distribution decreases). Such an impact of events is precisely what is predicted by belief learning models like the naive Bayesian model. Furthermore, this model takes account of biases in players' expectations. The naive Bayesian model predicts that players will be too optimistic when the empirical distribution of others' aggregate choices shifts to the left and it predicts that players will be too pessimistic if this distribution shifts to the right. In fact, in some experimental sessions the aggregate level of others' choices falls and in precisely those sessions over-optimism is observed.

Of course, at this point it cannot be excluded that a dynamic game theoretic model will be developed which does take account of the historical pattern observed in reported beliefs. The most difficult hurdle to take for dynamic game theoretic modelling seems to be the bias in the expectations. Most equilibrium concepts assume players to have unbiased expectations.

The naive Bayesian model not only organizes *reported expectations* better than static game theoretic models, it also takes better account of the *choices* whether or not to contribute. Assuming that players give a quantal response on the basis of the expected values of the alternatives, maximum likelihood estimations indicate that it is easier to rationalize expectations by the naive Bayesian model than by the Quantal Response Equilibrium model. Furthermore, the estimations for the naive Bayesian model suggest that players choose with moderately increasing precision over time. Similar estimates for the Quantal Response model are difficult to interpret, because they suggest an erratic pattern over time in the level of precision.

This study does not discriminate between different exponents of the class of belief learning models. In the analyses the naive Bayesian model has been used as the representative of this class. The strength of this model is that it generates precise predictions without the help of auxiliary assumptions. Somewhat less general exponents of the class of belief learning models have similar properties. The model of fictitious play generates very similar predictions and dynamics. One may argue that an advantage of the model of fictitious play is that it is less difficult to implement, and therefore, more realistic. In fact, it seems likely that most subjects have the cognitive abilities to keep track of the historical frequency distribution of past play as supposed by fictitious play. But this fact does not guarantee that they will *actually* keep track of historical frequency distributions. It seems very doubtful that any precise rule describes the updating process literally. What seems to be realistic is the common assumption underlying all exponents of the class of belief learning models, the assumption that players have a stationary view of the world: what happened in the past tells them what will happen in the future. They are not forward-looking in the sense that they predict how other players might change their behavior and try to strategically affect these changes. Subjects seem to use this stationarity assumption in an intuitive way for the adaptation of their beliefs, without the use of any precise rule.

It may be interesting to start thinking about how one can incorporate stochastic components in the belief updating rules, just as it has proven to be in the area of decision rules. The estimations for the generalized naive Bayesian model describing the means of the reported expectations suggest that actual players by and large update with similar speed as the model. But they also suggest that players differ in the errors made against the model.

6.5.2 Belief learning and the triangle hypothesis

There is a close connection between the class of belief learning models and the (psychological) triangle hypothesis. The triangle hypothesis was originally developed for the repeated prisoners' dilemma. In this game, individualists expect others to pursue an individualistic orientation as well, while cooperators expect others to pursue either a cooperative or an individualistic goal. As a consequence of these beliefs, individualists choose to defect while cooperators start with cooperating but adapt their preferred cooperative behavior if they learn that they are paired with an individualist. This hypothesis shares an implicit assumption with belief learning models. This common assumption is that when updating beliefs players do not think strategically. The triangle hypothesis assumes that both types (try to) learn the type of the other player by observing her or his behavior. A cooperative (defective) choice is interpreted as evidence for the position that the other pursues a(n) cooperative (individualistic) goal, and will continue to do so in the future. This implies a rather stationary view of the world. In fact, the triangle hypothesis might be interpreted as an application of the general idea of belief learning to the prisoners' dilemma.

There is one difference between the models, however. For the initial phase the triangle hypothesis predicts not only a difference in behavior but also a difference in beliefs between the two types. Cooperators expect others to pursue either an individualistic or a cooperative goal. Individualists expect others to only pursue an individualistic goal, and therefore they choose the selfish action all the time. This view does not need to be adapted since the own selfish behavior elicits defective choices of the other after a while even if the other actually pursues a cooperative goal. This difference in beliefs between types is not observed in the experiments reported here. The initial difference in beliefs does not seem to be a crucial ingredient for the triangle hypothesis, however. In fact, the implicit assumption that players pursue their goal myopically is sufficient. Recall that according to the triangle hypothesis, individualists choose the non-cooperative action at each stage, i.e., they do not anticipate the potential positive effect of a cooperative choice on the behavior of the other player.[7] If individualists pursue the selfish goal myopically, they will choose the defective action irrespective of their beliefs, and the same dynamics as originally expected will evolve.[8]

Finally, note that belief learning models are not only relevant for decision rules drawn from the expected utility approach. For example, individuals acting on the basis of fairness also need to form expectations about other players' behavior. If they want to match the average contribution level, or if they want to end up with earnings as similar as possible to those of other group-members, they need to form beliefs about the behavior of these others.

---

[7]It is acknowledged that from a rational point of view players *should* not consider playing the cooperative action in some situations, if they believe that others are individualistic as well. The backward induction hypothesis should hold in prisoners' dilemmas where rational individualistic players interact for a known finite number of periods. Therefore, in such a situation an individualist should choose the non-cooperative action in each period. However, if the interaction between the players is infinite, if the game is terminated at each period with a given probability or if there is uncertainty about the rationality of the other player, a rational individualistic player should consider the potential positive future effect of the cooperative choice (cf. Miller, 1990, for example).

[8]Of course, the lack of support for the prediction that initial beliefs differ between types might also be due to a difference in institutional setting. As noted in chapter 2, the game structure of public good games with a step-level production function resembles the game of chicken more than the prisoners' dilemma.

6.5.3 Belief learning and reinforcement learning

Although the emphasis in this study lies on belief learning, it cannot be excluded that an even simpler type of learning captures the essential features of the dynamics in behavior observed in the experiments. A simple reinforcement learning model is able to track the differences in behavior between the negative and the positive frame of the public good game. Reinforcement learning assumes that beliefs do not play a role in the choice-process of players. Players evaluate the success of their former action and the outcome of this evaluation determines whether they repeat their action or not. Successful outcomes tend to be repeated and unsuccessful ones tend to be abandoned.

The thought process is clearly simpler in reinforcement learning than in belief learning. But the resulting dynamics are not that different. This is not so surprising, if it is realized that a similar assumption forms the backbone of both types of learning. According to both there is an inherently constant element in people's view of the outside world. Reinforcement learning assumes that what is successful today will be successful tomorrow, just like belief learning assumes that the outcome of a game today will occur again tomorrow with increased probability. It is therefore often very difficult to discriminate between reinforcement learning and belief learning on the basis of choice patterns. Consider the public good game used in this study. If in the former period a player's contribution would have been critical to obtain the public good, the belief learning models predict that the player will increase her or his subjective probability that this outcome will occur again, and (s)he will be more inclined to contribute in this period. In the same situation the reinforcement learning model will also predict an increased probability of the cooperative choice. If the player contributed last period, (s)he will be satisfied with the choice, and tend to repeat it. If the player did not contribute, (s)he will not be satisfied with the choice and tend to switch to contribution in this period. A similar argument can be constructed for the case that in the former period of the game a player's contribution would not have been critical. The two models do not contradict each-other in the predicted choice patterns.

However, one might interpret the results on the *expectation formation process* as indirect evidence favoring belief learning. There is a relationship between expectations and behavior in the public good games studied here, and expectations evolve along patterns predicted by belief learning models. According to reinforcement learning, beliefs should not play any role at all in the explanation of players' choices.

6.5.4 Convergence to equilibrium and a stratification of games

One justification of the theoretical focus on the Nash equilibria of a game is based on the fact that the dynamics defined by very simple learning rules often converge to Nash equilibria.[9] This justification overlooks the fact that at present not very general results have been obtained on the convergence of learning rules, however. Perhaps it would be more fruitful to shift the theoretical attention to the study of the dynamics of empirically supported learning processes, as opposed to searching for learning processes that converge to a Nash equilibrium.

Probably, the lack of smooth convergence results makes many theorists feel uncomfortable about the subject of learning. However, one should keep in mind that learning rules do have one theoretical advantage over conventional game theory. Many game theoretic models suffer from the problem of a multiplicity of equilibria. Learning rules do not have such problems. In fact, learning rules may help solve the coordination problem present in many games, and they may do a better job than some of the refinement concepts (cf. Brandts and Holt, 1992).

This study does not mean to imply that strategic reasoning does not play any role at all in games. Strategic reasoning on a somewhat less sophisticated level seems very plausible. As already noted in chapter 2, subjects may anticipate what kind of choice another player will make given that (s)he applies a particular belief learning rule on her or his observations in the past. What a subject expects this other player to do may be a combination of the naive prediction based on the belief learning rule and the own observations on the one hand and of this limited strategic prediction on the other hand. Limited strategic thinking of this kind may prevent the dynamics to lock in on some of the rather pathetic examples of non-convergence of belief learning models. Some of these examples consist of cycles. Even quite naive subjects may detect such cycles after some time, and anticipate them. Such limited strategic anticipation could

---

[9] Of course, there are other justifications for the extensive use of Nash equilibria. From a theoretical perspective it will always remain an attractive concept, because it provides a concise summary of the strategic aspects of a game. But also at an empirical level, it is not a worthless concept. The Nash equilibria of a game remain useful bench-marks which may serve to provide a rough prediction of aggregate play. It is at least remarkable that in this study aggregate behavior by and large centers around one of the interior Nash equilibria or is attracted by the zero contribution equilibrium in all experimental treatments (or that it slowly converges to one of these equilibria). The other extreme point, where all players contribute to the public good, does not seem to have any attraction on aggregate play.

not be used by subjects in the present study, because they only received aggregate information about others' choices, and they could not deduce which player had observed which outcomes. To what extent subjects reason strategically in such a way may be an interesting question for future research.

Another factor exists which may facilitate a potential convergence process. The present study suggests that in particular the game theoretic assumption about consistent expectations is not fulfilled. Players' expectations about other players' behavior do not seem to be in equilibrium. Imitation may be an important factor for the materialization of consistent expectations in a game. Communication of beliefs among players might lead to common beliefs. Although this aspect is not formally incorporated in game theoretic modelling, it may be an important factor distinguishing games in the outside world from games in the laboratory. In the laboratory experimenters usually take a lot of trouble to guarantee anonymity and prevent communication among subjects. This procedure clearly prevents the possibility of social learning, which might increase the speed of a potential equilibrium selection process. Offerman and Sonnemans (1996) obtain an empirical result on the intermediating role of imitation in a setting without interaction between players. Imitation of beliefs occurs in their decision theoretic tasks. Decision-makers tend to adapt their beliefs in the direction of the beliefs of more successful decision-makers, even when all decision-makers base their beliefs on exactly the same information. Whether imitation also plays a role in games and whether it helps in the equilibrium selection process is an interesting question for future research.

The results in this study are specifically obtained for step-level public good games, and it is not likely that they will be transferable to *all* other kinds of games. In fact, it seems more likely that the level of strategic reasoning of players is a function of the perceived difficulty of a game. Strategic reasoning may be more common in easy games than in difficult games. The perceived difficulty of a game will increase with the number of players and with the number of Nash equilibria. It will also increase as the rules of the game are less clear to the players. In this respect the results obtained by Mookherjee and Sopher (1994) are instructive. They study a simple matching pennies game, a game with a unique Nash equilibrium where each of the two players chooses either of the two actions with probability 0.5. When they give subjects full information about the whole payoff matrix and all former moves by the opponent, the resulting play is best characterized as purely random (independently identically distributed) play. This is in agreement with Nash equilibrium play but not with learning models. The game is so easy that many subjects quickly understand that they have to outwit their opponent, and that their opponent tries to outwit them. The strategic aspect of the game is very obvious, and there is no coordination problem whatsoever. However, if they let subjects play the same game without information about the (potential) payoffs of the other player and without information of the opponent's former moves, the resulting play is better characterized by reinforcement learning.

It may be useful to sketch a map displaying different types of games. Each type of game tends to elicit a different set of behavioral rules for subjects. Easy games like the matching pennies game with full information could be best characterized by Nash equilibrium play. Difficult games with multiple players and multiple equilibria, like the public good game studied here, could be best characterized by belief learning. And extremely difficult games or badly defined games could be best characterized by reinforcement learning models. Experimental economics may be of great help in searching for the boundaries of each type of game.

6.6 Conclusions

This final section provides a brief sketch of a positive theory of behavior in (step-level) public good games. The evidence presented in this study suggests that any such theory should contain at least the following elements.

Environmental factors affect both beliefs and decision rules. The size of the group plays an important role in determining beliefs: in small groups individuals assess the probability of being critical higher than in large groups. The value and the frame of the public good affect the decision rule: a higher value of the public good and the positive (pubgood) frame both elicit more cooperative decision rules.

An individual's value orientation affects decision rules. Most people either pursue an individualistic or a cooperative goal. The social psychological idea that people pursue different goals may be translated to the economic expected utility approach in two ways. According to a first successful hypothesis, some individuals feel a cold-prickle and others a warm-glow when contributing. According to a second successful hypothesis, some individuals strive to be part of the in-group providing the public good, while others miss such a drive.

Decision rules describe how players choose given their beliefs. Individuals will sooner contribute when they estimate the probability of being critical to be higher. There is also a positive correlation between the probability of being redundant and the inclination to contribute.

Beliefs are formed adaptively. The outcome of the previous game affects the beliefs systematically. Belief learning models assuming that individuals have a stationary view on the behavior of other players take better account of beliefs than equilibrium models assuming that players have consistent beliefs.

Appendix A: Mathematical proofs

This appendix presents the proofs of the theorems and lemmas proposed in chapter 2. The first two proofs concern theorems of the game theoretic model with (homogeneous) expected value maximizers. The first theorem gives the condition for which three symmetric equilibria exist and it identifies the payoff dominant symmetric equilibrium. The second theorem describes the effect of an increase in group-size on the propensity to contribute. Recall that n denotes group-size and s denotes the threshold.

Theorem 2.1

Assume that $s>1$ and $n>s$. Let p_0^* represent the symmetric equilibrium where nobody contributes (i.e., $p_0^*=0$). If

$$\binom{n-1}{s-1}\left(\frac{s-1}{n-1}\right)^{s-1}\left(1-\frac{s-1}{n-1}\right)^{n-s} > \frac{c}{f(s)-c}\,, \qquad \text{A1}$$

two positive mixed strategies equilibria p_1^* and p_2^* with $0<p_1^*<p_2^*<1$ exist. In that case p_2^* yields a higher expected payoff than p_1^*, and p_1^* yields a higher expected payoff than p_0^*. □

Proof: first it is proven that under condition A1 two strictly positive symmetric equilibria exist. Define

$$f(p) = \binom{n-1}{s-1} p^{s-1} (1-p)^{n-s}\,, \qquad \text{A2}$$

the probability of being critical. In equilibrium,

$$f(p) = \frac{c}{f(s)-c}\,. \qquad \text{A3}$$

The maximum of $f(p)$ is reached for $p=(s-1)/(n-1)$:

$$f(0) = f(1) = 0\,; \qquad \text{A4}$$

$$0 < p < \frac{s-1}{n-1} \quad \Rightarrow \quad \frac{d}{d(p)} \; [f(p)] > 0 \; ; \qquad \text{A5}$$

$$\frac{s-1}{n-1} < p < 1 \quad \Rightarrow \quad \frac{d}{d(p)} \; [f(p)] < 0 \; . \qquad \text{A6}$$

Therefore, if condition A1 holds, two strictly positive symmetric equilibria exist (cf. figure 2.1). Now, define for each equilibrium strategy p_j with $j=1,2$:

$$A_j = (f(s)-c) \sum_{i=s}^{n} \binom{n}{i} p_j^{\,i} \, (1-p_j)^{n-i} \; ; \quad B_j = c - c*p_j \; . \qquad \text{A7}$$

A_j represents the expected payoff from the 'public account' and B_j the expected payoff from the 'private account'. It is clear that a player's expected payoff $E[\pi_j]$ for playing symmetric equilibrium p_j is equal to:

$$E[\pi_j] = A_j + B_j \; . \qquad \text{A8}$$

Assume that players play equilibrium p_2. Consider what happens if player k changes her strategy to p_1 while the others maintain strategy p_2. Her expected private payoff will be equal to B_1. Her expected public payoff will be higher than A_1, since the probability that the public good will be provided is higher if other players contribute with higher probability. By unilaterally deviating to p_1, player k can obtain an expected payoff higher than $E[\pi_1]$. Therefore, because p_2 is an equilibrium, the expected payoff $E[\pi_2]$ must be higher than $E[\pi_1]$. A similar line of reasoning leads to the conclusion that symmetric equilibrium p_1 yields a higher expected payoff than symmetric equilibrium p_0. ■

Theorem 2.3

Assume that $s>1$ and $n^*>s$. If p_1^* (p_1^{**}) and p_2^* (p_2^{**}) with $0<p_1^*<p_2^*$ represent the two mixed strategies equilibria when the number of players is equal to n^* (n^*+1), then

$p_1^{**} < p_1^*$ and $p_2^{**} < p_2^*$ (if p_1^{**} and p_2^{**} exist). □

Proof: to emphasize its dependence on group-size, define the probability of being critical as

$$f(n^*, p) = \binom{n^*-1}{s-1} p^{s-1} (1-p)^{n^*-s} . \qquad \text{A9}$$

From the proof of theorem 2.1 it appears that $f(n^*,p)$ reaches its maximum for $p=(s-1)/(n^*-1)$. Thus, if n^* increases, its maximum is obtained for a lower value of p. Furthermore,

$$p = \frac{s-1}{n^*} \Rightarrow f(n^*, p) = f(n^*+1, p) \qquad \text{A10}$$

$$0 < p < \frac{s-1}{n^*} \Rightarrow f(n^*, p) < f(n^*+1, p) \qquad \text{A11}$$

$$\frac{s-1}{n^*} < p < 1 \Rightarrow f(n^*, p) > f(n^*+1, p) . \qquad \text{A12}$$

This implies that for all n^*, $f(n^*,p)$ and $f(n^*+1,p)$ intersect at a value for p for which the latter is maximized. Theorem 2.3 follows immediately, as is illustrated in figure 2.1 in chapter 2. ■

The following three proofs concern the theorems of the game theoretic model for heterogeneous individuals. Theorems 2.4 and 2.5 assume the existence of two internally homogeneous individualists: (material) individualists contribute with probability p_1, while (material) cooperators contribute with probability p_2. Each player assigns an accurate probability q to the event that an arbitrary other individual is of the cooperative type. The polynomial representing the probability of being critical is the same for all individuals and equal to:

$$pol(p_1,p_2) = \sum_{k=0}^{n-1} \left(\binom{n-1}{k} q^k (1-q)^{(n-k-1)} * \right.$$

$$\left. \sum_{i=0}^{\min(s-1,n-k-1)} \binom{n-k-1}{i} p_1^i (1-p_1)^{(n-k-i-1)} \binom{k}{s-i-1} p_2^{(s-i-1)} (1-p_2)^{(k-s+i+1)} \right). \qquad \text{A13}$$

Theorem 2.4

Sufficient, although not necessary conditions for the uniqueness of the Bayesian Nash equilibrium in case 6 ($0<p_1<1$ and $p_2=1$) are:

$$\frac{q^{(s-1)}}{(1-q)} > \frac{(s-1)}{(n-s)} \qquad \text{A14}$$

$$f_i(s) > \frac{c}{\binom{n-1}{s-1} q^{s-1} (1-q)^{(n-s)}} + c \qquad \text{A15}$$

$$s < n; \quad 0 < q < 1 \qquad \text{A16}$$

□

Proof: (i) Inserting $p_1=0$ and $p_2=1$ in expression A13 yields:

$$pol(0,1) = \binom{n-1}{s-1} q^{s-1} (1-q)^{(n-s)} > \frac{c}{(f_i(s)-c)}, \qquad \text{A17}$$

because $f_i(s)$ is sufficiently large (inequality A15).

(ii) Inserting $p_1=1$ and $p_2=1$ in the same expression yields:

$$pol(1,1) = 0 < \frac{c}{(f_i(s)-c)}. \qquad \text{A18}$$

(iii) If it is true that $d(pol(p_1,1)/d(p_1) < 0$ for all p_1 between 0 and 1, then there is only one p_1 for which the Bayesian Nash equilibrium condition will hold and the proof is completed. This is true if and only if

$$\sum_{k=0}^{s-2} (s-k-1) \binom{n-1}{k} q^k(1-q)^{(n-k-1)} \binom{n-k-1}{s-k-1} p_1^{(s-k-2)}(1-p_1)^{(n-s)} - \sum_{k=0}^{s-1} (n-s) \binom{n-1}{k} q^k(1-q)^{(n-k-1)} \binom{n-k-1}{s-k-1} p_1^{(s-k-1)}(1-p_1)^{(n-s-1)} < 0 . \qquad \text{A19}$$

Rearranging terms and dividing left side and right side by $(1-p_1)^{(n-s-1)}$ yields:

$$\sum_{k=0}^{s-2}((1-p_1)(s-k-1)-p_1(n-s))\binom{n-1}{k}q^k(1-q)^{(n-k-1)}\binom{n-k-1}{s-k-1}p_1^{(s-k-2)} < (n-s)\binom{n-1}{s-1}q^{(s-1)}(1-q)^{(n-s)} . \qquad \text{A20}$$

Making use of the fact that

$$\frac{\binom{n-1}{k}\binom{n-k-1}{s-k-1}}{\binom{n-1}{s-1}} = \binom{s-1}{k} , \qquad \text{A21}$$

yields:

$$\sum_{k=0}^{s-2} ((s-k-1) - p_1(n-k-1)) \binom{s-1}{k} q^k (1-q)^{(n-k-1)} p_1^{(s-k-2)} < (n-s) q^{(s-1)} (1-q)^{(n-s)} \qquad \text{A22}$$

$$\Rightarrow \sum_{k=0}^{s-2} ((s-k-1)-p_1(n-k-1)) \binom{s-1}{k} \left(\frac{1-q}{q}\right)^{(s-k-1)} p_1^{(s-k-2)} < (n-s) \qquad \text{A23}$$

$$\Rightarrow \sum_{k=0}^{s-2}((s-k-1)-p_1(s-k-1))\binom{s-1}{k}\left(\frac{1-q}{q}\right)^{(s-k-1)} p_1^{(s-k-2)} < (n-s)\left(1+p_1 \sum_{k=0}^{s-2} \binom{s-1}{k}\left(\frac{1-q}{q}\right)^{(s-k-1)} p_1^{(s-k-2)}\right) . \qquad \text{A24}$$

Observing that

$$(s-k-1) \binom{s-1}{k} = (s-1) \binom{s-2}{k} , \qquad \text{A25}$$

yields:

$$\sum_{k=0}^{s-2} (s-1) \binom{s-2}{k} \left(\frac{1-q}{q}\right)^{(s-k-1)} p_1^{(s-k-2)} (1-p_1) <$$ A26

$$(n-s)(1+p_1 \sum_{k=0}^{s-2} \binom{s-1}{k} \left(\frac{1-q}{q}\right)^{(s-k-1)} p_1^{(s-k-2)}) .$$

This is certainly true if:

$$\left(\frac{1-q}{q}\right) (s-1) \sum_{k=0}^{s-2} \binom{s-2}{k} \left(\frac{1-q}{q}\right)^{(s-k-2)} < (n-s) \qquad \text{A27}$$

$$\Rightarrow \left(\frac{1-q}{q}\right) (s-1) \frac{\left(\sum_{k=0}^{s-2} \binom{s-2}{k} q^k (1-q)^{(s-k-2)}\right)}{q^{s-2}} < (n-s) . \qquad \text{A28}$$

A sufficient condition is therefore:

$$\frac{q^{(s-1)}}{(1-q)} > \frac{(s-1)}{(n-s)} \qquad \text{A29}$$

■

Theorem 2.5

Sufficient, although not necessary conditions for the uniqueness of the Bayesian Nash equilibrium in case 2 ($p_1=0$ and $0<p_2<1$) are:

$$\frac{(1-q)^{(n-s+1)}}{q} > \frac{(n-s)}{(s-1)} \qquad \text{A30}$$

$$f_c(s) > \frac{c}{\binom{n-1}{s-1} q^{s-1} (1-q)^{(n-s)}} + c \qquad \text{A31}$$

$$0 < q < 1; \quad s > 1 \qquad \text{A32}$$

□

Proof: (i) Inserting $p_1=0$ and $p_2=1$ in expression A13 yields:

$$pol(0,1) = \binom{n-1}{s-1} q^{s-1} (1-q)^{(n-s)} > \frac{c}{(f_c(s)-c)} , \qquad \text{A33}$$

as a result of inequality A31.
(ii) Inserting $p_1=0$ and $p_2=0$ in the same expression yields:

$$pol(0,0) = 0 < \frac{c}{(f_c(s)-c)} . \qquad \text{A34}$$

(iii) If it is true that $d(pol(0,p_2)/d(p_2) > 0$ for all p_2 between 0 and 1, then there is only one Bayesian Nash equilibrium for case 2.

$$\sum_{k=s-1}^{n-1} (s-1) \binom{n-1}{k} q^k (1-q)^{(n-k-1)} \binom{k}{s-1} p_2^{(s-2)} (1-p_2)^{(k-s+1)} - \sum_{k=s}^{n-1} (k-s+1) \binom{n-1}{k} q^k (1-q)^{(n-k-1)} \binom{k}{s-1} p_2^{(s-1)} (1-p_2)^{(k-s)} > 0 \qquad \text{A35}$$

$$\Rightarrow \sum_{k=s}^{n-1} ((1-p_2)(s-1) - p_2(k-s+1)) \binom{n-1}{k} q^k (1-q)^{(n-k-1)} * \binom{k}{s-1} (1-p_2)^{(k-s)} + (s-1) \binom{n-1}{s-1} q^{(s-1)} (1-q)^{(n-s)} > 0 \qquad \text{A36}$$

$$\Rightarrow \sum_{k=s}^{n-1} (s-1- p_2k) \binom{n-s}{n-k-1} q^k (1-q)^{(n-k-1)} (1-p_2)^{(k-s)} + (s-1) q^{(s-1)} (1-q)^{(n-s)} > 0 \qquad \text{A37}$$

$$\Rightarrow (s-1) - \sum_{k=s}^{n-1} (p_2k-s+1) \binom{n-s}{k-s+1} \left(\frac{q}{1-q}\right)^{(k-s+1)} (1-p_2)^{(k-s)} > 0 \qquad \text{A38}$$

$$\Rightarrow (s-1) - \sum_{k=s}^{n-1} (k-s+1)\binom{n-s}{k-s+1}\left(\frac{q}{1-q}\right)^{(k-s+1)}(1-p_2)^{(k-s)} + \sum_{k=s}^{n-1} (1-p_2)k \binom{n-s}{k-s+1}\left(\frac{q}{1-q}\right)^{(k-s+1)}(1-p_2)^{(k-s)} > 0 \qquad \text{A39}$$

$$\Rightarrow (s-1) - \sum_{k=s}^{n-1} (n-s)\binom{n-s-1}{k-s}\left(\frac{q}{1-q}\right)^{(k-s+1)}(1-p_2)^{(k-s)} + \sum_{k=s}^{n-1} k \binom{n-s}{k-s+1}\left(\frac{q}{1-q}\right)^{(k-s+1)}(1-p_2)^{(k-s+1)} > 0 \; . \qquad \text{A40}$$

This is certainly true if:

$$(s-1) - (n-s)\left(\frac{q}{1-q}\right) \frac{\left(\sum_{k=s}^{n-1} \binom{n-s-1}{k-s} q^{(k-s)} (1-q)^{(n-k-1)}\right)}{(1-q)^{(n-s)}} > 0. \qquad \text{A41}$$

A sufficient condition is:

$$(s-1) - (n-s)\left(\frac{q}{(1-q)^{(n-s+1)}}\right) > 0 \qquad \text{A42}$$

$$\Rightarrow \frac{(1-q)^{(n-s+1)}}{q} > \frac{(n-s)}{(s-1)} \qquad \text{A43}$$

■

Theorem 2.6

If there are *m* different types of individuals who all use the same transformation of the utility matrix (either all players are material cooperators, or all players are warm-glow cooperators, or all players are in-group cooperators), assimilation of behavior will result. In a Bayesian Nash equilibrium at most one type of player will randomize. All players with a smaller social utility component than this randomizing type will not contribute and all players with a greater social utility component will contribute for sure. □

Proof: define the subjective probability that the contribution of a player is critical for the provision of the public good as *P(s-1)*. In equilibrium, the players estimate this probability accurately. Estimations of the probability will be equal among individuals, because the probability that an arbitrary other individual will contribute is assumed to be independent of the own player's type. Consider the case that all players transform the utility matrix as material cooperators. Assume that in an equilibrium type *i* players randomize, then for these players:

$$P(s-1) \, * \, (f_i(s)-c) \, = \, c \, . \qquad \text{A44}$$

This implies for all types k with $f_k(s) < f_i(s)$:

$$P(s-1) \, * \, (f_k(s)-c) \, < \, c \, , \qquad \text{A45}$$

which means that all individuals of these types k will not contribute. Furthermore, for all types j with $f_j(s) > f_i(s)$:

$$P(s-1) \, * \, (f_j(s)-c) \, > \, c \, , \qquad \text{A46}$$

which means that all individuals of these types j will contribute for sure. The proofs for the cases where all individuals are warm-glow cooperators or all individuals are in-group cooperators are similar. ■

The following proofs concern the theorems and lemmas proposed for the naive Bayesian belief learning model. Some of the results are well known (e.g., theorem 2.7 and 2.8 are also given in Press, 1989, p.39), but it is hard to find proofs in the literature. Therefore, independent proofs are given here.

First, it is useful to prove the following lemma which is not mentioned in the main text:

Lemma A.1

$$\int_0^1 \theta^y \, (1-\theta)^z \, d\theta \, = \, \frac{1}{\binom{y+z}{y} \, (y+z+1)} \, , \qquad \text{A47}$$

if y and z are positive integers. □

Proof:

$$\int_0^1 \theta^y(1-\theta)^z \, d\theta \, = \, \left[\frac{1}{y+1} \, \theta^{y+1}(1-\theta)^z\right]_0^1 \, + \int_0^1 \frac{z}{y+1} \, \theta^{y+1}(1-\theta)^{z-1} \, d\theta \qquad \text{A48}$$

$$= \frac{z}{y+1} \left(\left[\frac{1}{y+2} \theta^{y+2}(1-\theta)^{z-1} \right]_0^1 + \int_0^1 \frac{z-1}{y+2} \theta^{y+2}(1-\theta)^{z-2}\, d\theta \right) \qquad \text{A49}$$

$$= \frac{z}{y+1} \frac{z-1}{y+2} \cdots \frac{1}{y+z} \int_0^1 \theta^{y+z}\, d\theta \qquad \text{A50}$$

$$= \frac{z!\ y!}{(y+z)!\ (y+z+1)} = \frac{1}{\binom{y+z}{y}(y+z+1)} \qquad \text{A51}$$

■

Players think that other players invariably contribute with unknown probability θ. Players start with an uninformative prior distribution of θ when no information about other players' behavior has been revealed yet: the prior distribution is assumed to be the uniform *[0, 1]* distribution with density $\pi(\theta) = I_{[0,1]}(\theta)$. A player observes realizations of others' behavior. Denote the k observations from the (assumed) binomial distribution by $x_1, \ldots, x_k$ and the sum of these observations by $s_k = x_1 + \ldots + x_k$. The density of the posterior distribution of θ given these observations is denoted by $\pi(\theta \mid x_1, \ldots, x_k)$ and the density of the distribution of x conditional on θ by $f(x \mid \theta)$, where x can take values 0 to $n-1$. The posterior distribution is a beta distribution and can be derived using Bayes' rule for continuous distributions.

Theorem 2.7

$$\pi(\theta \mid x_1, \ldots, x_k) = \pi(\theta \mid s_k) = [k(n-1)+1] \binom{k(n-1)}{s_k} \theta^{s_k} (1-\theta)^{k(n-1)-s_k} \qquad \text{A52}$$

□

Proof: the theorem can easily be proven with induction. Bayes' rule says that:

$$\pi(\theta|x_1,..,x_k) = \frac{f(x_k|\theta)\ \pi(\theta|x_1,..,x_{k-1})}{\int_0^1 f(x_k|\theta)\ \pi(\theta|x_1,..,x_{k-1})\ d(\theta)} . \qquad \text{A53}$$

First, it is shown that equation A52 holds for $k=1$. Making use of lemma A.1,

$$\pi(\theta|x_1) = \frac{\binom{n-1}{x_1}\ \theta^{x_1}\ (1-\theta)^{n-1-x_1}}{\binom{n-1}{x_1}\ \frac{1}{\binom{n-1}{x_1}}\ \frac{1}{n}} = n\ \binom{n-1}{x_1}\ \theta^{x_1}\ (1-\theta)^{n-1-x_1} . \qquad \text{A54}$$

Next, assume that theorem 2.7 holds for $k=l$, does it also hold for $k=l+1$?

$$\pi(\theta|x_1,..,x_{l+1}) =$$

$$\frac{\binom{n-1}{x_{l+1}}\ \theta^{x_{l+1}}\ (1-\theta)^{n-1-x_{l+1}}\ (l(n-1)+1)\ \binom{l(n-1)}{s_l}\ \theta^{s_l}\ (1-\theta)^{l(n-1)-s_l}}{\int_0^1 \binom{n-1}{x_{l+1}}\ \theta^{x_{l+1}}\ (1-\theta)^{n-1-x_{l+1}}\ (l(n-1)+1)\ \binom{l(n-1)}{s_l}\ \theta^{s_l}\ (1-\theta)^{l(n-1)-s_l}\ d(\theta)} \qquad \text{A55}$$

$$= \frac{(l(n-1)+1)\ \binom{n-1}{x_{l+1}}\ \binom{l(n-1)}{s_l}\ \theta^{s_l+x_l+1}\ (1-\theta)^{(l+1)(n-1)-s_l-x_{l+1}}}{(l(n-1)+1)\ \binom{n-1}{x_{l+1}}\ \binom{l(n-1)}{s_l}\ \frac{1}{(l+1)(n-1)+1}\ \frac{1}{\binom{(l+1)(n-1)}{s_l+x_{l+1}}}} \qquad \text{A56}$$

$$= ((l+1)(n-1)+1)\ \binom{(l+1)(n-1)}{s_{l+1}}\ \theta^{s_{l+1}}\ (1-\theta)^{(l+1)(n-1)-s_{l+1}} \qquad \text{A57}$$

■

It is easily seen that the posterior distribution does not depend on the particular order of the k observations, but only on the sum s_k of the observations. From the posterior distribution of θ the density of the predictive distribution $g(y \mid s_k)$ for a new observation y can be derived.

Theorem 2.8

$$g(y|s_k) = \frac{k(n-1)+1}{(n-1)(k+1)+1} \binom{k(n-1)}{s_k} \frac{\binom{n-1}{y}}{\binom{(n-1)(k+1)}{s_k+y}} \qquad \text{A58}$$

$$E[y|s_k] = \frac{(n-1)(s_k+1)}{k(n-1)+2} \qquad \text{A59}$$

$$var[y|s_k] = \frac{(n-1)(s_k+1)[k(n-1)+n+1][k(n-1)-s_k+1]}{[k(n-1)+2]^2[k(n-1)+3]} \qquad \text{A60}$$

□

Proof:

$$g(y|s_k) = \int_0^1 f(y|\theta)\ \pi(\theta|s_k)\ d(\theta) \qquad \text{A61}$$

$$= \int_0^1 \binom{n-1}{y} \theta^y (1-\theta)^{n-1-y} (k(n-1)+1) \binom{k(n-1)}{s_k} \theta^{s_k} (1-\theta)^{k(n-1)-s_k} d(\theta) \qquad \text{A62}$$

$$= (k(n-1)+1) \binom{n-1}{y} \binom{k(n-1)}{s_k} \int_0^1 \theta^{s_k+y} (1-\theta)^{(n-1)(k+1)-s_k-y} d(\theta) \qquad \text{A63}$$

$$= \frac{k(n-1)+1}{(n-1)(k+1)+1} \binom{k(n-1)}{s_k} \frac{\binom{n-1}{y}}{\binom{(n-1)(k+1)}{s_k+y}}\ ; \qquad \text{A64}$$

$$E[y|s_k] = \sum_{y=0}^{n-1} \frac{k(n-1)+1}{(n-1)(k+1)+1} \binom{k(n-1)}{s_k} \frac{\binom{n-1}{y} y}{\binom{(n-1)(k+1)}{s_k+y}} \qquad \text{A65}$$

$$= \frac{k(n-1)+1}{(n-1)(k+1)+1} \binom{k(n-1)}{s_k} (n-1) \sum_{y=1}^{n-1} \frac{\binom{n-2}{y-1}}{\binom{(n-1)(k+1)}{s_k+y}} \qquad \text{A66}$$

$$= \frac{k(n-1)+1}{(n-1)(k+1)+1} \binom{k(n-1)}{s_k} (n-1) \sum_{j=0}^{n-2} \frac{\binom{n-2}{j}}{\binom{(n-1)(k+1)}{s_k+j+1}} . \qquad \text{A67}$$

In order to calculate the sum-part of the last expression, substitute *(n-2)=t*; $s_k+1=s_l$ and $(k(n-1)+1)/(n-2)=r$ and use the fact that the probabilities of the predictive distribution sum up to 1 to get:

$$\sum_{j=0}^{n-2} \frac{\binom{n-2}{j}}{\binom{(n-1)(k+1)}{s_k+j+1}} = \sum_{j=0}^{t} \frac{\binom{t}{j}}{\binom{t(r+1)}{s_l+j}} = \frac{t(r+1)+1}{(tr+1)\binom{tr}{s_l}} = \frac{(n-1)(k+1)+1}{(k(n-1)+2)\binom{k(n-1)+1}{s_k+1}}. \qquad \text{A68}$$

Substituting this expression for the sum in A67 yields:

$$E[y|s_k] = \frac{k(n-1)+1}{(n-1)(k+1)+1} \binom{k(n-1)}{s_k} (n-1) \frac{(n-1)(k+1)+1}{(k(n-1)+2) \binom{k(n-1)+1}{s_k+1}} \qquad \text{A69}$$

$$= \frac{(n-1)(s_k+1)}{k(n-1)+2} ; \qquad \text{A70}$$

$$E[y(y-1)|s_k] = \sum_{y=0}^{n-1} \frac{k(n-1)+1}{(n-1)(k+1)+1} \binom{k(n-1)}{s_k} \frac{\binom{n-1}{y} y(y-1)}{\binom{(n-1)(k+1)}{s_k+y}} \qquad \text{A71}$$

$$= \frac{k(n-1)+1}{(n-1)(k+1)+1} \binom{k(n-1)}{s_k} (n-1)(n-2) \sum_{y=2}^{n-1} \frac{\binom{n-3}{y-2}}{\binom{(n-1)(k+1)}{s_k+y}} \qquad \text{A72}$$

The sum-part of the expression can be calculated by substituting *(n-3)=t*; $s_k+2=s_l$ and $(k(n-1)+2)/(n-3)=r$:

$$= \frac{k(n-1)+1}{(n-1)(k+1)+1} \binom{k(n-1)}{s_k} (n-1)(n-2) \sum_{j=0}^{n-3} \frac{\binom{n-3}{j}}{\binom{(n-1)(k+1)}{s_k+j+2}} . \qquad \text{A73}$$

$$\sum_{j=0}^{n-3} \frac{\binom{n-3}{j}}{\binom{(n-1)(k+1)}{s_k+j+2}} = \sum_{j=0}^{t} \frac{\binom{t}{j}}{\binom{t(r+1)}{s_l+j}} = \frac{t(r+1)+1}{(tr+1)\binom{tr}{s_l}} = \frac{(n-1)(k+1)+1}{(k(n-1)+3)\binom{k(n-1)+2}{s_k+2}} . \qquad \text{A74}$$

Substituting this expression for the sum in expression 73 yields:

$$E[y(y-1)\,|\,s_k] = \frac{k(n-1)+1}{(n-1)(k+1)+1}\binom{k(n-1)}{s_k}(n-1)(n-2)\frac{(n-1)(k+1)+1}{(k(n-1)+3)\binom{k(n-1)+2}{s_k+2}} \qquad \text{A75}$$

$$= \frac{(n-1)(n-2)\ (s_k+1)\ (s_k+2)}{(k(n-1)+2)\ (k(n-1)+3)} \ ; \qquad \text{A76}$$

$$var[y\,|\,s_k] = E[y^2\,|\,s_k] - (E[y\,|\,s_k])^2 \qquad \text{A77}$$

$$= E[y(y-1)\,|\,s_k] + E[y\,|\,s_k] - (E[y\,|\,s_k])^2 \qquad \text{A78}$$

$$= \frac{(n-1)(n-2)(s_k+1)(s_k+2)}{(k(n-1)+2)(k(n-1)+3)} + \frac{(s_k+1)(n-1)}{k(n-1)+2} - \frac{(s_k+1)^2(n-1)^2}{(k(n-1)+2)^2} \qquad \text{A79}$$

$$= \ldots = \frac{(n-1)(s_k+1)(k(n-1)+n+1)(k(n-1)-s_k+1)}{(k(n-1)+2)^2\ (k(n-1)+3)} \qquad \text{A80}$$

■

The following two theorems (2.9 and 2.10) and lemma (2.1) concern the 'belief learning pattern' and describe how players' beliefs are affected by new information. Theorem 2.9 is a general result. Theorem 2.10 and lemma 2.1 are derived specifically for binomially distributed variables. Finally, lemma 2.2 describes a limit result if group-size grows beyond bounds.

Theorem 2.9

Given the density of the prior distribution $\pi(\theta)$ with $0 \leq \theta \leq 1$, the old observations $x_1,\ldots,x_k$ and the new observation y it holds that:

$$g(y|x_1,..,x_k,\ y) \geq g(y|x_1,..,x_k) \qquad \text{A81}$$

□

Proof: after the observations $x_1,\ldots,x_k$ the posterior distribution is $\pi(\theta\,|\,x_1,..,x_k)$, implying

$$g(y|x_1,..,x_k) = \int_0^1 f(y|\theta)\ \pi(\theta|x_1,..,x_k)\ d(\theta)\ . \qquad \text{A82}$$

Now the new event y is observed, so that

$$g(y|x_1,..,x_k,\ y) = \int_0^1 f(y|\theta)\ \pi(\theta|x_1,..,x_k,\ y)\ d(\theta) \qquad \text{A83}$$

$$= \frac{\int_0^1 \pi(\theta|x_1,..,x_k)\ f(y|\theta)\ f(y|\theta)\ d(\theta)}{\int_0^1 \pi(\theta|x_1,..,x_k)\ f(y|\theta)\ d(\theta)}\ . \qquad \text{A84}$$

Thus,

$$g(y|x_1,..,x_k,\ y) \geq g(y|x_1,..,x_k) \Leftrightarrow \qquad \text{A85}$$

$$\frac{\int_0^1 \pi(\theta|x_1,..,x_k)(f(y|\theta))^2 d(\theta)}{\int_0^1 \pi(\theta|x_1,..,x_k)f(y|\theta)d(\theta)} \geq \int_0^1 \pi(\theta|x_1,..,x_k)f(y|\theta)d(\theta) \Leftrightarrow \qquad \text{A86}$$

$$\int_0^1 \pi(\theta|x_1,..,x_k)(f(y|\theta))^2 d(\theta) \geq [\int_0^1 \pi(\theta|x_1,..,x_k)f(y|\theta)d(\theta)]^2 \Leftrightarrow \qquad \text{A87}$$

$$E_\theta[(f(y|\theta)^2] \geq (E_\theta[f(y|\theta)])^2 , \qquad \text{A88}$$

which is true because $h(x)=x^2$ is convex so that the Jensen inequality holds (e.g., Mood, Graybill and Boes, 1985, pp 72). ■

Theorem 2.10

Assume that the events $x_1,...,x_k$ summing up to s_k have been observed from an (assumed) binomial $(n\text{-}1,\theta)$ distribution with unknown θ. The new observation is x_{k+1}. It holds that:

$$E[y|s_k+x_{k+1}] \geq E[y|s_k] \Leftrightarrow x_{k+1} \geq E[y|s_k] \qquad \text{A89}$$

□

Proof: using theorem 2.8,

$$E[y|s_k+x_{k+1}] \geq E[y|s_k] \Leftrightarrow \frac{(n-1)(s_k+x_{k+1}+1)}{(k+1)(n-1)+2} \geq \frac{(n-1)(s_k+1)}{k(n-1)+2} \Leftrightarrow \qquad \text{A90}$$

$$s_k+x_{k+1}+1 \geq \frac{(s_k+1)(k(n-1)+n+1)}{k(n-1)+2} \Leftrightarrow \qquad \text{A91}$$

$$x_{k+1} \geq \frac{(s_k+1)(n-1)}{k(n-1)+2} = E[y|s_k] \qquad \text{A92}$$

■

Lemma 2.1

$g(y\,|\,s_k)$ converges to *bin* $(n\text{-}1,\theta)$ if k approaches ∞ and if others contribute with constant probability θ. □

Proof: if x_i is binomially distributed, then the moment generating function of x_i is known to be equal to

$$m_{x_i}(t) = (\theta e^{t} + 1 - \theta)^{(n-1)} . \qquad \text{A93}$$

For s_k the moment generating function can be derived using theorem 9, p.192 in Mood, Graybill and Boes (1985):

$$s_k = \sum_{i=1}^{k} x_i \Rightarrow m_{s_k}(t) = \prod_{i=1}^{k} m_{x_i}(t) = (\theta e^{t} + 1 - \theta)^{k(n-1)} , \qquad \text{A94}$$

from which it becomes clear that s_k is binomially *[k(n-1), θ]* distributed. Thus,

$$E[s_k] = k(n-1)\theta \; ; \quad var[s_k] = k(n-1)\theta(1-\theta) \qquad \text{A95}$$

and according to the central limit theory s_k/k has as asymptotic distribution:

$$\lim_{k\to\infty} \frac{s_k}{k} \sim N \left[(n-1)\theta, \frac{(n-1)\theta(1-\theta)}{k}\right] , \qquad \text{A96}$$

so that s_k/k degenerates to $(n-1)\theta$. Now,

$$\lim_{k\to\infty} g(y|s_k) = \lim_{k\to\infty} \binom{n-1}{y} \frac{k(n-1)+1}{(n-1)(k+1)+1} \frac{\binom{k(n-1)}{s_k}}{\binom{(n-1)(k+1)}{s_k+y}} \qquad \text{A97}$$

$$= \lim_{k\to\infty} \binom{n-1}{y} \frac{(n-1+\frac{1}{k})}{(n-1+\frac{n-1}{k}+\frac{1}{k})} * \qquad \text{A98}$$

$$\frac{\dfrac{\binom{k(n-1)}{s_k}}{(k(n-1)+n-1)..(k(n-1)+1)(k(n-1))!}}{(s_k+y)..(s_k+1)s_k!(k(n-1)+n-1-s_k-y)..(k(n-1)-s_k+1)(k(n-1)-s_k)!}$$

$$= \lim_{k\to\infty} \binom{n-1}{y} \frac{(n-1+\frac{1}{k})}{(n-1+\frac{n-1}{k}+\frac{1}{k})} *$$

$$\frac{(\frac{s_k}{k}+\frac{y}{k})..(\frac{s_k}{k}+\frac{1}{k})(n-1+\frac{n-1}{k}-\frac{s_k}{k}-\frac{y}{k})..(n-1-\frac{s_k}{k}+\frac{1}{k})}{(n-1+\frac{n-1}{k})..(n-1+\frac{1}{k})} \quad \text{A99}$$

$$= \binom{n-1}{y} \frac{((n-1)\theta)^y \ (n-1-(n-1)\theta)^{n-1-y}}{(n-1)^{n-1}} \quad \text{A100}$$

$$= \binom{n-1}{y} \frac{((n-1)\theta)^y}{(n-1)^y} \frac{(n-1-(n-1)\theta)^{n-1-y}}{(n-1)^{n-1-y}} \quad \text{A101}$$

$$= \binom{n-1}{y} \theta^y \ (1-\theta)^{n-1-y} \quad \text{A102}$$

■

Lemma 2.2

Let $0<\theta<1$. If $n\to\infty$, then $g(y|s_k)\to 0$, $\forall y$, i.e., if group-size grows beyond bounds, and if other players contribute with probability θ, with θ strictly between 0 and 1, then the Naive Bayesian's predicted probability of any specific event approaches 0. □

Proof: using theorem 2.8,

$$\lim_{n\to\infty} g(y|s_k) = \lim_{n\to\infty} [\frac{k(n-1)+1}{(n-1)(k+1)+1} \binom{k(n-1)}{s_k} \frac{\binom{n-1}{y}}{\binom{(n-1)(k+1)}{s_k+y}}] \quad \text{A103}$$

$$= \frac{k}{k+1} \lim_{n\to\infty} [\frac{(n-1)!}{(n-1-y)!} \frac{[k(n-1)]!}{[k(n-1)-s_k)]!} \frac{[(n-1)(k+1)-(s_k+y)]!}{[(n-1)(k+1)]!} \frac{(s_k+y)!}{s_k! \ y!}] \quad \text{A104}$$

$$= \frac{k}{k+1} \lim_{n\to\infty} [\frac{(n-1)(n-2)...(n-y)}{[(n-1)(k+1)][(n-1)(k+1)-1]...[(n-1)(k+1)-y+1]} * \qquad \text{A105}$$

$$\frac{[k(n-1)][k(n-1)-1]...[k(n-1)-s_k+1]}{[(n-1)(k+1)-y]...[(n-1)(k+1)-s_k-y+1]} \binom{s_k+y}{y}] \leq$$

(the first y terms after the limit sign converge to $(k+1)^{-y}$. Making use of the fact that if $y \geq x$, then $x/y \geq (x-1)/(y-1)$, one can implement upper bounds for the subsequent s_k terms)

$$\leq \frac{k}{k+1} [\frac{1}{k+1}]^y \lim_{n\to\infty} ([\frac{k(n-1)}{(n-1)(k+1)-y}]^{s_k} \binom{s_k+y}{y}) = \qquad \text{A106}$$

$$= c \lim_{n\to\infty} ([\frac{k+1}{k} - \frac{y}{k(n-1)}]^{-s_k} \binom{s_k+y}{y}). \qquad \text{A107}$$

Note that

$$\lim_{n\to\infty} \frac{s_k}{n-1} = k\theta. \qquad \text{A108}$$

Therefore, the expression in A107 is equal to:

$$= c \lim_{n\to\infty} ([\frac{k+1}{k}]^{-k\theta(n-1)} [1+\frac{-yk\theta}{k+1} \frac{1}{k\theta(n-1)}]^{-k\theta(n-1)} \binom{k\theta(n-1)+y}{y}) \qquad \text{A109}$$

$$= c\, e^{\frac{yk\theta}{k+1}} \lim_{n\to\infty} [(\frac{k+1}{k})^{-k\theta(n-1)} \binom{k\theta(n-1)+y}{y}]. \qquad \text{A110}$$

The binomial coefficient after the limit sign $\sim O(n^y)$. This term increases to ∞ slower than the first term decreases to 0. Repeated application of the rule of de l'Hospital shows that the limit tends to 0. ■

Appendix B: Experimental instructions

This appendix contains a sample of the experimental instructions for subjects. First, section B1 provides the instructions for the decomposed game technique measuring value orientations in the public good experiments. A measure of a subject's value orientation was obtained before the public good experiment started. Section B.2 discusses the instructions for some of the public good treatments and the related game against nature. This discussion includes the explanation of the scoring rule for the elicitation of beliefs.

B.1 Decomposed game technique

The first part of the instructions of the decomposed game technique were given in a handout and were read aloud by one of the two experimenters (text in italics was not in the instructions):

For the next twenty-four questions you will be asked to make choices with monetary consequences. In twenty-four situations you will have to choose between two options: Option A and Option B.

For each option **two amounts** will be displayed: one amount you will receive or pay **yourself and** one amount that the **'other'** will receive or pay. The 'other' is another participant with whom you are paired in the experiment. The pairing is random (determined by a lottery) and secret: during and after the experiment you will **not** know with whom you have been paired.

During the experiment you will not get any information about the choices made by the participant with whom you are paired. Nor will the participant with whom you are paired get any information about your choices.

Your total payoff is the sum of the amounts that you make in each round. Each round you receive or pay the sum of the amount that you assign to yourself and the amount that 'the other' assigns to you. The sum of the amounts assigned to you by 'the other' is only revealed to you after the second experiment *(the public good experiment)* has ended.

The amounts in this experiment are denoted in Francs. Your earnings will be paid to you after the second experiment has ended in Dutch guilders according to the exchange rate **1 Franc = f 0,30**. The payoff will be private. Your payoff is your own business: you don't have to talk about it to anybody.

It is not allowed to speak with other participants or to communicate in any other way. If you want to ask a question, raise your hand.

Table B.1

24 questions of the decomposed game technique

	Option A		Option B	
Question	Amount Self	Amount Other	Amount Self	Amount Other
1	+15,00	+0,00	+14,50	-3,90
2	+14,50	-3,90	+13,00	-7,50
3	+13,00	-7,50	+10,60	-10,60
4	+10,60	-10,60	+7,50	-13,00
5	+7,50	-13,00	+3,90	-14,50
6	+3,90	-14,50	0,00	-15,00
7	0,00	-15,00	-3,90	-14,50
8	-3,90	-14,50	-7,50	-13,00
9	-7,50	-13,00	-10,60	-10,60
10	-10,60	-10,60	-13,00	-7,50
11	-13,00	-7,50	-14,50	-3,90
12	-14,50	-3,90	-15,00	0,00
13	-15,00	0,00	-14,50	+3,90
14	-14,50	+3,90	-13,00	+7,50
15	-13,00	+7,50	-10,60	+10,60
16	-10,60	+10,60	-7,50	+13,00
17	-7,50	+13,00	-3,90	+14,50
18	-3,90	+14,50	0,00	+15,00
19	0,00	+15,00	+3,90	+14,50
20	+3,90	+14,50	+7,50	+13,00
21	+7,50	+13,00	+10,60	+10,60
22	+10,60	+10,60	+13,00	+7,50
23	+13,00	+7,50	+14,50	+3,90
24	+14,50	+3,90	+15,00	0,00

The continuation of the decomposed game technique was computerized. On the upper left part of each screen a box was displayed for option A. In the box were two bars, one to display the amount available to oneself and the other to display the amount available for the other. If an amount was positive, the bar was above the x-axis and the color of the bar was green. If an amount was negative, the bar was below the x-axis and the color of the bar was red. The length of the bar was an indication of the magnitude of the amount. The amounts themselves were also written in the box. On the upper right part of the screen a similar box was displayed for option B. Before subjects made the actual choices, they read an example explaining the potential outcomes of one question in detail. Each subject proceeded at her or his own pace and got an opportunity to reconsider each choice before the next question was posed. In table B.1 the 24 choices are summarized in Francs. Each subject made the 24 choices in a (different) random order.

B.2 Public good games and nature

Here, a sample of the instructions of treatment high-5 is provided as example of the type of instructions in the public good games. Instructions were computerized and subjects proceeded at their own pace. After a short introduction about how to use the computer, the instructions continued with the rules of the game.

The experiment will last twenty periods. Each period you will be assigned to a new group of five persons. The composition of the groups changes from period to period. You will not know the identity of the other members of your group in any period, nor will any other participant know the identity of her or his group-members. The assignment to the groups is made randomly. The probability that you will meet exactly the same people in a group twice, is zero.

In each period you will be asked to make two decisions. First, you will be asked whether you want to buy a marker or not (decision A). Then, you will be asked to estimate the probabilities of how many of the others in your group will buy a marker (decision B).

DECISION A: You will make the decision whether or not to buy a marker. In this example the COSTS of buying a marker will be equal to 75 cents. During the experiment the COSTS will be a different amount. The COSTS of buying a marker are equal for everybody and will not change in the twenty periods.

If you buy a marker in a period, you will not literally receive a marker. You will get a revenue depending on the number of members of your group that buys a marker. This revenue will be called the GROUP-REVENUE, because it is equal for everyone in a group. Your payoff in this part of the experiment, your MARKER-PAYOFF, will be equal to the GROUP-REVENUE, if you decided not to buy a marker, and will be equal to the GROUP-REVENUE minus the COSTS if you decided to buy a marker.

Your decision whether or not to buy a marker will not be revealed to the other participants.

GROUP-REVENUE TABLE: As already mentioned, the GROUP-REVENUE for a group depends on the total number of participants in a group that buy a marker. The GROUP-REVENUE will be presented in a GROUP-REVENUE TABLE. Here you see an example of such a table for an imaginary case.

Table B.2
Group-revenue table

number of markers	0	1	2	3	4	5
group-revenue	30	40	50	140	180	200

The table will not change during the experiment. Each participant will have the same table, but it will be a different table from the one presented here. The format of the table will be the same but the amounts will differ. (...)

Next, an example was given explaining in detail how the GROUP-REVENUE table should be read. Subjects had to answer some questions testing their understanding before they proceeded with the instructions on decision B.

DECISION B: The second decision you will be asked to make in each period concerns your estimation of the probabilities about the number of OTHER people in your group that will buy a marker. Before you are told how many participants in your group bought a marker, you are asked to estimate the probability that exactly 0, 1, 2, 3 or 4 of the others will buy a marker. You are asked to report these probabilities in percentages. These 5 percentages should add up to 100%.

NOTE: this question concerns the number of markers bought by the OTHERS in your group, EXCLUDING YOUR OWN CHOICE.

You will receive a payoff dependent on your reported probabilities and the actual number of markers bought by the others in your group: the PROBABILITY-PAYOFF. This payoff is calculated on the basis of a formula. It is not important that you have (mathematical) insight in this formula. But it is important to know that your expected PROBABILITY-PAYOFF is maximized if you report probabilities truthfully. It is to your advantage to report probabilities honestly. It will never be the case that your PROBABILITY-PAYOFF is negative. Other participants will not get to know your reported probabilities, and you will not know which probabilities are reported by the others.

For completeness the formula will be given in a handout. People who want to check the mathematical proof of the statement that for this formula the expected PROBABILITY-PAYOFF is maximized if the probabilities are reported seriously and honestly, will be given this proof after the experiment.

Again, subjects had to answer questions testing their understanding. The following text explaining details of the formula was given in a handout.

Reporting the probabilities

You will fill in the percentages which you assign to how many of the other participants in your group (so outside yourself!) choose to buy a marker. You will get a payoff which depends on the number of markers bought by the others in your group and on your reported percentages: the PROBABILITY-PAYOFF. For the remainder of the experiment it is not important that you have mathematical understanding of the formula which is used to calculate the probability-payoff.

In principle it is sufficient to know that your expected PROBABILITY-PAYOFF is maximal if you report probabilities truthfully (the proof of this statement is available on request after the experiment has ended). So, it is advantageous for you to report probabilities as honestly as possible!

Here is the formula for those who are interested: call the reported percentages P_i for $0 \leq i \leq 4$, where P_i denotes the reported percentage that i of the other group-members choose to buy a marker. Calculate $p_i = P_i/100$ for all i between 0 and 4. If j of the other group-members choose to buy a marker, with $0 \leq j \leq 4$, you will receive a PROBABILITY-PAYOFF (referred to as PP) equal to:

$$PP = 60 + 120*p_j - 60*(p_0^2+p_1^2+p_2^2+p_3^2+p_4^2)$$

Again, for the remainder of the experiment it is not important that you have mathematical understanding of this formula: when you have reported your probabilities and when everybody in your group has made the choice whether or not to buy a marker, you will automatically be told how high your PROBABILITY-PAYOFF is.

Figure B.1 shows the screen where subjects were asked to report probabilities. Then it was explained how they could recall information about their own results in earlier periods. Two practice periods were conducted where the decisions of the others were simulated, as explained to the subjects. In the practice periods subjects played for fictitious money.

Figure B.1
Screen where subjects were asked to report probabilities

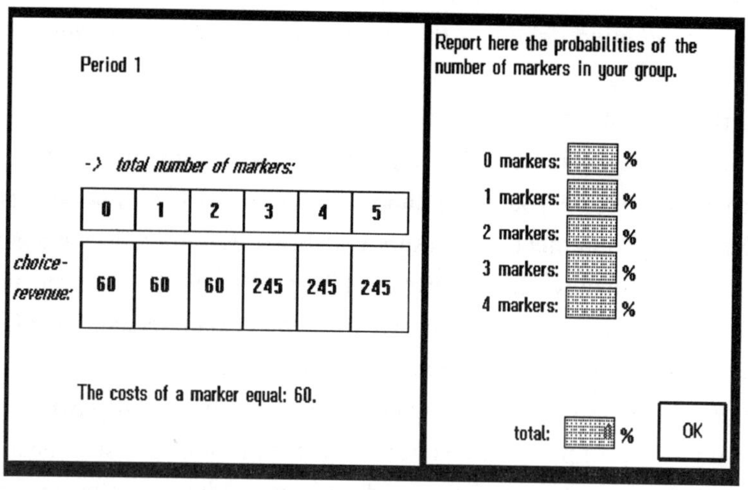

As explained in section 4.2, the decision to contribute was described differently in the partners treatments. Here, subjects chose between yellow and blue instead of between buying a marker or not. Besides a difference in the choice of words, the only difference between high-5 and pubgood was that in high-5 groups changed each period, while they remained constant in pubgood. The following is a translation of the summary of the instructions of the pubgood treatment. This summary was given to subjects in a

handout after they had read the computerized instructions.

The experiment will take 20 periods. During the whole experiment you will be in a group with the same participants.

Choosing between yellow and blue

Each period you will choose between yellow and blue. The amount related to yellow is -60 cent, the amount related to Blue is 0. Each group-member will get a payoff dependent on the number of yellow choices in your group: the GROUP-REVENUE.

Table B.3

group revenue table (pubgood)

	Number of yellow choices in the group					
	0	1	2	3	4	5
Group revenue	60	60	60	245	245	245

Amount related to a yellow choice: -60 cent
Amount related to a blue choice: 0 cent

If you choose blue, your choice-payoff will be equal to the GROUP-REVENUE. If you choose yellow, your choice-payoff will be equal to the GROUP-REVENUE minus the 60 cent (belonging to the yellow choice).

The summary continued with a description of the scoring rule. This description was similar to the description in high-5. The following is a translation of the summary of the instructions of the pubbad treatment.

The experiment will take 20 periods. During the whole experiment you will be in a group with the same participants.

Choosing between yellow and blue

Each period you will choose between yellow and blue. The amount related to yellow is -60 cent, the amount related to blue is 0. Each group-member will get a payoff dependent on the number of yellow choices in your group: the GROUP-REVENUE.

Table B.4
group revenue table (pubbad)

	Number of yellow choices in the group					
	0	1	2	3	4	5
Group revenue	185	185	185	0	0	0

Amount related to a yellow choice: 60 cent
Amount related to a blue choice: 0 cent

If you choose blue, your choice-payoff will be equal to the GROUP-REVENUE. If you choose yellow, your choice-payoff will be equal to the GROUP-REVENUE plus the 60 cent (related to the yellow choice).

In nature, the choices of group-members were replaced by random draws from a binomially distributed variable. This was explained as follows:

The experiment will last 20 periods. In the experiment there is an important role for a 'cage with balls'. In each period the cage is refilled with four new balls. Each ball is white or red. You are not told what the probability is that a ball is red. However, this probability is the same for each ball and this probability will not change during the experiment. At the end of each period the cage is emptied and refilled.

You will not literally see a cage. Imagine that the computer observes the cage and refills it in each period with red and white balls.

Then, decisions A and B were explained in a similar way as in high-5, and subjects' understanding of the rules was tested by having them answer some questions.

References

Alexander, R.D., 1987: *The Biology of Moral Systems*, Aldine de Gruyter, New York.

Andreoni, J., 1988: 'Why Free Ride? Strategies and Learning in Public Goods Experiments', *Journal of Public Economics* **37**, 291-301.

Andreoni, J., 1990: 'Impure Altruism and Donations to Public Goods: A Theory of Warm-Glow Giving', *Economic Journal* **100**, 464-477.

Andreoni, J., 1993: 'An Experimental Test of the Public Goods Crowding-Out Hypothesis', *American Economic Review* **83**, 1317-1327.

Andreoni, J., 1995a: 'Warm-Glow versus Cold-Prickle: The Effects of Positive and Negative Framing on Cooperation in Experiments', *Quarterly Journal of Economics* **110**, 1-22.

Andreoni, J., 1995b: 'Cooperation in Public-Goods Experiments: Kindness or Confusion?', *American Economic Review* **85**, 891-904.

Andreoni, J., and J.H. Miller, 1995: 'Auctions with Artificial Adaptive Agents', *Games and Economic Behavior* **10**, 39-64.

Aronson, E., P.C. Ellsworth, J.M. Carlsmith, and M.H. Gonzales, 1990: *Methods of Research in Social Psychology*, second edition, McGraw-Hill, Singapore.

Aumann, R., and A. Brandenburger, 1995: 'Epistemic Conditions for Nash Equilibrium', *Econometrica* **63**, 1161-1180.

Berger, J.O., 1980: *Statistical Decision Theory - Foundations, Concepts, and Methods*, Springer-Verlag, New York.

Boylan, R.T., and M.A. El-Gamal, 1993: 'Fictitious Play: A Statistical Study of Multiple Economic Experiments', *Games and Economic Behavior* **5**, 205-222.

Brandts, J., and C.A. Holt, 1992: 'An Experimental Test of Equilibrium Dominance in Signaling Games', *American Economic Review* **82**, 1350-1365.

Brandts, J., and C.A. Holt, 1993: 'Adjustment Patterns and Equilibrium Selection in Experimental Signaling Games', *International Journal of Game Theory* **22**, 279-302.

Brandts, J., and C.A. Holt, 1994: 'Naive Bayesian Learning and Adjustment to Equilibrium in Signaling Games', *Discussion Paper*, Universitat Autonoma de Barcelona.

Brandts, J., and A. Schram, 1996: 'Cooperative Gains or Noise in Public Goods Experiments: Applying the Contribution Function Approach', *Discussion Paper*, University of Amsterdam.

Brewer, M.B., and R.M. Kramer, 1986: 'Choice Behavior in Social Dilemmas: Effects of Social Identity, Group Size, and Decision Framing', *Journal of Personality and Social Psychology* **50**, 543-549.

Buunk, A.P., and R.W. Meertens, 1988: 'Wat is Sociale Psychology?' (What is Social Psychology?), in *Sociale Psychology* (Social Psychology), Meertens, R.W., and J. Von Grumbkow (eds.), Wolters Noordhoff, Groningen.

Caldwell, B.J., 1982: *Beyond Positivism*, Allen and Unwin, London.

Camerer, C., 1995: 'Individual Decision Making', in *The Handbook of Experimental Economics*, Kagel, J.H., and A.E. Roth (eds.), Princeton University Press, New Jersey.

Caporael, L.R., R.M. Dawes, J.M. Orbell, and A.J.C. van de Kragt, 1989: 'Selfishness Examined: Cooperation in the Absence of Egoistic Incentives', *Behavioral and Brain Sciences* **12**, 683-739.

Carter, J.R., and M.D. Irons, 1991: 'Are Economists Different and If So, Why?', *Journal of Economic Perspectives* **5**, 171-177.

Cooper, D., S. Garvin, and J. Kagel, 1994: 'Adaptive Learning vs. Equilibrium Refinements in An Entry Limit Pricing Game', *Discussion Paper*, University of Pittsburgh.

Crawford, V.P., 1995: 'Adaptive Dynamics in Coordination Games', *Econometrica* **63**, 103-143.

Davis, D.D., and C.A. Holt, 1993: *Experimental Economics*, Princeton University press, New Jersey.

Dawes, R.M., J. McTavish, and H. Shaklee, 1977: 'Behavior, Communication, and Assumptions About Other People's Behavior in a Commons Dilemma Situation', *Journal of Personality and Social Psychology* **35**, 1-11.

Dawes, R.M., J.M. Orbell, R.T. Simmons, and A.J.C. van de Kragt, 1986: 'Organizing Groups for Collective Action', *American Political Science Review* **80**, 1171-1184.

Dehue, F.M.J, C.G. McClintock, and W.B.G. Liebrand, 1993: 'Social Value Related Response Latencies: Unobtrusive Evidence for Individual Differences in

Information Processing', *European Journal of Social Psychology* **23**, 273-293.
Dowding, K.M., 1991: *Rational Choice and Political Power*, Edward Elgar Publishing Limited, Hants.
Dunning, D., D.W. Griffin, J.D. Milojkovic, and L. Ross, 1990: 'The Overconfidence Effect in Social Prediction', *Journal of Personality and Social Psychology* **58**, 568-581.
Dyer, D., J.H. Kagel, and D. Levin, 1989: 'A Comparison of Naive and Experienced Bidders in Common Value Offer Auctions: A Laboratory Analysis', *Economic Journal* **99**, 108-115.
Eichberger, J., 1995: 'Bayesian Learning in Repeated Normal Form Games', *Games and Economic Behavior* **11**, 254-278.
Eichberger, J., H. Haller, and F. Milne, 1993: 'Naive Bayesian Learning in 2x2 Matrix Games', *Journal of Economic Behavior and Organization* **22**, 69-90.
El-Gamal, M.A., and D.M. Grether, 1994: 'Are People Bayesian? Uncovering Behavioral Strategies', *Discussion Paper*, Caltech.
El-Gamal, M.A., R.D. McKelvey, and T.R. Palfrey, 1994: 'Learning in Experimental Games', *Economic Theory* **4**, 901-922.
Ellison, G., and D. Fudenberg, 1993: 'Rules of Thumb for Social Learning', *Journal of Political Economy* **101**, 612-643.
Ellison, G., and D. Fudenberg, 1995: 'Word-of-Mouth Communication and Social Learning', *Quarterly Journal of Economics* **110**, 93-125.
Erev, I., and A.E. Roth, 1996: 'On the Need for Low Rationality, Cognitive Game Theory: Reinforcement Learning in Experimental Games with Unique, Mixed strategy Equilibria', *Discussion Paper*, University of Pittsburgh.
Fehr, E., G. Kirchsteiger, and A. Riedl, 1993: 'Does Fairness Prevent Market Clearing? An Experimental Investigation', *Quarterly Journal of Economics* **108**, 437-459.
Fischer, G.W., 1982: 'Scoring-Rule Feedback and the Overconfidence Syndrome in Subjective Probability Forecasting', *Organizational Behavior and Human Performance* **29**, 352-369.
Frey, B., 1992: *Economics as a Science of Human Behavior*, Kluwer, Dordrecht.
Friedman, D., and S. Sunder, 1994: *Experimental Methods - A Primer for Economists*, Cambridge University Press, New York.

Fudenberg, D., and D.M. Kreps, 1993: 'Learning Mixed Equilibria', *Games and Economic Behavior* **5**, 320-367.

Gale, J., K.G. Binmore, and L. Samuelson, 1995: 'Learning to Be Imperfect: The Ultimatum Game', *Games and Economic Behavior* **8**, 56-90.

Gibbons, R., 1992: *A Primer in Game Theory*, Harvester Wheatsheaf, New York.

Gradstein, M., and S. Nitzan, 1990: 'Binary Participation and Incremental Provision of Public Goods', *Social Choice and Welfare* **7**, 171-192.

Grether, D.M., 1992: 'Testing Bayes Rule and the Representativeness Heuristic: Some Experimental Results', *Journal of Economic Behavior and Organization* **17**, 31-57.

Grether, D.M., and C.R. Plott, 1979: 'Economic Theory of Choice and the Preference Reversal', *American Economic review* **69**, 623-638.

Grether, D.M., and C.R. Plott, 1984: 'The Effects of Market Practices in Oligopolistic Markets: An Experimental Examination of the Ethyl Case', *Economic Inquiry* **22**, 479-507.

Griesinger, D.W., and J.W. Livingston, 1973: 'Toward a Model of Interpersonal Motivation in Experimental Games', *Behavioral Science* **18**, 173-188.

Griffin, D., and A. Tversky, 1992: 'The Weighing of Evidence and the Determinants of Confidence', *Cognitive Psychology* **24**, 411-435.

Güth, W., and S. Nitzan, 1993: 'Are Moral Objections to Free Riding Evolutionary Stable?', *CENTER Discussion Paper* No. 9302, Tilburg University.

Harless, D.W., and C.F. Camerer, 1994: The Predictive Utility of Generalized Expected Utility Theories', *Econometrica* **62**, 1251-1289.

Harsanyi, J., 1977: *Rational Behavior and Bargaining Equilibrium in Games and Social Situations*, Cambridge University Press, London.

Heckman, J., and B. Singer, 1984: 'A Method for Minimizing the Impact of Distributional Assumptions in Econometric Models for Duration Data', *Econometrica* **52**, 271-320.

Hey, J.D., 1991: *Experiments in Economics*, Basil Blackwell, Oxford.

Hey, J.D., and C. Orme, 1994: 'Investigating Generalizations of Expected Utility Theory Using Experimental Data', *Econometrica* **62**, 1291-1326.

Hogarth, R.M, and H.J. Einhorn, 1992: 'Order Effects in Belief Updating: The Belief Adjustment Model', *Cognitive Psychology* **24**, 1-55.

Hogarth, R.M, and M.W. Reder (eds.), 1987: *Rational Choice: The Contrast Between Economics and Psychology*, The University of Chicago Press, Chicago.

Isaac, R.M., K. McCue, and C. Plott, 1985: 'Public Goods Provision in an Experimental Environment', *Journal of Public Economics* **26**, 51-74.

Isaac, R.M., D. Schmidtz, and J. Walker, 1988: 'The Assurance Problem in a Laboratory Market', *Public Choice* **62**, 217-236.

Jordan, J.S., 1993: 'Three Problems in Learning Mixed-Strategy Nash Equilibria', *Games and Economic Behavior* **5**, 368-386.

Kahneman, D., and A. Tversky, 1979: 'Prospect Theory: An Analysis of Decision Under Risk', *Econometrica* **47**, 263-291.

Kelley, H.H., and A.J. Stahelski, 1970: 'Social Interaction Basis of Cooperators' and Competitors' Beliefs About Others', *Journal of Personality and Social Psychology* **16**, 66-91.

Kerr, N.L., 1989: 'Illusions of Efficacy: The Effects of Group Size on Perceived Efficacy in Social Dilemmas', *Journal of Experimental Social Psychology* **25**, 287-313.

Kim, O., and M. Walker, 1984: 'The Free Rider Problem: Experimental Evidence', *Public Choice* **43**, 3-24.

Komorita, S.S., 1987: 'Cooperative Choice in Decomposed Social Dilemmas', *Personality and Social Psychology Bulletin* **13**, 53-63.

Komorita, S.S., and J.M. Barth, 1985: 'Components of Reward in Social Dilemmas', *Journal of Personality and Social Psychology* **48**, 364-373.

Komorita, S.S., and P. Carnevale, 1992: 'Motivational Arousal vs. Decision Framing in Social Dilemmas', in *Social Dilemmas: Theoretical Issues and Research Findings*, Liebrand, W.B.G., D.M. Messick, and H.A.M. Wilke (eds.), Pergamon Press, Oxford.

Koomen, W., 1988: 'Het Onderzoeksinstrumentarium van de Sociaal-Psycholoog' (The Research Instruments of the Social Psychologist), in *Sociale Psychology* (Social Psychology), Meertens, R.W., and J. Von Grumbkow (eds.), Wolters Noordhoff, Groningen.

Kreps, D.M., and R. Wilson, 1982: 'Reputation and Imperfect Information', *Journal of Economic theory* **27**, 253-279.

Kuhlman, D.M., C. Camac, and D.A. Cunha, 1986: 'Individual Differences in Social

Orientation', in *Experimental Social Dilemmas*, Wilke, H., D. Messick, and C. Rutte (Eds.), Verlag Peter Lang, New York.

Kuhlman, D.M., and D.L. Wimberley, 1976: 'Expectations of Choice Behavior Held by Cooperators, Competitors, and Individualists Across Four Classes of Experimental Games', *Journal of Personality and Social Psychology* **34**, 69-81.

Ledyard, J.O., 1995: 'Public Goods: A Survey of Experimental Research', in *The Handbook of Experimental Economics*, Kagel, J.H., and A.E. Roth (eds.), Princeton University Press, New Jersey.

Lichtenstein, S., and P. Slovic, 1971: 'Reversals of Preference between Bids and Choices in Gambling Decisions', *Journal of Experimental Psychology* **89**, 46-55.

Liebrand, W.B.G., 1984: 'The Effect of Social Motives, Communication and Group Size on Behaviour in an N-Person Multi Stage Mixed Motive Game', *European Journal of Social Psychology* **14**, 239-264.

Luce, R.D., 1959: *Individual Choice Behavior - A Theoretical Analysis*, John Wiley & Sons, New York.

Maddala, G.S., 1983: *Limited-Dependent and Qualitative Variables in Econometrics*, Cambridge University Press, New York.

Marwell, G., and R. Ames, 1981: 'Economists Free Ride, Does Anyone Else? Experiments on the Provision of Public Goods', *Journal of Public Economics* **15**, 295-310.

McClintock, C.G., and W.B.G. Liebrand, 1988: 'Role of Interdependence Structure, Individual Value Orientation, and Another's Strategy in Social Decision Making: A Transformational Analysis', *Journal of Personality and Social Psychology* **55**, 396-409.

McFadden, D., 1974: 'Conditional Logit Analysis of Qualitative Choice Behavior', in *Frontiers of Econometrics*, Zarembka, P. (ed.), Academic Press, New York.

McFadden, D., 1976: 'Quantal Choice Analysis: A Survey', *Annals of Economic and Social Measurement* **5**, 363-390.

McKelvey, R.D., and T.R. Palfrey, 1995: 'Quantal Response Equilibria for Normal Form Games', *Games and Economic Behavior* **10**, 6-38.

Messé, L.A., and J.M. Sivacek, 1979: 'Predictions of Others' Responses in a Mixed-Motive Game: Self Justification or False Consensus?', *Journal of Personality and Social Psychology* **37**, 602-607.

Messick, D.M., H. Wilke, M.B. Brewer, R.M. Kramer, P.E. Zemke, and L. Lui, 1983: 'Individual Adaptations and Structural Change as Solutions to Social Dilemmas', *Journal of Personality and Social Psychology* **44**, 294-309.

Metrick, A., and B. Polak, 1994: 'Fictitious Play in 2 x 2 Games: A Geometric Proof of Convergence', *Economic Theory* **4**, 923-933.

Milgrom, P., and J. Roberts, 1991: 'Adaptive and Sophisticated Learning in Normal Form Games', *Games and Economic Behavior* **3**, 82-100.

Miller, G., 1990: 'Managerial Dilemmas', in *The limits of Rationality*, Schweers Cook, K., and M. Levi (eds.), University Press, Chicago.

Miller, J.H., and J. Andreoni, 1991: 'Can Evolutionary Dynamics Explain Free Riding in Experiments?' *Economics Letters* **36**, 9-15.

Mood, A.M., F.A. Graybill, and D.C. Boes, 1985: *Introduction to the Theory of Statistics*, third edition, McGraw-Hill, Singapore.

Mookherjee, D., and B. Sopher, 1994: 'Learning Behavior in an Experimental Matching Pennies Game', *Games and Economic Behavior* **7**, 62-91.

Murphy, A.H., and R.L. Winkler, 1970: 'Scoring Rules in Probability Assessment and Evaluation', *Acta Psychologica* **34**, 273-286.

Nowak, M., and K. Sigmund, 1993: 'A Strategy of Win-Stay, Lose-Shift that Outperforms Tit-For-Tat in the Prisoner's Dilemma Game', *Nature* **364**, 56-58.

Nyarko, Y., M. Woodford, and N.C. Yannelis, 1994: 'Bounded Rationality and Learning', *Economic Theory* **4**, 811-820.

Offerman, T., 1994: 'Different Preferences Regarding the Voluntary Provision of Step-Level Public Goods: A Game Theoretical Approach', *Discussion Paper*, University of Amsterdam.

Offerman, T., and A. Schram, 1993: 'Selfishness, Rationality and Orientation Re-examined: Evidence from Economic and Psychological Experiments', *Discussion Paper*, University of Amsterdam.

Offerman, T., A. Schram, and J. Sonnemans, 1996: 'Quantal Response Models in Step-Level Public Good Games', forthcoming in *European Journal of Political Economy*.

Offerman, T., and J. Sonnemans, 1996: 'Learning by Experience and Learning by Imitating Successful Others', forthcoming in *Journal of Economic Behavior and*

Organization.

Offerman, T., J. Sonnemans, and A. Schram, 1995: 'Belief Learning in Public Goods Games: Sophisticated Strategists versus Naive Bayesians', *TRACE Discussion Paper*, TI 95-132, University of Amsterdam.

Offerman, T., J. Sonnemans, and A. Schram, 1996: 'Value Orientations, Expectations and Voluntary Contributions in Public Goods', *Economic Journal* **106**, 817-845.

Olson, M., 1971: *The Logic of Collective Action*, Harvard University Press, Cambridge Massachusetts.

Ostrom, E., R. Gardner, and J. Walker, 1994: *Rules, Games, and Common-Pool Resources*, University of Michigan Press, Michigan.

Palfrey, T.R., and J.E. Prisbey, 1993: 'Altruism, Reputation and Noise in Linear Public Goods Experiments', *Discussion Paper*, Caltech.

Palfrey, T.R., and H. Rosenthal, 1988: 'Private Incentives in Social Dilemmas', *Journal of Public Economics* **35**, 309-332.

Palfrey, T.R., and H. Rosenthal, 1991: 'Testing Game-Theoretic Models of Free-riding: New Evidence on Probability Bias and Learning', in *Laboratory Research in Political Economy*, Palfrey, T.R. (ed.), University of Michigan Press, Ann Arbor.

Partow, Z., and A. Schotter, 1993: 'Does Game Theory Predict Well for the Wrong Reasons?', *Discussion Paper*, RR 93-46, New York University.

Potters, J., and F. Van Winden, 1995: 'Comparative Statics of a Signaling Game: An Experimental Study', forthcoming in *International Journal of Game theory*.

Press, S.J., 1989: *Bayesian Statistics: Principles, Models and Applications*, Wiley, New York.

Pruitt, D.G., 1967: 'Reward Structure and Cooperation: the Decomposed Prisoner's Dilemma Game', *Journal of Personality and Social Psychology* **7**, 21-27.

Pruitt, D.G., 1970: 'Motivational Processes in the Decomposed Prisoner's Dilemma Game', *Journal of Personality and Social Psychology* **14**, 227-238.

Pruitt, D.G., 1981: *Negotiation Behavior*, Academic Press, New York.

Pruitt, D.G., and M.J. Kimmel, 1977: 'Twenty Years of Experimental Gaming: Critique, Synthesis and Suggestions for the Future', *Annual Review of Psychology* **28**, 363-392.

Rapoport, A., 1988: 'Provision of Step-Level Public Goods: Effects of Inequalities of

Resources', *Journal of Personality and Social Psychology* **54**, 432-440.

Raub, W., and C. Snijders, 1995: 'Gains, Losses and Cooperation in Social Dilemmas: The Effects of Risk Preferences, *ISCORE Paper* No. 31, Utrecht University.

Robinson, J., 1951: 'An Iterative Method of Solving a Game', *Annals of Mathematics* **54**, 296-301.

Ronis, D.L., J.F. Yates, and J.P. Kirscht, 1989: 'Attitudes, Decisions, and Habits as Determinants of Repeated Behavior', in *Attitude Structure and Function*, Pratkanis, A.R., S.J. Breckler, and A.G. Greenwald (eds.), Lawrence Erlbaum Associates, Hillsdale.

Roth, A.E., 1993: 'The Early History of Experimental Economics', *Journal of the History of Economic Thought* **15**, 184-209.

Roth, A.E., and I. Erev, 1995: 'Learning in Extensive-Form Games: Experimental Data and Simple Dynamic Models in the Intermediate Term', *Games and Economic Behavior* **8**, 164-212.

Schmalensee, R., 1976: 'An Experimental Study of Expectation Formation', *Econometrica* **44**, 17-41.

Schram, A., and J. Sonnemans, 1995: 'Voter Turnout and the Role of Groups: Participation Game Experiments', forthcoming in *International Journal of Game theory*.

Selten, R., 1991: 'Evolution, Learning, and Economic Behavior', *Games and Economic Behavior* **3**, 3-24.

Selten, R., and J. Buchta, 1994: 'Experimental Sealed Bid First Price Auction with Directly Observed Bid Functions', *Discussion Paper* B270, University of Bonn.

Shapley, L., 1964: 'Some Topics in Two-Person Games', in *Advances in Game Theory, Annals of Mathematical Studies* **5**, 1-28.

Simon, H.A., 1987: 'Rationality in Psychology and Economics' in *Rational Choice*, Hogarth, R.M., and M.W. Reder (eds.), The University of Chicago Press, Chicago.

Smith, C.A.B., 1961: 'Consistency in Statistical Inference and Decision', *Journal of the Royal Statistical Society*, Series B, **23**, 1-25.

Smith, V.L., 1989: 'Theory, Experiment and Economics', *Journal of Economic Perspectives* **3**, 151-169.

Smith, V.L., and J.M. Walker, 1993: 'Monetary Rewards and Decision Cost in Experimental Economics', *Economic Inquiry* **31**, 245-261.

Sonnemans, J., A. Schram, and T. Offerman, 1996: 'Public Good Provision and Public Bad Prevention: The Effect of Framing', forthcoming in *Journal of Economic Behavior and Organization.*

Sugden, R., 1984: 'Reciprocity: The Supply of Public Goods through Voluntary Contributions', *Economic Journal* **94**, 772-787.

Suleiman, R., and A. Rapoport, 1992: 'Provision of Step-Level Public Goods with Continuous Contribution', *Journal of Behavioral Decision Making* **5**, 133-153.

Tajfel, H., and J.C. Turner, 1986: 'The Social Identity of Intergroup Behavior' in *Psychology of Intergroup Relations*, Worchell, S., and W.G. Austin (eds.), Nelson-Hall, Chicago.

Taylor, D.M., and F.M. Moghaddam, 1994: *Theories of Intergroup Relations - International Social Psychological Perspectives*, second edition, Praeger, Westport.

Trivers, R.L., 1971: 'The Evolution of Reciprocal Altruism', *Quarterly Review of Biology* **46**, 35-57.

Vallone, R.P., D.W. Griffin, S. Lin, and L. Ross, 1990: 'Overconfident Predictions of Future Actions and Outcomes by Self', *Journal of Personality and Social Psychology* **58**, 582-592.

Van Dijk, E., and H. Wilke, 1995: 'Coordination Rules in Asymmetric Social Dilemmas: A Comparison between Public Good Dilemmas and Resource Dilemmas', *Journal of Experimental Social Psychology* **31**, 1-27.

Van Lange, P.A.M., 1992: 'Confidence in Expectations: A Test of the Triangle Hypothesis', *European Journal of Personality* **6**, 371-379.

Van Lange, P.A.M., 1995: 'Social Value Orientations: A Brief Note', *Discussion Paper*, Free University, Amsterdam.

Van Lange, P.A.M., and D.M. Kuhlman, 1994: 'Social Value Orientations and Impressions of Partner's Honesty and Intelligence: A Test of the Might Versus Morality Effect', *Journal of Personality and Social Psychology* **67**, 126-141.

Warr, P.G., 1982: 'Pareto Optimal Redistribution and Private Charity', *Journal of Public Economics* **19**, 131-138.

Weimann, J., 1994: 'Individual Behaviour in a Free Riding Experiment', *Journal of*

Public Economics **54**, 185-200.

Wong, S., 1987: 'Positive Economics' in *The New Palgrave Dictionary of Economics*, Eatwell, J., M. Milgate, and P. Newman (eds.), The Macmillan Press Limited, London.

Wright, W.F., and M.E. Aboul-Ezz, 1988: 'Effects of Extrinsic Incentives on the Quality of Frequency Assessments', *Organizational Behavior and Human Decision Processes* **41**, 143-152.

Yamagishi, T., and K. Sato, 1986: 'Motivational Bases of the Public Goods Problem', *Journal of Personality and Social Psychology* **50**, 67-73.

Subject Index

advantage of experiments 8
altruism 23, 30, 41, 45, 58, 175, 176
anomaly (~ies) 4, 11, 137, 138, 163
appropriate level for testing 16
assimilation of behavior 45, 91, 145, 198
attitude(s) 4, 8, 17, 18, 26, 67, 68, 75-78, 81, 82, 117, 120, 164, 173, 178, 181
auxiliary
  ~assumption(s) 8, 51, 54, 116, 125, 182
  ~hypotheses 81
backward looking 58
Bayesian learning 60, 128
behaviorally equivalent 63
belief learning
  ~pattern 51, 54, 55, 64, 127, 128, 132, 133, 136, 137, 162, 204
  naive~ 60
  sophisticated~ 60
best response(s) 28, 48-50, 58, 60, 99, 126, 128, 147, 163
boundedly rational players 61
casino-heuristic 137
chicken game 25
cognitive
  ~considerations 61
  ~processes 4, 6
cold-prickle 117, 188
common
  ~knowledge 42, 45, 126
  ~pool 33, 85, 86, 113, 114, 116, 118
communication of beliefs 187
computational abilities 53, 55, 57, 126, 127
conjugate family 52, 56
conservatism 56, 140
conservative 16, 108, 110
consistency 70, 71, 77, 89, 90, 122, 123, 146, 180
consistent expectations 42, 50, 187
cooperator(s)
  in-group~ 27, 28, 31, 45, 59, 63, 97, 98, 100-102, 105, 106, 121, 179, 198, 199
  material~ 27, 28, 31, 34, 35, 41, 45, 63, 64, 97-101, 102, 105, 176, 179, 198
  warm-glow~ 27, 28, 30, 31, 34, 45, 47, 63, 97, 98, 101-104, 106, 121, 155, 174, 198, 199
Cournot rule 57, 58
criterium of symmetry 38
critical
  probability of being~ 25, 39, 42,

59, 64, 93, 95, 97, 105, 112, 113, 115, 116, 120, 122, 123, 131, 152, 171, 188, 189, 191, 193
decision rules
deterministic ~ 143
decision theoretic 139, 177, 181, 187
decomposed game
~technique 18, 68, 71, 73, 77, 78, 82, 104, 120-123, 145, 146, 170, 173, 174, 179, 180, 211, 212
distribution(s)
beta ~ 52, 53, 148, 200
binomial ~ 48, 51, 133, 138, 200
Dirichlet ~ 56
non-informative ~ 137
posterior ~ 51, 52, 56, 105, 148, 174, 200, 201, 205
predictive ~ 52-54, 127, 150, 201, 203
prior ~ 35, 51, 53, 57, 60, 132, 137, 148, 200, 205
stationary ~ 154
dominance 12, 13, 38
elicitation of beliefs 68, 87, 108, 211
end-period effect 114
environment
changes in the ~ 17, 18, 39, 41, 58, 64, 82, 170-172
stability of the ~ 62
equilibrium
~selection 6, 161, 164, 187
Bayesian Nash ~ 42-45, 164, 194, 196-198
Nash ~ 6, 35-38, 42-45, 47, 49, 51, 126, 161, 164, 186-188, 194, 196, 197, 198
evolution 58, 61, 120, 170, 172, 176, 177
~ary forces 174
expected utility
~hypothesis 27, 28, 63, 97-99
~theory 26, 98
~with noise hypothesis 30, 99, 100
~with noise theory 29
expected value
~hypothesis 25, 26, 28, 30, 31, 94-96
~theory 25
~with noise hypothesis 30, 31, 99, 100
~with noise theory 29
experimental realism 9, 77
external validity 9, 10
externalities
negative ~ 23, 33, 82, 171
positive ~ 22, 82, 171
fairness 31, 179, 184
false consensus hypothesis 24, 25, 32, 62, 81, 90, 94, 107, 120, 170

favorable state of the world
130, 131
fictitious play 51, 54, 57-60,
137, 138, 182, 183
forward looking 58
framing 17, 33-35, 63, 82, 84,
89, 113, 115, 117,
121, 123, 170
free-rider 5
futile
probability of being ~
105, 121
game against nature 55, 75, 77,
126-130, 133, 134,
136, 137, 139,
162-164, 181, 211
game theoretic model(s)
dynamic ~ 35, 36, 40,
49, 164, 182
static ~ 36, 48, 54, 55,
126, 132, 133, 137,
152, 162, 163, 182
group-composition
variability of the ~ 17,
39, 40, 64, 82, 85,
89, 108
history
~-dependence 125
homegrown beliefs 51
imitation 62, 187
in-group (*see* cooperators)
~biasing effect 176
incentive compatible mechanism
11, 26, 67, 68
incomplete information 36, 41
independent measure(s) 18, 68,
81, 120, 178
inertia 160, 161
insurance 76
interaction
~between players 16,
58, 63, 129, 154,
170, 175, 187
~between subjects 16,
18, 122, 131, 163
interdisciplinary
~approach 3
~study 19
investment
~decision(s) 20-22, 131
~game(s) 75, 130
kin altruism 175, 176
level of
~precision 29, 30, 152,
182
~rationality 29, 47, 49,
58, 102, 152
lottery mechanism 74
manipulation of subjects 14, 15
methodological individualism 4,
5
monetary incentives 12, 70, 71
monotonicity 12
motivational vector(s) 69-71,
94, 123, 145, 173
multi-modal distributions 137,
138
mundane realism 9
naive Bayesian
~learning 60
optimism 182
optimistic 55, 64, 67, 132, 133,
162, 182
order effects 56, 57, 143
overconfidence 75, 138
Pareto optimum 25, 121
parsimony 4, 30, 31, 63, 177
partners mode 83-85, 88, 90,
91, 94, 95, 105,
113, 121,

123, 128, 133, 135
Pavlov-hypothesis 31
payoff dominance 38
perceived difficulty 138, 181, 187
pessimistic 55, 64, 127, 133, 182
player(s)
full ~ 86-88, 93, 95, 108
simple ~ 86-88, 108
positive theory 18, 167, 169, 170, 188
primacy 56, 57, 140, 141, 143, 163
prisoners' dilemma 23-25, 34, 51, 173, 183, 184
prospect theory 33, 34, 63, 116, 117
Pruitt's hypothesis 33, 34, 63, 88, 116, 117
public
~ bad(s) 33-35, 63, 84-86, 88, 89, 113-120, 122, 123, 129, 154, 158-162, 171, 172
~ payoff 84, 87, 109, 123, 170, 192
public good game
definition of the ~ 19
quantal response 28-30, 36, 46-48, 58, 99, 101, 128, 144, 146-150, 155, 178, 181, 182
~ equilibrium 46-48, 144, 146-149, 181, 182
~ naive Bayesian model 146, 147
questionnaire(s) 11, 14, 71-73, 76, 77, 88, 117-119, 136, 159
~ and oral interviews 14
random
~ ization 8
~ model 150-152
rational expectations 35, 47, 63
realism 4, 9, 10, 77
recency 56, 57, 140, 163
reciprocal altruism 175, 176
reciprocity 31, 175
redundant
probability of being ~ 59, 98, 105, 189
refinement(s) 37, 51, 151, 186
reinforcement learning 18, 22, 49, 60-62, 64, 118, 120, 129, 154, 155, 158, 159, 160, 161, 164, 170, 172, 181, 185, 188
replicator dynamics 60, 61
representativeness
~ (of beliefs) 10, 56, 140
~ of subjects 10
response mode 56
risk-attitude(s) 26, 75-78
salience 12
satisfaction 118, 119, 122, 129, 154, 155, 158-161, 172
scoring rule 18, 68, 72-74, 78, 86, 120, 211, 217
logarithmic ~ 73
quadratic ~ 68, 72, 73, 86
spherical ~ 73
strictly proper ~ 72
simulations 60, 104, 125, 129,

153-161, 164
social
~facilitation 6
~identity theory 27, 176
~learning 187
~utility component 27, 45, 46, 174, 178, 198
sociality hypothesis 176
spectator(s) 32, 81, 84, 86-88, 107, 108
strangers mode 83, 84, 91, 94, 95, 105, 121, 123, 128, 132, 133, 135
strategic anticipation 60, 186
strategically equivalent 33, 63, 82, 85, 113, 114, 121, 129, 171
subject mode 84, 85, 95, 108-110, 113, 121
subjective interdependency 88, 117
tit-for-tat strategy 15
treatment effect(s) 8, 89, 110, 113, 115, 121
triangle hypothesis 23-25, 62, 90, 91, 94, 107, 120, 181, 183, 184
trigger strategies 49
uni-modal distributions 137
utility transformation 99, 102, 158
value orientation
altruist(s) 23
competitor(s) 23, 24, 28, 89
cooperator(s) 23-25, 27, 28, 30, 31, 34-36, 41-45, 47, 59, 62-64, 71, 72, 89, 90-106, 109, 110, 114-116, 120-122, 132, 134, 155, 173-177, 179, 183, 184, 193, 198, 199
individualist(s) 23-25, 28, 36, 42-44, 62, 71, 72, 89-96, 104-106, 109, 110, 114, 120-122, 132, 134, 173-175, 177, 183, 184, 193
warm-glow (*see* cooperators)
zero-likelihood problem 46

Author index

Aboul-Ezz 13
Alexander 175
Ames 180
Andreoni 23, 27, 30, 33, 34, 41, 61, 62, 83, 158, 178
Aronson 9
Aumann 35, 126
Barth 35
Berger 56
Boes 206, 207
Boylan 50
Brandenburger 35, 126
Brandts 50, 51, 58, 175, 186
Brewer 35
Buchta 62
Buunk 5
Caldwell 4
Camerer 33, 75, 177
Caporael 26, 27, 176
Carlsmith 9
Carnevale 35
Carter 180
Cooper 50
Crawford 58
Davis 9, 11, 75
Dawes 26, 27, 32, 41, 67, 107, 176
Dehue 173
Dowding 4
Dunning 138
Dyer 11
Eichberger 50, 51, 60
Einhorn 56
El-Gamal 50, 56, 164
Ellison 62
Ellsworth 9
Erev 61, 62
Fehr 175
Fischer 76
Frey 4
Friedman 6, 8, 11, 12
Fudenberg 50, 57, 62
Gale 61, 62
Gibbons 49
Gonzales 9
Gradstein 36, 38
Graybill 206, 207
Grether 7, 13, 56, 76
Griesinger 68
Griffin 138
Güth 175
Haller 60
Harless 33, 177
Harsanyi 38
Heckman 45, 99
Hey 7, 10, 12, 73, 177
Hogarth 4, 56
Holt 9, 11, 50, 51, 58, 75, 186
Irons 180
Isaac 41, 180
Jordan 50, 60
Kagel 11
Kahneman 33
Kelley 23, 24, 68
Kerr 41
Kim 14
Kimmel 34

Kirchsteiger 175
Kirscht 62
Komorita 35
Koomen 14
Kramer 35
Kreps 36, 50, 57
Kuhlman 22-24, 173
Ledyard 13, 26, 41, 110, 117
Levin 11
Lichtenstein 13
Liebrand 21, 23, 68, 90, 173
Livingston 68
Luce 28
Maddala 29
Marwell 180
McClintock 23, 173
McCue 180
McFadden 28, 29
McKelvey 28, 36, 46, 47, 146, 163, 164
McTavish 32, 107
Meertens 5, 6
Messé 32
Messick 32
Metrick 50, 60
Milgrom 49, 50, 57, 58, 141
Miller 61, 62, 184
Milne 60
Moghaddam 27, 176
Mood 206, 207
Mookherjee 50, 187
Murphy 72, 73
Nitzan 36, 38, 175
Nowak 31
Nyarko 35
Offerman 13, 41, 50, 91, 152, 187
Olson 4, 5, 19
Orbell 27, 176
Orme 177
Ostrom 33
Palfrey 28, 30, 36, 41, 45-47, 67, 68, 133, 146, 163, 164
Partow 50
Plott 6, 7, 13, 180
Polak 50
Potters 9, 50
Press 52, 199
Prisbey 30
Pruitt 33, 34, 63, 88, 116, 117
Rapoport 26, 41, 67, 68
Raub 33
Reder 4
Riedl 175
Roberts 49, 50, 57, 58, 141
Robinson 60
Ronis 62
Rosenthal 41, 45, 67, 68, 133
Roth 6, 61, 62
Sato 32
Schmalensee 138
Schotter 50
Schram 13, 50, 68, 91, 152, 175, 180
Selten 6, 61, 62
Shaklee 32, 107
Shapley 60
Sigmund 31
Simon 4
Singer 45, 99
Sivacek 32
Slovic 13
Smith 6, 13, 37, 74
Snijders 33
Sonnemans 50, 68, 91, 152, 180, 187
Sopher 50, 187
Stahelski 23, 24, 68
Sugden 175

Suleiman 26, 41, 67, 68
Sunder 6, 8, 11, 12
Tajfel 27, 176
Taylor 27, 176
Trivers 175
Turner 27, 176
Tversky 33, 138
Vallone 138
Van De Kragt 27, 176
Van Dijk 35
Van Lange 22, 23, 173, 174
Van Winden 9, 50
Walker 13, 14
Warr 27
Weimann 15, 41
Wilke 35
Wilson 36
Wimberley 23, 24
Winkler 72, 73
Wong 169
Wright 13
Yates 62